Literary Criticism and Cultural Theory
Outstanding Dissertations

edited by
William E. Cain
Wellesley College

A Routledge Series

Other Books in This Series:

A COINCIDENCE OF WANTS
The Novel and Neoclassical Economics
Charles Lewis

MODERN PRIMITIVES
*Race and Language in Gertrude Stein,
Ernest Hemingway, and Zora Neale
Hurston*
Susanna Pavloska

PLAIN AND UGLY JANES
*The Rise of the Ugly Woman in
Contemporary American Fiction*
Charlotte M. Wright

DISSENTING FICTIONS
*Identity and Resistance in the
Contemporary American Novel*
Cathy Moses

PERFORMING LA MESTIZA
*Textual References of Lesbians of Color
and the Negotiation of Identities*
Ellen M. Gil-Gomez

FROM GOOD MA TO WELFARE QUEEN
*A Genealogy of the Poor Woman in
American Literature, Photography and
Culture*
Vivyan C. Adair

ARTFUL ITINERARIES
*European Art and American Careers in
High Culture, 1865–1920*
Paul Fisher

POSTMODERN TALES OF SLAVERY
IN THE AMERICAS
From Alejo Carpenter to Charles Johnson
Timothy J. Cox

EMBODYING BEAUTY
*Twentieth-Century American Women
Writers' Aesthetics*
Malin Pereira

MAKING HOMES IN THE WEST/INDIES
*Constructions of Subjectivity in the
Writings of Michelle Cliff and Jamaica
Kincaid*
Antonia Macdonald-Smythe

POSTCOLONIAL MASQUERADES
*Culture and Politics in Literature, Film,
Video, and Photography*
Niki Sampat Patel

DIALECTIC OF SELF AND STORY
*Reading and Storytelling in Contemporary
American Fiction*
Robert Durante

ALLEGORIES OF VIOLENCE
*Tracing the Writings of War in Late
Twentieth-Century Fiction*
Lidia Yuknavitch

VOICE OF THE OPPRESSED IN THE LANGUAGE
OF THE OPPRESSOR
*A Discussion of Selected Postcolonial
Literature from Ireland, Africa and
America*
Patsy J. Daniels

EUGENIC FANTASIES
*Racial Ideology in the Literature and
Popular Culture of the 1920's*
Betsy L. Nies

THE LIFE WRITING OF OTHERNESS
Woolf, Baldwin, Kingston, and Winterson
Lauren Rusk

FROM WITHIN THE FRAME
Storytelling in African-American Fiction
Bertram D. Ashe

THE SELF WIRED
*Technology and Subjectivity in
Contemporary Narrative*
Lisa Yaszek

THE SPACE AND PLACE OF MODERNISM
*The Russian Revolution, Little Magazines,
and New York*
Adam McKible

THE FIGURE OF CONSCIOUSNESS
*William James, Henry James, and
Edith Wharton*
Jill M. Kress

WILL THE CIRCLE BE UNBROKEN?
Family and Sectionalism in the Virginia Novels of Kennedy, Caruthers, and Tucker, 1830–1845

John L. Hare

LONDON AND NEW YORK

Published in 2002 by
Routledge
711 Third Avenue, New York, NY 10017

Published in Great Britain by
Routledge
2 Park Square, Milton Park, Abingdon, Oxfordshire OX14 4RN

First issued in paperback 2014
Routledge is an imprint of the Taylor & Francis Group, an informa business

Copyright © 2002 by Taylor & Francis Books, Inc.

All rights reserved. No part of this book may be reprinted or reproduced or utilized in any form or by any electronic, mechanical, or other means, now known or hereafter invented, including photocopying and recording, or in any information storage or retrieval system, without written permission from the publishers.

Cataloging-in-Publication Data is available from the Library of Congress

ISBN 978-0-415-94157-0 (hbk)
ISBN 978-0-415-76236-6 (pbk)

To My Family
Virginia Derhaag Hare
James Julian Hare
Matthew John Hare

Contents

Preface	*ix*
Chapter One Introduction	*1*
Chapter Two Generational Progress in *Swallow Barn*	*13*
Chapter Three "An Ardent Desire": *Kentuckian in New-York*	*31*
Chapter Four Authority and Affection: *Cavaliers of Virginia*	*51*
Chapter Five Whigs and Covert Missions: *Horse-Shoe Robinson*	*69*
Chapter Six Birthright and Authority: *George Balcombe*	*89*
Chapter Seven The Family Restructured: *The Partisan Leader*	*107*
Chapter Eight Mistaken Identity: *Rob of the Bowl*	*127*
Chapter Nine To the West: *Knights of the Horse-shoe*	*143*
Chapter Ten Conclusion	*163*

vii

viii	*Contents*
Notes	*173*
Works Cited	*179*
Index	*185*

Preface

The novels of John Pendleton Kennedy, William Alexander Caruthers, and Nathaniel Beverley Tucker represent an almost undiscovered treasure of the literary history of the antebellum United States. Most observers regard them as insignificant, pallid imitations of Sir Walter Scott's romances; those who find them more worthy of note have often examined them against the backdrop of the South's Lost Cause, which was neither a cause nor lost in the 1830s and 1840s when the novels originally appeared. But these novels captured reasonable audiences because they offered intriguing stories. Moreover, the authors, professional men of the Middle States, included in their works proposals for the United States to navigate the perilous times of the Jacksonian period.

These novels catered to a wide range of interests. *Swallow Barn* and *Kentuckian in New-York* offered readers views of life in various sections of an expanding country in which travel was still difficult. *Cavaliers of Virginia, Rob of the Bowl, Horse-Shoe Robinson,* and *Knights of the Horseshoe* included swashbuckling stories of the historical past. *George Balcombe* revolved around a young man's attempt to reclaim his birthright. *The Partisan Leader,* like the political novels of the twentieth century, dramatized the political tensions of the author's times. Arguably, the elements of later plantation novels and historical romances are all present in these works: southern belles and chivalric gentlemen abound, surrounded by wise elders, loyal (and often humorous) subordinates, appealing children, and scurrilous villains.

But the novels are more than entertaining reading. John Pendleton Kennedy, William Alexander Caruthers, and Nathaniel Beverley Tucker were urbane members of the professional class in the middle states of Virginia and Maryland. They were aware of the leading role that Virginia had played in colonial settlement, the Revolutionary War, and the founding of the United States, and they believed that the middle states were to have a continuing role in leading the nation, particularly in times like the Jacksonian era—rich with opportunity, but also fraught with peril. Moreover, Virginia and Maryland had begun the transition from agriculture to industry earlier than other southern states. They were thus uniquely positioned to chart the course that they expected other states would have to follow to preserve the Union and intersectional good will. In their novels, they proposed a *via media* that relied not on political trading in compromises but on a shared conceptualization of society.

Their conceptualization had its roots in ideas that had come from England with the early colonists almost two centuries before these novelists were born. First among these was the notion that society comprised people of differing aptitudes and interests. In this organic view of society, everyone had a different part to play, and all of the parts were necessary to the functioning of the whole. Some members of society had the abilities required to lead the whole—that is, they could balance and harmonize the contending interests. In doing so, they approximated the role of a father in a family or an aristocratic leader in a community.

Under their leadership, the other members of the society would recognize their interdependency and common purpose, and they would be bound by affection. In this regard, the authors of the Virginia novels extended the familial paradigm beyond its English core. They did so in part out of necessity because their country was facing questions concerning the nature of the bonds among the states. Here again, familial relationships served as metaphors: the bonds among states could be discussed as innate and fraternal or voluntary and marital. While the novels present a range of types of relations—parent-child, sibling, adoptive, and marital—they also reinforce regularly that the foundation of peace and prosperity is the faithfulness of the leaders of society.

This focus is not surprising. These authors lived in an era when the last of the Revolutionary leaders had died; that is, leaders with powerful credentials were no longer available. The question of what qualities leaders should possess was, for the first time, a serious question. Andrew Jackson came to the presidency without the political pedigree or experience of those who preceded him in the White House, and he was vastly different from his predecessors in his social and geographic origins. Although his role in winning the War of 1812—the second war for independence—might be debated, his victory at New Orleans (after the war had actually ended) increased national pride and made him a national figure. While he possessed charisma as a result of this victory and could appeal to the newly broadened electorate, some of his actions before and during the early part of his presidency raised questions about his leadership style and the balance of powers among the branches of the national government.

These novels, in short, are not simplistic escapist romances but rather carefully constructed proposals of a framework in which sectional tensions could be resolved. But the authors' pleas for moderation were lost in the

Preface

increasingly strident debates over specific issues. Sectional divisions became more pronounced. Troops on both sides invoked familial metaphors, calling themselves "a band of brothers" on one side and assuring their support to "Father Abraham" on the other. The outcome of four years of fratricidal war would be a painful national reconstruction that failed to resolve the fundamental questions that had led to the war. As time passed, these novels came to be seen as romantic escapism. But the authors who wrote them had not written to record what was; they hinted in part at what might be.

This study examines the use of familial ideology in these novels. It draws on a close reading of the texts informed by contemporary reviews and relevant material from the papers of the authors as well as secondary sources on the history of the Jacksonian era. In the time since I completed this work as a dissertation under direction of R. Gordon Kelly at the University of Maryland, no new scholarship concerning these works or authors has appeared.

I cannot hope to adequately acknowledge the encouragement I received from friends, students, and colleagues during my study of these novels. In the American Studies department at the University of Maryland, Gordon Kelly was the kind of advisor every doctoral candidate should have— patient, insightful and probing, but never intrusive. The members of my committee, Hasia Diner, Jo Paoletti, Lewis Lawson, and Myron Lounsbury brought the same deft touch to their questions and comments. Gary Pittenger, now retired, vied with Bryant Davis at Montgomery College— Germantown Campus for the dubious distinction of being my chief cheerleader, sounding board, and devil's advocate. But as with any work of this kind, my deepest gratitude goes to my family. Julian Hare, my father, died before this work was begun, but he taught me to love books, ideas, and history. I hope that what my sons, James and Matt, learned by watching my experience as a student will somehow repay them for the times when they had to tiptoe around so that I could work. Had it not been for the confidence of my wife, Virginia, I never would have been in a position to start the work that led to this study, and had it not been for her absolute certainty that I would finish and the work would be good, I never would have finished it.

CHAPTER ONE

Introduction

Although the Virginia novels of the ante-bellum period have sometimes been disregarded as pale imitations of Sir Walter Scott's historical romances, they offer an important resource for those who wish to understand better how national tensions may have appeared to some of the gentry in the middle states during the Jacksonian 1830s and early 1840s. In these novels, John Pendleton Kennedy, William Alexander Caruthers, and Nathaniel Beverley Tucker used the family as a paradigm for examining such questions as the seriousness of national political tensions, the structure of society, the nature of authority, and the relationship of the states to the central government. Nevertheless, these novels have received only brief treatment from literary scholars and critics and almost none from historians. Moreover, when attempting to place these works in historical context, literary scholars have focused on their treatments of slavery, apparently accepting the conventional assumption that slavery was at the root of all sectional difference. This has led to some curious patterns in the discussion of these novels. For example, while the novels do include some slave characters, these are seldom functional figures in terms of plot advancement or the development of central figures.[1] And in the early to mid-1830s, when most of the works considered here were written, the anti-slavery movement was only in the early stages of a campaign to end slavery gradually through moral suasion. The existing literary studies, then, read the novels against the background of what Kennedy, Caruthers, and Tucker may not have considered the most pressing problem of their day.

A particularly curious characteristic of literary study of these novels is that not one of the sources consulted in the research for this study treats the novels of Kennedy, Caruthers, and Tucker in chronological order based on date of publication and in the context of the political tensions and issues associated with the middle period of American history. On the contrary, most of the studies done to date have treated the works of these three authors separately: Kennedy's works followed by Caruthers's works and then Tucker's works, each author's works discussed briefly in chronological order. As a result, any sense of change over time is weakened in these accounts—a considerable loss because Kennedy, Caruthers, and Tucker all incorporated into their works implicit and explicit references to matters of public discussion. These include internal improvements, relations with Native Americans, slavery, sectionalism, party formation, political candidates, and western expansion. Thus isolated from the immediate historical context, these novels are more likely to appear as indications of the authors' romantic yearnings to escape from the realities of their day into a more idyllic setting. This isolation also allows modern critics and scholars to conduct their studies in the context of the concerns and values of their own times, treating slavery, for example, as a key issue in *Swallow Barn* (1832), even though the anti-slavery movement was not yet nationally organized at the time of the novel's composition and publication.

Vernon L. Parrington led the way in this thinking in his *Romantic Revolution in America, 1830–1860* (1927), arguing that these novelists had been overlooked for too long because of their association with a lost cause—although the cause was neither defined nor lost when the works were written. As he saw it, the period between 1812 and 1860 was the national adolescence of the United States, "a period of extravagant youth, given over to a cult of romanticism that wrought as many marvels as Aaron's rod" (vii). This view, as we will see in considering *Swallow Barn,* is one with which John Pendleton Kennedy would have agreed readily. Much of the strength of Parrington's examination of these works derives from his willingness to see the works as products of the generally optimistic (if contentious) Jacksonian era and to set aside some of the tensions that arose later.

Parrington, however, identified Southern culture as distinctive from Northern culture, and he identified Virginia and South Carolina as "germinal centers of [a singular] southern culture" from which arose distinctive ways of thinking. As we shall see, this strong association of Virginia with the South is conspicuously different from the sectional representations presented in Caruthers's *Kentuckian in New-York* (1834) and implied in Nathaniel Beverley Tucker's *The Partisan Leader* (1836). Parrington saw the Virginians of the Jacksonian period as breaking ranks with their predecessors, Jefferson and Madison, and prizing romance over sentiment and exuberance over dignity—as romantics, in other words. He saw Tucker as the leader in this escapist and defensive movement, a man who "richly embodied all the picturesque parochialisms that plantation life encouraged" and sought "to arouse Virginia to its peril before the jaws closed upon it." But Tucker's works possessed for Parrington "no savor of humor or pleasantry of satire" because the Virginian "had so long and bitterly brooded over the supposed wrongs of Virginia that he had lost all sense of

Introduction 3

proportion" (33–35). Caruthers, on the other hand, "had pretty well rid himself of the intense and narrow parochialisms that restricted the sympathies of Beverley Tucker" as a result of his travels. This, according to Parrington, accounted for Caruthers's opposition to slavery as well as to city mobs (39–43). Parrington saw John Pendleton Kennedy as "very like Caruthers in temperament and gifts, a liberal in all his sympathies" and "an agreeable representative of the *ante bellum* Southerns, an American Victorian . . . standing midway between the northern radical and the southern Fire Eater" (44). These authors, he argued, depicted in their works a plantation aristocracy that was hospitable, individualistic, kind to black people and tolerant of most poor whites, fond of the outdoor life, and filled with community spirit.

Parrington's conclusions are difficult to dispute, yet the organization of his work may have led him to overlook important relationships among the works. Parrington treats Tucker first, Caruthers second, and Kennedy third, implicitly suggesting that the three authors composed or published their novels in this order even though the actual order is more complex but generally the reverse.[2] Set against a stronger historical context and treated in order of publication dates, the novels still bear out some of the distinctions that Parrington saw, but they also indicate that Tucker's earnest alarm was rooted in more substantial and enduring concerns than his hatred of Martin Van Buren or fear for a Virginian way of life.

Jay Broadus Hubbell took the next step in calling attention to the writers of the South with *The South in American Literature* (1954). This encyclopedic work has its roots in the old study of literature in historical context—the assumption that literary works directly reflect their authors and the historical milieus of those authors. Accordingly, for Hubbell, John Pendleton Kennedy becomes "less Southern and more national," just as his native Baltimore became less Southern and more industrial. (481). Similarly, for Hubbell, Caruthers's works reflect that the author was "a Presbyterian, a Whig, an optimist, and an enthusiastic believer in the manifest destiny of the American republic" (497), and Beverley Tucker, because of his years in Missouri during the statehood and compromise controversies of 1819–20, came to see the Union as a curse and "became a Virginian of the Virginians [conspicuously lacking] Caruthers' desire to promote intersectional good will" (424). While there is much useful information to be gleaned from Hubbell's work, his approach leaves opens some serious questions. What, for example, was the South and to what extent did these authors see themselves as part of the region? As we shall see, they may well have seen themselves as men of the middle states. Both Kennedy and Caruthers wrote from nationalistic perspectives, and even the most strident of the three, Tucker, was not a Union man but saw himself as a Virginian first with only a secondary and conditional allegiance to a region. Thus, the three authors, for their disagreements on many issues, very likely would have had little argument with the notion that their state or region had a special role to play in the Union. But at the same time, they would have agreed more strongly with the idea that the gentry throughout all of the states had a particularly important leadership role in society. That role being fulfilled, regional and state loyalties would strengthen the nation instead of dividing it. To argue too quickly that these are *Southern* authors may leave a commentator wrestling with whether one of them is a typical or atypical example—and if an author diverges from the norm that a commentator has established for the region or state, does that author become an exception to the norm, or does he represent the norm for some new and distinct type?

William R. Taylor took on the matter of sectionalism in *Cavalier and Yankee: The Old South and the American National Character* (1961), a myth-symbol examination proceeding from the premise that "By 1860, most Americans had come to look upon their society and culture as divided between a North and a South, a democratic, commercial civilization and an aristocratic, agrarian one," and on both sides, they sought to define an acceptable national character that could accommodate the desirable characteristics of both (xv). While this premise seems to share some of the potential weaknesses noted previously, Taylor recognized that the North and South were subject to the same historic forces, and he held that the South consciously differentiated itself from the North by attempting to create a set of values that isolated the region from the increasingly materialistic, impersonal, and dominant North (xix–xx). The authors, then, became for Taylor more or less representative men of their times, working out their identities and the national character in the pages of their novels. Within this framework, Kennedy, whose fortune and success depended upon the city of Baltimore, came to revere the Virginian way of life of which he wrote in *Swallow Barn*. Taylor considers his novels as an effort to create for himself an aristocratic Anglo-Saxon cultural identity that would replace his mercantile Scots-Irish background (167–172). Likewise, Caruthers, whose Scots-Irish mercantile background differed from Kennedy's primarily in its geographic locus, sought to create a cavalier culture for himself, even though he ultimately came to see that the cavalier was not fitted for American life—because American life, for him, was life on the frontier (134–144). Taylor acknowledged that Tucker was a "professional Southerner" (in the sense of one whose working identity is organized around his identification with the region) and the "only [one of the authors he considered who] spoke from the point of view of the professional Southerner and Tidewater aristocrat, . . . [but] even he wrote with eighteen years in Missouri fresh in his mind" (143). Nevertheless, Taylor held that Tucker recognized that the effete eastern cavalier could survive only by learning some of the frontiersman's skills.

Taylor's formulation leaves intact the sectional identities to which twentieth-century readers are accustomed—North, South, and West—but again,

Introduction 5

the question arises of whether the authors saw themselves in these terms. Moreover, Taylor leaps from the authors' personal discomfort with their own cultural backgrounds and their desires to claim distinction to the presumed national search for identity, and this is a substantial leap indeed.

More recent scholars, such as Ritchie Watson (in *The Cavalier in American Fiction* (1985)) and Kathryn Seidel (in *The Southern Belle in the American Novel* (1985)) have sought to expand on Taylor's work. Watson examined the cavalier figure in Virginia fiction and argued that this figure did not recreate a historical class but rather portrayed ideals of masculine virtue that prevailed during the time when the authors wrote their works (ix). He argued that Virginian fiction could be studied without consideration of what went on in other states and regions and still produce "insights into the defensive and uncritical attitude that nearly all southerners have adopted on occasion toward their region" (xi–xii), a shaky supposition at best because it seems to conflate Virginia and the South. Moreover, the authors we are considering here do not present a singular view of the cavalier figure. One can argue, for example, that both Governor Berkley and his adversary, Nathaniel Bacon, in Caruthers' *Cavaliers of Virginia,* are cavalier figures, but they are very different men evoking different responses from readers.

Watson credits Caruthers and John Esten Cooke with development of the cavalier figure (34), which leaves one wondering just how to account for Ned Hazard, the knight errant of *Swallow Barn.* Kennedy appeared to Watson as a developer of figures who mixed reality with the cavalier ideal in their fiction and were part of a dying way of life.[3] Caruthers, on the other hand, developed cavalier figures that represented, rather than a dying way of life, the physician-author's own optimistic, nationalistic, liberal point of view, and his figures contrast with Douglas Trevor, the chivalric figure of Beverley Tucker's novel, *The Partisan Leader* (113, 109). One of Watson's most important contributions, however, is the recognition that the cavaliers exist alongside of yeoman figures who often prove more successful in some respects than the aristocrats and allow such authors as Caruthers to present a more democratic view (121–122).

Watson's readings of individual works offer some useful insights, as long as one checks facts carefully, but his argument weakens when he explains that the image of the Southern aristocrat made the South appear to Northerners as a strange and exotic culture fundamentally incompatible with the culture of the North (146). Much of his argument turns on the national progression toward Civil War; indeed, he entitles one section of his work "Virginia Fiction and the Coming of the Civil War" (144). He lays a weak foundation indeed on which to believe that Kennedy and Caruthers, both of whom had extensive connections in the North, would have been so unfamiliar with the Northern *mentalité* as to overlook that readers in the section where their works were published would regard their

6   *Will the Circle be Unbroken?*

cavalier figures as based upon fact and indicative of irreconcilable differences between the two sections.

Kathryn Seidel focused on the Southern belle, a figure she described as a young, unmarried woman, living on a great plantation with her widowed father, sixteen or seventeen years of age, and marriageable. The belle is "exuberant, a bit vain, and rather naïve"—and in many instances, she represents the South itself (3, xiii). Since the origin of the belle with Bel Tracy in *Swallow Barn,* Seidel argues, there have come to be two very different belle figures: the pure maiden on a pedestal and the depraved nymphomaniac, and the traits of the belle in any particular novel depend upon and reflect the author's view of the South (xi–xii). Seidel's interest lay not so much in the belles of any particular period but in the progression of belles that began with Bel Tracy in Kennedy's *Swallow Barn* and continued to the works of Gail Godwin more than a century and a half later. As a result, she wrote of only one of the novels with which we are concerned here. Nevertheless, she makes one observation that is critical to the present study: "During the first half of the nineteenth century, . . . the home was elevated to the status of a sacred refuge from the corrupt world; the home became the temple of civilization's most cherished values and virtues" (4–5). Given this, she says, "The plantation owner and his family ruled legitimately because of their 'noble blood.' His sons and daughters were by analogy princes and princesses in their dominions" (5). As we shall see, some Southern Whigs of the 1830s, like their pre-Revolutionary counterparts, saw the home as a microcosm and the relations of its inhabitants as representative of the relations between the household and the state.

All of these readings relate in some way to the idea of convention. Parrington and Hubbell, one can argue, held that slavery and agrarianism were conventions of life that differentiated the South from the North. For Taylor, Watson, and Seidel, figures in the literature of the period or region were conventions; that is, they were recurring figures that identified that literature with its period and region. The present study, however, requires a somewhat different view of convention, one that can go beyond simple identification and description of the recurring motif or metaphor and accommodate the dynamism of history.

Paisley Livingston points out that critics have defined convention in various ways. In this case, it is important to recognize that any recurring, non-necessary, and non-natural feature in a series of literary works may be considered as a convention (67). According to Livingston, however, conventions are patterns of behavior (including linguistic behavior) that arise from the cultural expectations that authors share with their intended audiences, and they allow resolution of complex problems by invoking meetings of the minds that have occurred in previous similar circumstances (71). In his conceptualization, the conventions or deviations from conventions in texts reflect the intentions of the authors of those texts; consequently, those

Introduction

studying the texts can consider those works as a form of mediation between an author and readers who are both familiar with the convention (73). That is, "we would try to explain a particular textual feature by linking it to an author's reasons . . . , just as we might try to explain a reader's reception of the text in terms of the reader's reasons, reasons that typically include various inferences about the author's mental states" (74). In pursuing such explanations, it is important to bear in mind that the authors were seeking to express ideas that might be controversial in ways that would accommodate diverse points of view as broadly as possible (77–78). For purposes of this study, family relationships and rituals are conventions—patterns of life that authors believed they and their readers shared.

Livingston's discussion of convention defines the concept, but it does not establish a method of inquiry that will lead through the literary and historical contexts. For that, I have drawn upon the dramaturgical method used by Rhys Isaac in *The Transformation of Virginia*. Isaac pointed out that it was necessary, in the study of history, to identify the key structures or relationships in the extant accounts of an event and to reduce them to essentials. This could be done by treating incidents involving these structures as rituals and examining them in detail. As he put it, "The theater model serves to emphasize the formalities that govern so much of social life. The shared meanings with which settings, costumes, roles, and styles are invested serve at once as limiting constraints on the actors and as channels through which effective—indeed powerful and coercive—communications can be directed" (351).

Moreover, Isaac argued for the careful examination of metaphors, pointing out that "culture is composed of interlocking sets of paradigms, or metaphors, that shape participants' perceptions by locating diverse forms of action on more or less coherent maps of experience" (347).

Livingston's conceptualization and Isaac's method seem particularly applicable to the present undertaking. In all of the novels included in this study, some familial relationship serves as a focal point. That is, the authors call upon a previous meeting of the minds—the family experience of the reader as well as an existing familial paradigm, an established literary deployment of the family—to address a complex set of issues concerning relations among those who governed and those who were governed. While these authors sometimes referred to contemporary problems and issues, they usually avoided making these matters central to their novels. As we will see, these references appear to be offhand hints or reminders that the time in which the novel is set bears some relation to the time in which the original readers encountered it. By using the family, the only institution in which every person participates in some way, the authors were calling upon a well-established way of looking at the state. This familial paradigm has been described by Melvin Yazawa in *From Colonies to Commonwealth: Familial Ideology and the Beginnings of the American Republic* (1985).

8   *Will the Circle be Unbroken?*

Yazawa has pointed out that one conventional way of describing relationships between the ruler and the subject during the colonial era was in terms of the family. That is, the family was a microcosm of the structure of the organic community in which each member had a different but vital role to play and all members were knit together, as John Winthrop expressed it, by affection under direction of the head, the father or ruler (9). This familial paradigm, according to Yazawa, carried a massive store of cultural information. It defined schematically the obligations that people had to each other, the origin of those obligations, and how those obligations were to be discharged (12–14). First, it held that society was hierarchical and organic, binding all of its members with bonds of affection (9, 2). This affection was not simply a matter of liking or loving others; it was founded upon a shared recognition of interdependency that embraced desire, hope, gratitude, joy, grief, hatred, and anger. This made society and the ties that bound its members extremely complex, but these ties could still be explained readily because society and its institutions, especially the church and the commonwealth, were macrocosms of the family (2).

Maintaining the order of society and ensuring that members all contributed to the common good demanded a ruler, just as maintaining the order and productivity of the family demanded a father. This ruler-father had to recognize that his exalted position and greater power and wealth made him answerable to God as well as the polity. He had to do more good than others, and he had to endeavor to sort out the confusion that had plagued mankind since Adam's fall (13). Superiors in the family and the state had to manage the affairs entrusted to them by God with a fatherly tenderness and a careful regard for the lives and welfare of their subordinates, even sacrificing themselves for their subordinates if necessary (23). They were also to comport themselves with humility, modesty, sincerity, self-denial, diligence, watchfulness, justice, benevolence, prudence, and constancy, always being prepared to answer to God and the polity for their actions. In addition to this faithfulness, rulers and fathers had to avoid the greater temptations to which they were subjected, and they had to avoid an inordinate sense of self-importance, or pride (24–25). When they did all of this, they would inspire in their subordinates a public spirit and moral reformation, and this, in turn, would lead to health, happiness, peace, and prosperity (26). Ruler-fathers who did not manifest this faithfulness might become tyrants, and if they did not uphold their obligations to their subordinates, their subjects might come to regard the filial fear of displeasing the ruler as a conditional obligation (27).

As Yazawa describes it, this paradigm placed a premium upon demeanor, the rituals of subservience that indicated inward filial respect and discipline (36). Such apparently trivial acts as the removal of hats and bowing in the presence of superiors were important for two reasons: First, these acts required attentiveness to one's social environment and duty and thus

Introduction

limited opportunities for vice and profaneness to claim uncultivated minds; second, they provided an indication of parental success in child-rearing, indicating that parents were instilling in their children a proper respect for order and restraint (38–39). Here again, the familial paradigm operated upon superiors as well as subordinates. As children and subordinates were bound to demonstrate filial regard through their demeanor, superiors were to exercise restraint in discipline, loathing misdeeds while pitying and demonstrating empathy for the wrongdoer (45). They were to recognize that harsh punishment only aroused a selfish desire to avoid pain while mild and rational correction aroused a wish in the offender to avoid giving further offense to an affectionate ruler or parent (45, 47). Affectionate discipline would address the reason of the offender and show that the superior's will was reasonable; thus, it would inspire the affections of the offender and forestall further misbehavior (48). In addition, discipline that was unduly severe, particularly in the commonwealth, might alienate the very affections that were supposed to bind people together. It could make compliance servile and selfish rather than filial and communitarian (58).

Drawing on the literature of the Colonial and Revolutionary periods, Yazawa pointed out that the familial paradigm of the colonial era cast England as the Mother Country of the colonies and the monarch as ruler-father of the empire, and it suggested that the colonies, like children, would mature and leave the home of their parent (87, 89). As English restrictions and impositions on the colonies increased in the mid-eighteenth century, the colonists came to regard themselves as affectionate and dutiful children who had been unjustly punished by a parent whom they loved (92). This led to the breakup of the imperial family and a new republican social order. While some revolutionaries associated this order with youthful vigor, frugality, justice, kindness, and courage, they also feared that youth would give way, in time, to avarice, luxury, pride, and idleness (99). It was critical that Americans establish domestic virtues that would allow them to exploit America's natural advantages. But republican emphasis on rational law seemed to replace personal integrity with legal honesty, and the organic view of society seemed cyclical—and therefore subject to decline (108–109). Republicanism depersonalized authority, Yazawa argued, and discretion in government seemed too monarchical and arbitrary to be tolerated (112). Moreover, in a republic, citizens were connected to the law and the state—not directly to their fellow citizens (143). Yazawa held that the early decades of the nineteenth century shored up faith in the durability of the republic, and the republican paradigm destroyed the familial paradigm of order, affection, filial fear, and paternal faithfulness (190, 194). The republican world cherished instead autonomy, personal independence, and equality (194).

Although Yazawa suggested that the familial paradigm disintegrated in the early years of the Republic, it appears to have persisted into the

Jacksonian era—and perhaps later. Peter Bardaglio, in *Reconstructing the Household: Families, Sex, and the Law in the Nineteenth-Century South* (1995), included no reference to Yazawa's work. Nevertheless, he argued that "as important as the household was as a private institution in the Victorian South, it was even more important as a political institution in the broadest sense; it not only constituted the chief vehicle for the exercise of power in southern society but also served as the foundation of southern public beliefs and values" (xi).

While acknowledging affectionate love between spouses and between parents and their children, Southerners still held patriarchal rule as crucial to the direction of family—and, by extension, of the republic. According to Bardaglio, this social order, which seems to me very consistent with Yazawa's familial paradigm, began to crumble until elite Southerners came to regard secession as the only means of separating themselves from the pressures that were weakening their domestic order. His examination of Southern family law led him to this "household theory of secession" (xiv), a theory that secession was a defensive enterprise aimed at protection of a social structure represented by the household and in which chattel slavery was a necessary feature.

The novels considered in the present study cover a period from roughly 1828 to roughly 1841, and for the most part, they cannot be taken to support strongly the household theory of secession. Nevertheless, they do suggest that the familial paradigm remained in effect, at least in the minds of some authors, well into the nineteenth century. As we will see, Kennedy, Caruthers, and Tucker all addressed the relationship of leaders to the polity, and all expected from presidents the affection and faithfulness that their predecessors had expected from monarchs and royal governors. They presented leaders who resembled the representations of Andrew Jackson in the anti-Jacksonian literature of the time, and those representations of the Jacksonian figure in the novels ignore the needs and interests of those they lead, just as the unfaithful ruler in Yazawa's familial paradigm. Similarly, these anti-Jacksonian representative figures fail to arouse among their people the public spirit necessary to unify the polity. To this extent, the familial paradigm continued as Yazawa presented it.

But the familial paradigm that Yazawa identified in colonial materials, for all of the cultural knowledge that it carries, considers family as no more than the relationship between parent and child. Family was far more, as Bardaglio suggests, and the authors recognized its other dimensions. To cite briefly two examples, family was, for the authors treated in this study, in part a process by which wealth and wisdom were accumulated and passed on to new generations. In *Swallow Barn,* for example, Kennedy shows Frank Meriwether and Ned Hazard removing obstacles that had hindered the preceding generation. Moreover, the generation that followed them appears in the novel to be learning lessons that will allow the pattern of

Introduction

improvement to continue. That is, they are shown adding to and transmitting the accumulated wisdom of the family. In *George Balcombe,* Tucker built his plot around an idealized ruler-father figure, the title character, whose work in the novel is to ensure that the accumulated wealth of a family passes to the next generation. William Napier cannot regain his inheritance from his grandfather Raby on his own because he lacks the abilities that Balcombe has developed. While Napier gains some of these skills during the novel, Balcombe, as ruler-father of an extended family, must identify the common interests of the family members and use those interests to motivate their cooperation in some dangerous undertakings. Napier must learn this from Balcombe before he can assume his inheritance and rightful place in the community.

Similarly, families do not simply burst on the scene. They come into being through a process in which prospective partners evaluate each other and make somewhat reasoned decisions to marry or are drawn to each other by mystical and apparently irresistible forces. In the process, parents may expose prospective partners' strengths or weaknesses in an effort to influence courtship and marriage decisions. This is particularly important if we are to apply the familial paradigm to the United States in the Jacksonian era because so much of the political controversy of the time had to do with how the Union had come to exist and the nature of the bonds among states and the central government. When Caruthers ended *Kentuckian in New-York* with multiple marriages, he was not simply tying up the loose ends of the plot; rather, he was using several happy couples to indicate what qualities were necessary to maintaining national unity. It is no accident that the novel ended not simply with marriages, but with marriages that joined partners from different regions. Still, these marriages are simple matters based on a mystical romantic attraction, and we shall see that the novel ignores such thorny issues as where the newlyweds will live and how they will deal with differences that arise because of their different backgrounds.

Similarly, the families of the nineteenth century more often than not included siblings, and the sibling relationship served as an alternative model of the Union, one in which the states were not voluntarily joined but were joint participants in a common destiny. This becomes particularly apparent in *The Partisan Leader,* where political differences over the nature of the Union and the desirability of secession divide two sets of brothers. And for all of Beverley Tucker's outspoken advocacy of secession, one must wonder why, at the end of the work, the plot does not end with the rescue of either brother from the danger that secession imposed.

In the end, the Virginian novelists of the Jacksonian period used the familial paradigm to examine schematically some of the crucial issues of their day. While the paradigm offered them a way of simplifying complex relationships and relieved them of spelling out the details of why those rela-

12   *Will the Circle be Unbroken?*

tionships worked or should have worked as shown in the novels, it failed in the end. First, it was most effective when a singularly imposing figure was at the head of the government. It worked well, then, when the President of the United States was the only holder of that office to lend his name to an era of American history. For good or ill, while Jackson was in office, his presence organized the support and opposition on every issue, and the familial paradigm could readily incorporate his characterization. With his retirement, his successors—even Van Buren, who was generally considered a consummate strategist—were unable to exert similar force on the issues, and the paradigm did not facilitate discussion of their executive style. Moreover, the debates of Jackson's time were not entirely sectional matters nor even partisan matters. The parties, in the modern sense of the word, did not exist until Jackson, Van Buren, and their associates began developing partisan apparatus in the mid-1830s. While states recognized some similarities, their loyalties were not clearly specified. A novel such as *The Kentuckian in New-York* could offer to spell out what sectional alignments ought to be only in a time when these alignments were neither clearly nor rigidly defined. While sibling relations and marriage relations could serve as models of relations among states or groups of people, they proved less successful as models of sections or parties. As a result, the familial paradigm weakened. It was no longer possible to simplify issues by treating them schematically, and the possibility of dividing a house—a noble lineage—became slightly greater.

CHAPTER TWO

Generational Progress in
Swallow Barn

Swallow Barn, John Pendleton Kennedy's first book-length work, appeared in 1832, at a time when national tensions had not begun to harden into lasting divisions but could be represented as stages in national development. The author, in his preface to that first edition, wrote that his work was not a novel but rather "a rivulet of story wandering through a broad meadow of episode" (vii). In 1853, when the second edition was published and tensions were somewhat higher, he again claimed that the book was not a novel, but a work "interchangeably partaking of the complexion of a book of travels, a diary, a collection of letters, a drama, and a history" (11). Nevertheless, *Swallow Barn,* originally conceived as a book of epistolary essays, was carefully unified by plot, and the careful plotting permitted Kennedy to address the political tensions of the time within the framework of the family. For Kennedy, such issues were not conflicts between states or sections, but stages in shaking off the past and moving toward the future, and in *Swallow Barn,* he presented three generations of a family and showed them dealing with a long-standing problem, a legal quibble over a relatively useless tract of land. In the end, his novel used the family to suggest that the Union could accommodate tensions so long as all involved maintained their tolerance and sense of perspective under the leadership of men who had at heart the good of the community.

When Kennedy began collecting material for *Swallow Barn* in 1828, he may have intended to write a series of essays about the extension of the old Tidewater aristocratic order into the part of the Virginian upcountry with which he was most familiar, the area around Martinsburg in what is now West Virginia (Bohner 319). To represent this old order, he created the Meriwether family (in early drafts called the Oldstock family) of Swallow Barn: Frank; his wife, Lucretia; and their seven children (among whom only the three adolescents, Lucy, Victorine, and Rip, are identified by name). They share the plantation with Edward (Ned) Hazard, Lucretia's

13

14   *Will the Circle be Unbroken?*

brother, and Prudence, Frank's spinster sister. The essays were to be unified by a narrator named Mark Littleton, a New York cousin of the Hazards.

Mark's visit coincides with the reemergence of a long-standing tension in the community around the slightly run-down Swallow Barn plantation. The boundary between Swallow Barn and an adjacent plantation, The Brakes, is in dispute. For nearly fifty years, Isaac Tracy, who owns The Brakes, has pursued a lawsuit against the owners of Swallow Barn over a tract of land along this boundary. Two generations earlier, the land had belonged to Isaac's father, who had sold it to Ned's grandfather, Edward, for use as a millpond. The soil, however, proved too porous for this purpose, and Hazard had to abandon the project (Kennedy 130–142). The tract of land, known as the Apple-pie Branch, was also too marshy for crops, so it lay unused until Isaac Tracy decided that it would be satisfactory for pasturage of his cattle. At that point, he initiated a suit against Edward Hazard based on the premise that the original sale had been for a specific purpose and became void if the land was not used for that purpose (148–149). The suit had continued for years, and "Mr. Tracy [has been] completely driven out of every intrenchment of law and fact; which . . . set him into a more thorough and vigorous asseveration of his first principles" (150). Nevertheless, the Meriwethers and Hazards have continuously remained on friendly terms with Tracy, his daughters, Bel and Catharine, his son Ralph, and their kinsman, Harvey Riggs. These neighbors even remained friendly when the families found themselves on opposite sides during the Revolutionary War, with the Tracys supporting the British and the Hazards supporting independence. By the time of the novel, the suit has become little more than a disruptive nuisance that takes the principals away from their customary work, and to resolve the matter, Frank Meriwether proposes to Tracy that it be arbitrated by mutual friends, attorneys Philpot Wart (representing Meriwether) and Singleton Swansdown (representing Tracy) (151). Unbeknownst to Tracy, Meriwether has decided that the long sequence of suit and countersuit has become intolerably burdensome and has instructed Wart to end the matter by ensuring that the arbitration places the land in Tracy's possession.

Swansdown and Wart carefully review all of the legal papers that the quarrel has generated, but the case ultimately requires that they visit the tract and determine whether the dam that formed the millpond was destroyed suddenly or eroded gradually (203, 204, 205). This inquiry forces them to search the swamp for evidence on this point, and they return with a decision contrary to what the courts have held for fifty years: The disputed land belongs to Isaac Tracy and the Brakes. This gives Isaac possession of the land that he has tried to claim, and the ruling is precisely what Frank Meriwether had sought as an end to the nuisance. Still, although it provides the occasion for a celebration, the settlement may not be permanent. At the end of the book, Isaac says he wishes that the matter

Generational Progress in Swallow Barn   *15*

could be reviewed again, even though the result of the arbitration by Wart and Swansdown produced the effect that he sought from the first. Although he is satisfied with the result, he wishes the settlement to incorporate language validating one of his assertions that was tangential to the arbitration.

Isaac's wish to return to the legal issue, however, is not fulfilled. Readers and Mark Littleton have known since the earliest reference to the lawsuit that one of the Swallow Barn slaves, "'Mammy Diana, who is a true sibul [sic], has uttered a prophecy which runs thus—'That the landmarks shall never be stable until Swallow Barn shall wed The Brakes'" (91). This final resolution depends on the courtship of Ned Hazard and Isaac Tracy's daughter, Bel, and that courtship forms the second plot of the work. While the lawyers have sought to resolve the ownership of Apple-pie Branch, Ned has managed to make a fool of himself in Bel's eyes by allowing her to catch him singing her name loudly in the woods (85). The misdeed seems inconsequential, but Bel, an unmarried woman on a somewhat remote plantation, has little with which to occupy herself except attention to the mannerly details of life and the reading of chivalric novels. The careless singing of her name suffices to offend her, and the question of her relationship with Ned hangs in the balance through most of the novel.

After the arbitration of the legal case, however, the romantic plot takes hold. In her efforts to approximate the life of a heroine from one of her novels, Bel has attempted to train and outfit a marsh hawk for falconry. Her success, however, has been limited to the outfitting, and when she first attempts to hunt with the hawk, the bird seizes the opportunity to escape (228–231). Ned, recognizing an opportunity to restore himself to Bel's good graces, volunteers to find the bird, and with the assistance of Littleton, Wilful (his spaniel), and some of the people of the neighborhood, he succeeds. Bel is ecstatic at the return of her hawk, and she grants Wilful the freedom of her parlor for his role in the rescue and warms to the courtship of Ned, the Knight of the Hawk (371–373). Encouraged and counseled by Littleton and Harvey Riggs, a kinsman of the Tracys, Ned attempts with some success to appear more serious and settled in Bel's presence, and the two are married shortly after Mark leaves Swallow Barn (389–392, 396, 504). When Isaac speaks of reopening the lawsuit over Apple-pie Branch, Ned, now speaking as his son-in-law, dissuades him from doing so (505–506). The interests of Swallow Barn and The Brakes have become fused, and the passage of Ned and Bel from frivolous courtship to marriage and stability places Ned in a position of increased influence with Isaac. As a son-in-law, he can ensure that Isaac will not raise the suit over the long-disputed tract of land again.

Swallow Barn was a popular work when it was published. Despite a cholera epidemic that forced some booksellers to close for a time, roughly 1500 copies, or three-fourths of the first printing, sold in the first nine months after publication. A pirated edition appeared in London, and a Swedish edition was published by 1835 (Bohner, 72–73). Nevertheless, the work has attracted relatively little attention from modern scholars and critics. Vernon Parrington recognized it as the earliest successful novel of plantation life and commented on the idyllic setting and romantic treatment of slavery (28, 50). Jay Hubbell argued that it is "a more faithful picture of Virginia life than a romantic novel could have been" (492). On the other hand, Jan Bakker, one of Kennedy's more recent commentators, classified the work as a romantic novel that represents the plantation as an idealized pastoral environment. According to Bakker, Kennedy, with his recognition of economic realities and the potential of cities, viewed the passing of the Virginia plantation with mixed emotions; the plantation was, in other words, the antithesis of "the rise of socially leveling Jacksonian democracy, unseemly urban and rural development and mechanization, and abrasive North-South sectionalism" (41). William R. Taylor read the work as Kennedy's way of addressing his ambiguities about his mercantile class origins and genteel aspirations (168–169). J. V. Ridgely saw Kennedy's first novel as essentially conservative but interesting because the author "saw the possibilities in contrasting southern and northern cultures" (40). All of these readings posit that the central issue of the times was the increasing tension between North and South—even though sectional allegiance was only weakly established while Kennedy was writing. While this tension is only one part of the novel, it overlooks Kennedy's nationalist views, which were well established by this time. Kennedy's modern commentators also overlook that he and his readers may have viewed their times as being far more complex than modern readers imagine them to have been. In short, all of these readings could benefit from better understanding of Kennedy's family circumstances and his views on the host of social, economic, and political changes taking place around him in the late 1820s and early 1830s.

John Pendleton Kennedy's experiences in a close and durable family led him to perceive the family as a stable (but not static) entity founded on affection, mutual assistance, and toleration, and he saw the Union in similar terms.[1] Kennedy's experience almost surely led him to regard the family as founded upon mutual affection between husband and wife. His father, John Kennedy, was an Irish immigrant who had come to Philadelphia in 1784 to join his two brothers in their business of supplying copper to shipbuilders (Bohner 4). The novelist's mother, Nancy Pendleton, was the daughter of a family distinguished in Virginia and in South Carolina. This marriage across social and economic distances offered no obvious benefits to either partner. Neither parent nor son commented on this, but the social ties of the aristocratic Piedmont woman could not have been useful to her new husband in his Baltimore mercantile business, and the marriage to a recently arrived immigrant Irishman of the mercantile class could not raise

Generational Progress in Swallow Barn   *17*

her status or standard of living. Consequently, it seems safe to say that John Pendleton Kennedy's parents married on the basis of affection. The Kennedy marriage, like the marriage of Bel Tracy and Ned Hazard, also appears to have involved a degree of tolerance on the part of both partners. John Pendleton Kennedy recalled that his mother had been the real authority in the family (Bohner 3–4)—a role in which Bel can be cast rather easily on the basis of her imperious behavior as a single woman. This suggests that Kennedy's ideas concerning familial roles were not based on some fixed standard that established male dominance, but rather on continuing negotiation and interpretation.

The Kennedy family of Baltimore seems to have been quite durable. In an era when death still disrupted many nuclear families and promoted the formation of complex blended families (such as we shall see in considering Nathaniel Beverley Tucker), John and Nancy Kennedy both survived to old age and remained in Baltimore until John Pendleton, their eldest son, was a relatively successful lawyer and politician (Bohner 223). They saw all four of their sons survive to adulthood, and when the couple retired to western Virginia, their three younger sons, all adults, moved with them while John Pendleton remained in Baltimore (74). This stability made Kennedy's experience of family different from those of the other authors considered here, both of whom experienced disruption of some familial ties. In light of this difference, it is not surprising that Kennedy's work reflects a more permanent view of the family, and by extension, an interpretation of the familial paradigm that treats the Union as similarly permanent.

This familial durability, in Kennedy's experience, extended beyond the nuclear family, but it did not make the family static. On the contrary, Kennedy's experience impressed on him that roles in a family necessarily changed over time. He was able to attend college in Baltimore only because his Kennedy uncles in Philadelphia provided financial assistance when his father went bankrupt in 1804 and when the growing family of John and Nancy Kennedy needed a larger home in 1809 (Bohner 11–13). In time, the author would continue this pattern, making loans on occasion to his brothers and assisting his Pendleton cousins in their efforts to launch literary careers even when their political views were very different from his own (223, 189–190). And Kennedy's family ties expanded to include his in-laws, as well: Even after the death of his first wife, he and her father remained friendly and often traveled together (59–61), and he was heavily involved in the business operations of his second wife's father (63–67). In short, John Pendleton Kennedy's definition of family was flexible and functional, not rooted in any single principle such as honor or paternalism, but on the members' wish to perpetuate an affectionate and supportive relationship regardless of adversity. A man of John Pendleton Kennedy's experience, then, would reasonably regard familial relationships as enduring and mutually supportive.

18   *Will the Circle be Unbroken?*

To claim that John Pendleton Kennedy saw his family experience as a rags-to-riches success story would be speculative; nevertheless, he undoubtedly recognized that his life as a prosperous lawyer, man about town, politician, and novelist was very different from that of his father. His uncles had made possible his father's immigration and business start in America, and the economic base that his family had established enabled him to take his place in Baltimore. While the author had no children who survived infancy, his actions in assisting various relatives indicate that he experienced the family as a broad network that existed to promote the development of all of its members. That development was a part of the natural order of things; that is, it occurred as members took advantage of opportunities different from those available to previous generations and other members and responded to circumstances that were also different from those of their contemporaries. Taking this view, Kennedy would have found merit in the words of John Adams: "I must study politics and war, that my sons may have liberty to study mathematics and philosophy, geography, natural history and naval architecture, navigation, commerce and agriculture, in order to give their children the right to study painting, poetry, music, architecture, statuary, tapestry, and porcelain" (Adams).

In this formulation, the acts of one generation enable the progress of the next, and the potential of the individual is connected to that of his family and the state. The first step in national development, then, was to establish the framework of government through politics and to provide for defense. This done, people could turn their attention to the production of goods for sale rather than subsistence, and the next generation would have the leisure and economic prosperity to enjoy the arts. Adams's letter containing this quotation had not been published when Kennedy was writing *Swallow Barn*, but the novel indicates that the two men would have agreed that the individual's fortune was connected to that of the state and that families and states evolved through stages. This idea of generational progression is part of the familial paradigm as described by Melvin Yazawa (99, 100), but Kennedy's view, as we shall see, is more positive than most of the theorists of the Revolutionary generation who believed that nations were born, matured, and died.

During the 1820s, Kennedy came to favor the development of manufactures, internal improvements supported by the central government, and emancipation of slaves, all measures that he regarded as ultimately beneficial to all states and regions (Bohner 47–48, 50–51, 66). During the same period, however, his personal experiences and observations of the political process convinced him that these measures could occur only when men of integrity led the nation and the electorate had developed the political maturity to put national interests above personal and regional considerations. In *Swallow Barn,* this belief emerges through the tale of a legal issue that cannot be resolved within the established legal process. On the contrary, the

Generational Progress in Swallow Barn   *19*

matter of Apple-Pie Branch cannot be finally resolved until "Swallow Barn shall wed the Brakes," and that marriage, in turn, depends upon the maturation—a change of head and heart—of the characters involved. Kennedy suggests that this reading may be extended to national political and social matters through the careful planting of characters who represent different stages of life as well as apparently offhanded references to some of the important political matters of the day.

Kennedy's belief in the evolution of the state emerges clearly in the novel at two points in particular: The first relates the appearance and demeanor of servants at the dinner that celebrates conclusion of the lawsuit. In that passage, Kennedy writes that "A bevy of domestics, in every stage of training, attended upon the table, presenting *a lively type of the progress of civilization, of the march of intellect*" (Kennedy 326–327, italics added). While this passage continues with a lengthy discussion of how the servants are dressed, the later passage, in which Mark Littleton discusses slavery, makes clear that the progression is not simply one of apparel nor is it limited to African Americans. Kennedy, in this later passage speaking through Mark, holds that slavery "is a transition state in which we see [African Americans] . . . ," a position that he regards as proven by history to be "inevitably a temporary phase of human condition." Frank, who seems also to speak for Kennedy in this passage, holds that slavery is "theoretically and morally wrong" and he believes that *in time*, society will find a way of emancipating slaves without injustice or inhumanity to freedmen or the rest of society (453–456). Clearly, then, *Swallow Barn* expresses Kennedy's belief in the perfection of society over time. The future, then, will be better than the past and present.

While such a view seemed quite reasonable to Kennedy, he saw by the late 1820s that the progress he expected was not occurring smoothly on the national—or perhaps even the state—level. Relatively free from external threats since the end of the War of 1812, Americans had attempted to address internal issues. One such issue was the authority of the Federal government, particularly with respect to the generation and use of revenue. Certainly canals and roads (and later, railroads) would benefit many Americans in the long term, but did the Federal government have authority to spend money on such improvements? Kennedy, like John Quincy Adams and Henry Clay, believed that the authority was implicit in the general welfare clause of the Constitution, but Andrew Jackson, who was elected President at about the time when Kennedy began writing *Swallow Barn*, took another view. He did not question the efficacy of Federal funding for improvements, but he believed that a Constitutional amendment was necessary to make this support legal. Kennedy, an experienced lawyer and state legislator, recognized the problems and delays that could arise as amendments were written and debated in legislatures and interpreted in courts; indeed, he dramatized some of the foibles of this process by relat-

20   *Will the Circle be Unbroken?*

ing in detail the writing of the agreement concerning Apple-pie Branch in
Swallow Barn (240–247). Moreover, he knew all too well that the electorate sometimes seemed to be motivated by narrow self-interest. After all,
he had lost his seat in the Maryland Assembly because of his support for a
canal between western Maryland and Washington, D.C. His Baltimore
constituents had believed that this proposed canal would benefit the development of Washington and Alexandria as trading centers at the expense of
their own city.

To examine minutely Kennedy's views on the issues of the late 1820s is
beyond the scope of this work; one passage from his journal serves to indicate the frustration that the author felt, not so much with the course of government, but with the way in which the issues were addressed. In late
September 1830, Kennedy recorded that he had taken up *Swallow Barn*
"with the purpose of writing the last impression for the press."[2] Two sentences later, after a passing reference to one of his political essays, his frustration emerged:

> The election contest is now going on but I take no part in it. I am disgusted
> with the glaring meannesses of the time and the perpetual struggle to cre-
> ate distinctions between the higher and lower orders of the people. The
> struggle at present is to give influence and power to the mob at the sacri-
> fice of the peace of society and the most valuable principles of the
> Constitution. South Carolina threatens disunion, and they proceed almost
> to the verge of Treason. I would put down this spirit of rebellion if need
> be with the bayonet.
>
> Jackson's Maysville message, respecting the *veto* is the most absurd state
> paper I ever read, and will consign him to oblivion. His party is execrable.
> While on the other hand Clay is electioneering among the people for the
> presidency in every way calculated to excite disgust. My objections to the
> veto being known, an overture was made to me from the Clay party here
> to bring me out for the legislature and afterwards for Congress upon con-
> dition that I would vote for Clay but with no other pledge. This I declined
> as I am not willing to be made a fool of by either party. Clay's tariff prin-
> ciples I like, but my objections to him are too deep from other considera-
> tions to allow me to become his advocate although I do not say that I may
> not in the choice of evils be compelled to vote for him against the anti-tar-
> iff candidate for the Presidency (Kennedy Journal, italics in original).

Kennedy objects, in this passage, to the meanness of the times—the narrow self-interest of South Carolinians in opposing the tariff of 1828 as well
as the absurdity of Jackson's thinking on the veto of the Maysville road and
the ambition of Henry Clay to be President. Kennedy's journals suggest
repeatedly that he enjoyed the process of political debate and expected all
parties to accept the outcome of legislative process. Following this thinking, Jackson should have accepted the Maysville Road act, and the South
Carolinians should have accepted the tariff of 1828 as representing the outcome the mature debate focused on the interests of the nation as a whole.

Generational Progress in Swallow Barn   *21*

Although in 1830 South Carolina had not yet nullified the tariff, it was already clear that the election of which Kennedy spoke would place advocates of nullification in power in the state. By the same token, Jackson's use of the veto also struck some Americans—and, very likely, John Pendleton Kennedy—as a refusal to accept the outcome of the deliberative and legislative process. A similar refusal occurs in *Swallow Barn,* when Isaac Tracy insists upon returning to the courts with the same issue over a fifty-year period. Particularly when Tracy wishes to reopen the matter after gaining title to the land, it seems that he, like Jackson and the Nullifiers, is more concerned with specific outcomes than with the integrity of the process. In a dynamic, maturing nation, such narrowness could prove a serious problem. Consequently, Kennedy believed that when contending parties did not accept the outcome of an established process, unusual measures, such as the proposed use of force in South Carolina or the manipulated arbitration in *Swallow Barn,* might be necessary to bring about a resolution.

Kennedy's objection to Clay, as indicated in his journal, was not a matter of disagreement on policy or principle; on the contrary, it had to do with what Kennedy regarded as Clay's unstatesmanlike efforts to secure the presidency for himself. That is, Kennedy was objecting to Clay as a man who was misusing the political process—which had been designed to serve the polity—to serve his own interests. In this respect, Clay resembles Isaac Tracy, who embroils his neighbors in an extended progression of lawsuits in his effort to get control of a piece of swampy land—and then, when he has control of the land, wishes to reopen the matter to ensure that the record reflects what he believes it should reflect.

Kennedy had supported Andrew Jackson for President in 1828, but he objected to Jackson's veto of the Maysville Road bill. The latter is of particular interest with respect to *Swallow Barn* because Jackson's veto turned on a highly technical reading of the Constitution, just as Philly Wart's resolution of the lawsuit turns on an obscure point of law. The bill provided for the Federal government to support building of a segment of the interstate National Road even though that segment lay entirely within the boundaries of Kentucky. The National Road ran westward from Baltimore into Kentucky, and any extension of it would facilitate travel and trade at least in Maryland, Virginia, and Kentucky. Nevertheless, Jackson declared the Maysville extension to be an intrastate improvement. By calling the veto absurd, Kennedy suggested that his displeasure was with the narrow, abstract basis on which the veto rested as much as with its practical effect; that is, a narrow definition of *interstate,* in this instance, must have struck Kennedy as a semantic quibble that ignored the obvious pragmatic benefits of the road. For him, this was inadequate as a foundation for a decision of great practical importance.

In *Swallow Barn,* a similarly narrow distinction—whether the destruction of a dam was sudden or gradual—provides the basis for resolution of

22   Will the Circle be Unbroken?

the Apple-pie Branch matter. As in the case of the Maysville Road, the
results of an action are set aside to allow for consideration of issues that
have no real bearing on the outcomes. The dam has been destroyed; the
cause of the destruction has no bearing on whether the sale was only for a
specific purpose. Philly Wart's explanation of the legal principle involved
reflects the narrow, highly technical basis on which the issue is resolved:

> '[The] two contiguous estates were divided by the water-line or margin of
> the mill-dam on the side of The Brakes . . . [and] where a river holding the
> relation which this mill-dam occupied between these two estates, changes
> its course by slow and invisible mutations, so as to leave new land where
> formerly was water, then he to whose territory the accretions may be made
> in such wise, shall hold them as the gain or increment of his original stock.
> But if the river change its course by some forcible impulse of nature, as by
> violent floods, or the like, then shall he who suffers loss by such vicissi-
> tude, be indemnified by the possession of the derelict channel' (Kennedy
> 203–204).

This serves Philly's purpose of placing the land in Isaac's possession. It
overlooks that neither party has gained or lost anything of consequence
because neither has yet put the disputed tract to any productive use. To
resolve the matter, then, Wart and Swansdown must discover how the
course of the branch changed. As they do so, Kennedy provides some of
the comedy of the work, depicting the two lawyers plunging around in the
muck of a snake-infested swamp as they seek relevant evidence on this
point. (Of course, Wart's real intent seems to be to place Swansdown, who
is punctilious about his appearance and fearful of snakes, in a setting that
he will be eager to leave.) The most sympathetic characters in the work,
Ned Hazard and Frank Meriwether, are not really concerned with the
destruction of the dam; what matters to them is that, as Frank puts it, the
matter be disposed of in a way that precludes Tracy's reopening of the suit.
As Frank observes, "It is the interest of the commonwealth that there
should be an end of strife'" (Kennedy 187). Meriwether does not specify
how the end of conflict serves the interests of the commonwealth, but such
a protracted dispute must have distracted the principals from management
of their farms. Given the repeated appeals, the cost to the principals must
have been significant. On one level, then, the settlement of the matter
allows the parties to return to their regular business without fear of further
frivolous interruption or expense.

On another level, Frank indicates that the resolution of the matter serves
the broader community—the commonwealth. This is neither conflation
nor equation of the good of the individual with that of the state. While
Kennedy does not make the point explicitly, Frank's statement depends
upon an organic view of society—one of the foundations of the familial
paradigm. In the social organism, each member has a divinely appointed
function to fulfill, and any man-made disruption, such as the lawsuit, dis-

Generational Progress in Swallow Barn 23

tracts people from their functions. When the men involved are among the leading men of their community, as Frank and Isaac are, their distraction may have an effect through the entire community. Frank's recognition of this is entirely consistent with his place as a popular magistrate: As a good ruler-father, he recognizes and acts upon the interests of the community, even though he stands to lose some acreage in the process and the benefits to him are unspecified. Kennedy, during the writing of *Swallow Barn,* indicated in his journal that he was frustrated that people had perverted the political process so that it no longer served the real interests of people but was focused upon the interpretation of minutiae to serve the interests of a few prominent men. Consequently, it produced not commonweal, but strife. While the novel is not necessarily a direct indictment of the political climate of the times, it surely embodies some of Kennedy's frustration as well as his persistent belief that what he regarded as the meanness of the age would eventually pass—if political leaders understood their role in the national organism.

That Kennedy meant to use *Swallow Barn* to comment on the times—and that some readers took it as such commentary—is clear enough. Kennedy's choice as publisher, and the eventual publisher of the work, was Carey and Lea, successor to Mathew Carey. During the 1820's, Matthew Carey had established a reputation as a political maverick of sorts, a conservative who was willing to champion the cause of higher wages for workers (Schlesinger 131). In addition to gaining a reputation for social concern, Carey was among the earliest publishers to develop a national perspective: Based in Philadelphia, he had been a pioneer in developing the South Atlantic, Pennsylvania, and Ohio valley markets for the book trade (Charvat 78), and his firm had hardly become the most powerful publishing house in the United States by misjudging how readers would respond to a particular work. Carey recognized, as the publisher of the first successful American magazine, *American Museum,* that political sentiment would be a factor in reading selections, and he was well aware of the political overtones in *Swallow Barn.* Henry Carey, his son, very likely spoke for his aging father as well as himself when he praised *Swallow Barn* as a work that might overcome the animosity that some saw developing between North and South. He wrote to Kennedy that "If [*Swallow Barn*] should produce such a feeling as you desire you will have rendered a great service to the nation. Each portion of the Union looks with a feeling of dislike towards the other, when it requires only to know them better to see admirable qualities in every portion. The Yankee dislikes the Virginian and the Virginian despises the Yankee, when a stranger would find good reason to admire both" (Carey).

Just what feeling Kennedy desired to produce has been lost, but it is evident that he wished his novel to be read in the context of the political issues of the times. The work is laden with references to specific political and social matters, particularly in the earlier chapters through which the author establishes a relationship with readers and provides hints on how the work should be read. Mark Littleton visits Swallow Barn in the first place because he believes that his ignorance of Virginia is causing him to fall into prejudice against Southerners as less sophisticated and modern than Northerners; in doing so, he is acting against the ignorance of which Carey wrote. Similarly, Frank's wife, Lucretia, is not merely "a pattern of industry" or a notable housewife; instead of using these stock phrases to characterize her, Kennedy referred to national politics by calling her "the very priestess of the American system, for, with her, the protection of manufactures is even more of a passion than a principle" (Kennedy 39). Frank is characterized as "distempered with politics"—apparently as was the author who created him—but also convinced that "there [would] always be men enough in Virginia willing to serve the people" in public office. Like Kennedy, Frank opposed Adams in the 1828 campaign. He also is concerned about the manners of large cities and clings to agrarian ideals (Kennedy 32, 36).

In addition, Kennedy presents readers "Traces of the Feudal System," a chapter in which he discusses with considerable candor the economy and society of Virginia, pointing out in the process that Frank wonders whether people might be better off without such technological advances as steamboats—a question that Kennedy, who was much concerned with improving transportation, probably never considered seriously. Frank's rationale for this opposition to progress in transportation is that "it strikes deeper at the supremacy of the states than most persons are willing to allow. This annihilation of space . . . is not to be desired" (72–73). That is, transportation would make for easier exchange of goods and ideas, and the states would lose their claims to distinctiveness. This, in turn, might weaken the parts of the organism unable to perform their distinctive and necessary functions. Thus, Frank views technological progress as threatening the basis of society. Still, he recognizes that steamboats are a present reality and not likely to pass from the scene.

Finally, scattered throughout the work are allusions to the characters' and their ancestors' experiences in the Revolutionary War as well as discussion of the proper division of powers between state and federal government. These scattered references serve as reminders of the national political climate throughout the novel, particularly at the beginning and at the end—points at which readers might be particularly interested in the relationship between the novel and their own common-sense reality. The scattered references, however, do not necessarily fit together in any coherent way; many of them are simply one-line allusions. Kennedy did not offer solutions to controversies, although his journals indicate that he had strong views on the direction in which they should be resolved. Still, he had confidence that tensions would ease and problems would be resolved over time in keeping with his view that civilization was tending toward some desir-

Generational Progress in Swallow Barn   25

able end through constant improvement. In *Swallow Barn,* then, Kennedy's deployment of the familial paradigm is not simply a matter of how a dominant patriarchal figure and subordinate elements of society should relate to each other. Rather than representing the degeneration that the Revolutionaries had expected to occur in the organic community, Kennedy indicated that over time, generations would succeed each other, and within families—or nations—the stages of the life course would bring about gradual improvement, no matter how shortsighted the present leadership (or other available candidates) might seem.

Kennedy's confidence in this process of generational maturation shows up in his presentation of some of the principal characters. That is, by showing members of families at various stages in their life courses, Kennedy could show that each generation was able to bring about some improvement over its predecessor. This becomes clear when we consider the men of the Hazard-Meriwether family, Frank Meriwether, the generation currently holding power while lamenting the passage of the past; Ned Hazard, the generation rising to power; and Rip Meriwether, the generation that will presumably follow Ned's in leading the family and community.

While much of the story in *Swallow Barn* revolves around Ned Hazard, the head of the household and present ruler-father is, in fact, Frank Meriwether, husband of Ned's sister, Lucretia Hazard Meriwether. Frank came into possession of Swallow Barn (which previously belonged to Ned and Lucretia's father) by virtue of "having married Lucretia . . . and lifted some gentlemanlike encumbrances which had been sleeping for years upon the domain," which lay adjacent to his own land holdings (Kennedy 27). While much of the introduction of Frank, as we shall see, tends toward William R. Taylor's notion of the cavalier, it is clear that he has some of the business acumen associated with the Yankee figure. After all, it is he who takes the lead in setting up a sham arbitration to free himself from Isaac Tracy's lawsuits, and he has lifted encumbrances on Swallow Barn that Walter Hazard, Lucretia's father, could not remove. That is, Frank, the present generation in power, is capable of doing things that were not possible for its predecessors of Walter Hazard's generation.

Kennedy's introductory description of Frank sets up a comparison with Ned and Rip. Consequently, it rewards careful attention. The patriarch is a country gentleman about forty-five years old, apparently a successful planter. He is a cheerful and comfortable man with considerable interest in appearances:

> It is pleasant to see him when he is going to ride to the Court House on business occasions. He is then apt to make his appearance in a coat of blue broadcloth, astonishingly glossy, and with an unusual amount of plaited ruffle strutting through the folds of a Marseilles waistcoat. A worshipful finish is given to this costume by a large straw hat, lined with green silk. There is a magisterial fulness in his garments which betokens condition in

26   *Will the Circle be Unbroken?*

> the world, and a heavy bunch of seals, suspended by a chain of gold, jingles as he moves, pronouncing him a man of superfluities (Kennedy 31).

His magisterial public appearance corresponds with his position in the community: He represents the present generation in the prime of life, the generation that controls power and sets the course of the community.

Frank has settled opinions on a host of issues and is in that sense well prepared to set a direction, but he has not sought a position in government—a fact that "is considered rather extraordinary" although Kennedy never reveals *who* considers it extraordinary (32).[3] The reference here to what Frank has *not* done serves to call readers' attention to the larger world in which the novel is set. After a visit to Washington, Frank acquired a distaste for politics; moreover, he believes that no man should seek or decline public office. That is, a gentleman should not seek the power of office, but he is obligated to accept it when his neighbors offer it. Still, he expresses his opinions freely to all of his visitors (Kennedy 32, 34). Here again, the description is suggestive: There is no indication that the views so strongly expressed within the walls of Swallow Barn directly relate to what Meriwether does as a Justice of the Peace or voter. The real business of politics and administration is thus isolated from discourse about issues. Dining table debate is one thing; governing is quite another. In a sense, then, Kennedy indicates through this "very model of landed gentlemen" that the political process has partially broken down among the members of the generation who currently hold power, even as he describes the character who will bring the Apple-pie Branch issue a step closer to final resolution. In addition, Frank is provincial: he has never visited the North and seldom traveled outside of Virginia. His travels outside of his own county appear to be limited to winter visits to Richmond. He considers city people "hollow-hearted and insincere, and wanting in that substantial intelligence and virtue, which he affirms to be characteristic of the country" (Kennedy 34, 35). He suffers from an ignorance similar to that which Henry Carey decried in his 1832 letter to Kennedy and which Mark is traveling (and Ned has traveled) to overcome. This ignorance, however, must be distinguished from hatred; Kennedy, moving among relatives and business associates in the genteel circles of Philadelphia and Virginia and recognized as a visitor in both may not have seen much sectional animosity. He would have seen—and would see again—sectional ignorance: One example of this came from Henry Carey, who would, in July 1832, ask Kennedy to provide him information concerning the prices and living conditions of slaves in seven Southern states.

Ned Hazard invites Mark Littleton's visit to Swallow Barn, thereby showing an interest in intersectional relations that Frank sees as diminishing the sectional differences that increase the strength of the national organism. Thus less provincial than his brother-in-law, Ned is about thirty-three, and Kennedy gives him many of the appurtenances of a carefree

Generational Progress in Swallow Barn 27

young cavalier. He describes Ned's attire in detail, as he does Frank's, and Ned's evident interest in his appearance clearly connects the young man with his brother-in-law, the master of Swallow Barn. When ready for a morning ride, he wears "an olive frock, black stock, and yellow waistcoat, with a German forage-cap of light cloth, having a frontlet of polished leather, rather conceitedly drawn over his dark, laughing eye. This headgear gives a picturesque effect to his person, and suits well with his weatherbeaten cheek as it communicates a certain reckless expression that agrees with his character" (Kennedy 51).

Ned's apparel, then, is as fine as Frank's, but the two men create different impressions with their attire. These impressions are appropriate to the men's different stages in life. While Frank is magisterial, Ned is (when readers first encounter him) rakish. Like Frank, Ned is tall and faultless in appearance, and both men are shown to possess both firmness and flexibility in their dealings with Isaac Tracy. Still, Ned is not Frank: Twelve years younger and still single, he is better traveled and less provincial, and he has a sense of humor (Taylor 130). Unlike Frank, Ned expresses few political opinions, and his position in the community and household is based on his ability to move in a range of social circles rather than his possession of a magisterial demeanor. As we have observed, however, he has become "somewhat indispensable" to Frank in the operation of Swallow Barn, learning, perhaps, what his father was not able to teach him about financial management of a plantation. Thus he will become a better planter than his father, and he may prove a better community leader than Frank because he is better traveled. He has also maintained contact with his New York cousin, Mark Littleton, so it appears that he will be far less provincial than his brother-in-law.

This stylish young man is on his way to becoming a man of social stature similar to Frank, but with distinct differences. Kennedy emphasizes this by requiring Ned to wear less striking clothing and take on a more serious mien in order to win the hand of Bel Tracy. He passes through the five degrees of love, as Bel's cousin Harvey Riggs puts it, and the process through which he becomes her liege man involves study and conversation that takes into account her interests instead of remaining focused on his own (Kennedy 422, 396). By becoming more serious and marrying Bel, Ned enhances his status: In his last appearance, when he has taken up residence with his new bride at The Brakes, he has passed into a new stage of life. As a result, he is able to take control of matters when Isaac wishes to renew the lawsuit (Kennedy 506). Earlier in the work, Isaac refused to acknowledge Ned as an interested party, but at the end he takes pause from Ned's statement and recognizes, if reluctantly, that the matter of Apple-pie Branch is settled. In the process, he recognizes Ned's new stature in the community. Thus, Ned's progress toward full maturity suggests that he will, in time, match and may exceed Frank Meriwether as a planter and community leader.

To further underscore this progression, Kennedy also devotes considerable attention to Frank's adolescent son, Rip, and that attention cannot be justified by Rip's marginal role in the plot. It seems reasonable, however, as part of Kennedy's representation of a progression of generations. Rip's disheveled appearance stands in contrast to the fastidious attire of his father and his Uncle Ned. Although the boy seems to lack sartorial sensibility, his attire is utilitarian: His shirt serves as a pocket for food or pebbles, and his hat serves as a drinking vessel, a basket, a ball, a storage bin, and a gauntlet (Kennedy 41). His "nondescript skull cap" like the rest of his attire, is as appropriate for Rip as Frank's blue broadcloth coat and Marseilles waistcoat and Ned's olive frock and yellow waistcoat are for their respective wearers: Rip has not yet developed a clearly defined personal style that can be reflected in his dress. Young enough that he has no specific, responsible role in the family or community, his attire allows him to experiment with many roles. His apparent stylelessness is the most appropriate style for him.

Rip is impish, but his impishness seems to be a quality of the unformed character—moreover, his Uncle Ned, as a schoolboy, was no better (Kennedy 55–59). Kennedy describes in some detail some of the more notable foibles of Ned's academic career, and there appears to be no reason for him to do so until we realize that this detail makes possible further comparison between Ned and his nephew. Moreover, the comparison allows readers to conclude that Ned was once what Rip is in the present of the novel, and Rip eventually will become what Ned is, just as Ned will become what Frank is.

Rip's education appears to consist chiefly of accompanying the men on several occasions during the novel; this constitutes an important part of his preparation for the role that he will eventually occupy as a planter with his own plantation, family, and slaves. Moreover, Kennedy uses these occasions to set up other parallels between Rip and the older men. When Mark and Ned go fishing, Rip goes as well, accompanied by a slave child (Kennedy 106–107). The relationship between these two boys parallels the relationship between Frank and Carey, the African American stablemaster of Swallow Barn (Kennedy 37). Rip also accompanies the men of Swallow Barn when they go to the mill tract to pursue the legal case, and he is present with the adults before the dinner celebrating the end of the lawsuit (Kennedy 197, 317–318). Again, the comparability of Frank, Ned, and Rip is too strongly developed to be the result of chance. It is a part of Kennedy's design for the work. The plot could progress smoothly if Rip were not a part of the novel; consequently, his presence and limited role suggest that Kennedy wanted readers to be mindful of generational progression. To the extent that Kennedy linked Swallow Barn to contemporary social and political issues, the generational progression relates to the idea of national progress. The generation of the Founding Fathers was passing, as the deaths of Thomas Jefferson and John Adams in 1826 had made clear. New

Generational Progress in Swallow Barn   29

generations of leaders would have different aptitudes and shortcomings that related to the times in which they lived.

A similar pattern of generational comparison appears among the women: Lucretia Meriwether, Bel Hazard, Prudence Meriwether, and the Meriwether daughters, Lucy and Victorine. It is not necessary to explore these comparisons in detail; in most respects, they are very similar to those that Kennedy sets up among the central male figures in the novel. The most significant difference is that the young women, Victorine and Lucy, have the option of becoming wives like their mother or becoming spinsters such as Prudence and Catharine Tracy. What seems likely is that they will follow the path of their mother, Lucretia, and Bel. Kathryn Seidel has shown that Bel Tracy, in the course of the novel, passes through a period between the girlhood of Victorine and Lucy and the maturity of Lucretia Meriwether. As Seidel explains, "A young girl had few tasks other than to be obedient, to ride, to sew, and perhaps to learn reading and writing. . . . [She] was to stay home until such time as a suitable . . . marriage could be arranged for her. . . . After marriage, a girl was expected to become a hard-working matron who was supervisor of the plantation, nurse, and mother" (5–6).

While Seidel does not explicitly refer to Lucretia Meriwether in her discussion of how Bel Tracy establishes the model for the belle figure, the roles of supervisor, nurse, and mother fit perfectly the mistress of Swallow Barn. Through most of the novel, Bel, like Ned, appears to have little work to occupy her time, although Lucretia's example indicates that this will change when she marries. At twenty-three, Bel is older than Lucy and Victorine by almost a decade, and she has passed eighteen, the age at which young women were generally recognized as having reached their majority (Smith 243). As Seidel put it in her thorough summary of Bel's character, she

> "is motherless and has a father who dotes on her. She is exuberant, a bit vain, and rather naive. She is talented as a horsewoman and skilled in music. Proud of her aristocratic heritage, she has one flaw, 'a vein of romance in her composition'; she desires not just a man, but a 'gallant cavalier,' perhaps from the novels of Sir Walter Scott. . . . She is finally rescued from her fantasies by a stalwart lad, and the novel ends with their marriage" (Seidel 3–4).

This rescue silences Bel; after she agrees to marry Ned, she never makes another appearance in the novel. But the example of Lucretia indicates that Bel Tracy Hazard will probably become a notable plantation mistress, a priestess of the American System, and the moral center of her family.

The peace of the community is restored at the end of *Swallow Barn* because the boundary dispute is resolved. Frank has accomplished what his father-in-law could not, and the ties that unify the community have been strengthened with Ned's marriage to Bel. The legal wrangling has been resolved and an obstacle to the progress of all parties has been removed. But this *locus amoenis* is not yet perfected. The national issues to which Kennedy refers in the novel, however, remain to be resolved. Ned's generation and Rip's will have their own problems to settle. Still, the novel ends on a positive note, a clear indication that Frank's generation, with help from Ned's, has moved the community forward from the circumstances that Frank assumed when he came of age. As later works would suggest, however, this could occur only when leaders were faithful to their duties and their subordinates. The good-natured affability of Frank Meriwether could keep his parochialism from becoming a problem so long as he remained at Swallow Barn. Through such upheavals as the Nullification Crisis and the Bank War, some Americans would come to question whether Jackson in the White House was as out of place and far more dangerous than Frank might have been in political life.

In *Swallow Barn*, Kennedy offered no solutions to specific social or political problems. The problems confronting the nation were numerous and ill-defined, and the author was himself frustrated with the political leaders who were seeking to address those problems. As of the publication of the novel in 1832, issues that would be crises later had not yet emerged. Nothing had happened to promote strong sectional or ideological alignments, and Kennedy could still hope that in time, a new generation of leaders would resolve the issues that so confounded the leaders of the present, just as Frank has solved problems that had beset his predecessor as master of Swallow Barn. The novel, then, represents a baseline against which other novels of the period may be read and understandings of sectional tension may be traced. It also presents an optimistic note that would not sound so clearly for some time.

CHAPTER THREE

"An Ardent Desire":
Kentuckian in New-York

William A. Caruthers' first novel, *Kentuckian in New-York* (1834–35), reflects a higher level of sectional tension than Kennedy's *Swallow Barn*—and indeed, than all of the other works in this study except Tucker's *The Partisan Leader*. Between the publications of *Swallow Barn* and *Kentuckian in New-York*, the Nullification Crisis of 1832–33 had made the threat of disunion seem more menacing than ever before and prompted some people to perceive sectional alignments more strongly than they had in the past. Like many moderates, Caruthers believed—perhaps erroneously—that the crisis was a conflict between the North and South, and that the middle states of Virginia and Maryland could assist in drawing the Northern and Southern states together. Opposing interests would not interfere with a stronger union if all of the states simply recognized their interdependencies. In other words, he saw the states as bound by the kinds of interdependencies that characterized relationships in the familial paradigm. To make these points in *Kentuckian,* Caruthers used courtship and marriage to represent the process of Union: As three wealthy young men (two South Carolinians and a Virginian) travel outside of their native regions, they lose prejudices and find love and marriage. On their journeys, they must put aside their preconceptions and put contention behind them. They do not do this out of any rational expectation of gain but rather from an almost mystical sense of attraction and affection.

The seriousness and resolution of the Nullification Crisis surpassed the explanatory and prescriptive force of the familial paradigm. That paradigm was founded on an organic model of society, one in which each part of the whole relied upon and contributed to each other part. The tariff issue, however, suggested that such a model was inadequate because the measures necessary to the economic growth of the North appeared harmful, at least in the short term, to the South. The familial paradigm also relied upon the faithfulness of a ruler-father who could recognize and coordinate the inter-

32   *Will the Circle be Unbroken?*

ests of subordinates, thereby reminding them of their mutual dependency and encouraging a public spirit that served all. But Andrew Jackson, threatening to send Federal troops to South Carolina to enforce compliance, had, in effect, threatened to pit the states against each other. Moreover, the compromise developed by Henry Clay and John C. Calhoun to end the crisis was not a model of interdependency and public spirit recognized. There was in the crisis no leader who could be celebrated as a strong, wise ruler-father.

As we have seen, *Swallow Barn* was written before strong sectional alignments had developed among the states. Before the Nullification Crisis peaked in December 1832, the besetting problem of the Union (at least in the view of men like John Pendleton Kennedy) was not necessarily one of sectional discord but of national maturation; no issue, including the controversy over the Missouri Compromise of 1820, had simultaneously produced strong sectional alliances and confrontation between branches and levels of government. Despite brief threats, such as the Hartford Convention, the Union had seemed durable, and putting differences to rest permanently seemed to depend upon maturation, toleration, and the recognition of common interests (Feller 7–13). This was part of a positive, natural, and irresistible process; people could lament the loss of the past and seek to preserve its more attractive elements, but ultimately they would accept change with good will. A formulation of this sort was possible in a period when political parties and sectional alliances were weak, and it could be expressed by emphasizing the generational progression implicit in the familial paradigm. Between Kennedy's completion of *Swallow Barn* and the publication of the work, however, differences deteriorated into a genuine threat to the Union.

In the two years separating the publications of *Swallow Barn* and *The Kentuckian in New-York*, the nation faced what some historians regard as the most important constitutional crisis arising between the ratification of the Constitution and Bill of Rights and the Civil War: the Nullification Crisis of 1832–33 (Ellis 12). The issue was resolved through compromise, but it produced new political alliances that seemed strongly sectional and thus very different from the ideological or pragmatic alliances of the past. The evolution of these alliances was frightening: South Carolina passed an ordinance refusing to enforce the Tariff of 1828 and seemed to many Americans to be on the verge of secession. Other Southern states, including Virginia, were not necessarily sympathetic to nullification, but they were strongly opposed to Jackson's threatened use of Federal troops to enforce the tariff. Accordingly, they resolved to assist the South Carolinians in defending themselves if necessary. Jackson's allies in the North—including his Secretary of State, Martin Van Buren of New York—doubted that nullification was constitutional, as did many Virginians, and they had similar doubts about the constitutionality of the President's threats to use force without Congressional approval. The crisis that many saw as threatening

"An Ardent Desire": Kentuckian in New-York

the Union was averted when Jackson's most prominent political opponent, Henry Clay, a Kentuckian born in Virginia, offered a compromise tariff plan that neither side liked but both would accept out of what an act of the Virginia legislature referred to as "an ardent desire to preserve the peace and harmony of our common country" (Ellis 136). It is important to recognize that the emotionalism suggested by "ardent desire" existed also in courtship and marriage: the same language could be used to describe the attraction between man and woman. The legislative act, therefore, spoke not of a reasoned case in support of maintaining the Union, but of a mystical, passionate drive approaching a compulsion to do so.

While political issues such as the tariff and internal improvements could be divisive forces, they were not the only issues dividing the United States in the early 1830s. Daniel Feller has pointed out that Americans of this era were at odds over a host of social and cultural issues, including utopianism, penal and educational reform, religion, and structures of business and labor. They possessed a "sense of possibility [that] inspired optimism and exuberance . . . [but] also imparted an earnest and even terrible urgency. Decision would produce losers as well as winners" (Feller 12). *The Kentuckian in New-York* captures this generalized tension and uses courtship and marriage to suggest that some of the tensions might be resolved by recalling the mystical forces that led to the formation of the Union. The states, by this time, had begun to drift apart, it seemed. Nullification, to some, seemed tantamount to secession. To others, the central government's increasing power seemed divisive.

The Kentuckian in New-York is the work of William A. Caruthers, a Virginian who was married to a Georgian woman and at the time living in New York City. Perhaps the most unusual feature of the novel is that it ends with marriages joining eight characters who represent the North and South (in two marriages), the middle states and the South, and the West and the middle states. *Kentuckian* does not fit established genres; like many travel books in its day, it uses the epistolary form so that characters can reflect upon their surroundings as they travel in unfamiliar territory, but it is also a novel of manners that reports the differences (and similarities) between Northerners and Southerners. In addition, it is a gothic love story in which relationships between the principal male and female characters, like those among the states, are portrayed as being founded on mysterious attractions, dependency, and unflagging persistence in the face of danger, uncertainty, and frustration. The characters' acceptance of these destined relationships leads them to marriage and, presumably, happiness; because the characters represent different sections, the novel celebrates the unification of the states without calling for any sacrifice of state or sectional identity.

The contemporary reviewers of *Kentuckian* did not all recognize this theme in Caruthers' work, perhaps because the intersectional novel was a new type at the time. When *Kentuckian* first appeared, *American Quarterly*

Review, a strongly nationalistic magazine published in Philadelphia, attacked the sectional stereotypes in the work while recognizing that the novel included some fine passages (Davis 124–125). *Waldie's,* another Philadelphia magazine, and the *New-York American* found the work unremarkable, calling attention to weak characterization (Davis 125). There were, however, favorable reviews that acknowledged weaknesses but attributed them to the author's inexperience. The *New York Transcript* praised Caruthers' knowledge of the sections of which he had written as well as his impartial treatment of regional differences, which suggests that the reviewer placed the book in the travel narrative genre. The *New York Times* found the novel clever and praised the Kentuckian's droll remarks (Davis 126–127). *Knickerbocker,* in the most positive review that the work received, praised Caruthers' reflections upon "'prominent American topics'" (quoted in Davis 128). Apparently, reviewers who did not see sectional identity as a danger could praise the novel for representing sectional differences accurately and even-handedly; reviewers who were strongly nationalistic saw danger in calling attention to sectional differences, but they apparently overlooked the marriages that occurred—despite these differences—at the end of the novel.

Modern scholars have had similar problems in dealing with the scope of Caruthers' work. Vernon Parrington was struck by the characters' ability to sense impending conflict over sectional views on the national economy (40–42), although "national economy," in Parrington's usage, appears to mean only slavery. Curtis Carroll Davis saw the work as "an epistolary novel of manners depicting the America of 1832 . . . in a way that won a preponderance of critical approval up and down the Atlantic seaboard" (105) as well as one that was important because the primary male characters represented "an authentic, though not now widely recognized area of the South," Caruthers' native Shenandoah Valley region (113). Jay Hubbell argued that *Kentuckian* was of interest to modern readers because of "Caruthers' contribution to intersectional good will" (498), although he accepted Davis's assertion that "of the four hundred and forty-two pages in the two small volumes of *The Kentuckian,* [only] fifteen are concerned with socio-political issues in general and with the slavery question in particular" (Davis 112). William R. Taylor identified the work as a novel of manners, but he recognized that it transcended simple classification and argued that it pointed out how North, South, and West might benefit from association with each other—obliterating, in the process, sectional identities and taking on a singular national identity (188–190). J. V. Ridgely gave the work only a few lines as a mildly successful sentimental romance, but he believed that the variety of settings and the attack on the abuses of slavery made the work "an early example of the 'intersectional novel'" (44).

All of these readings, contemporary and modern alike, leave out significant portions of the work. In doing so, they accept a narrow definition

"An Ardent Desire": Kentuckian in New-York

of intersectionalism, and that definition leads them—as Davis has done explicitly—to overlook the breadth of Caruthers' concern with problems of sectional identity and national union. If we recognize that the plot revolves around intersectional courtships and marriages, we can see more clearly what the *Knickerbocker* reviewer found praiseworthy—the discussion of a range of American topics of the early 1830s. In such a discussion, strongly individualized characters could prove a liability, distracting readers from consideration of national and regional concerns; the characters would, however, have to be associated with sections. The title of the work, *The Kentuckian in New-York, or The Adventures of Three Southerns*, further suggests that Caruthers meant to deal in types rather than specific individuals. The generic terms *Kentuckian* and *Southerns* invite readers to consider the primary characters as typical and representative of sections. Moreover, the characters represent Virginia, New York, and South Carolina—states that were centers of regional political power.

Consequently, and despite the apparent expectations of reviewers, Caruthers' characters in the work are weakly individualized. The principal male character, Victor Chevillere, is a South Carolinian recently graduated from college. While Victor is, by birth, a Cotton South aristocrat, he has been educated in Virginia and thereby has come in contact with young men of similar class from different regions of the country. Along the way, he has lost most of his sectional prejudices and developed an abhorrence for such prejudices, even when he sees them in close friends. One such friend is the other central male character, Beverley Randolph, Victor's college roommate. Beverley is a Virginian and only slightly less aristocratic than Victor. Unlike Victor, however, he does not seem to have left his native state until after college, and his resulting prejudice against Yankees is sufficient to be a matter of concern to Victor. These two characters carry on much of the narration of the novel through their letters to each other, and there is little practical difference between them. William R. Taylor saw Victor, the South Carolinian, as an archetypal Whig, arguing for retention of sectional identity, nationwide harmony among the sections, personal moderation, and self-control (189). Beverley, in the final analysis, combines Victor's virtues with other admirable characteristics: objectivity, courage, and optimism. Nevertheless, Victor and Beverley are not fully developed characters; as we shall see in other Caruthers heroes, they may be described as "'little more than animated ideals'" (Cowie, quoted in Davis 150). They simply represent their class and states, as do the other aristocratic men in the work, South Carolinian Augustus Lamar and the New Yorkers Hazelhurst (whose sister Isabel marries Augustus Lamar) and Arthur (who is also a college friend of Victor, Augustus, and Beverley).

The women of the novel are also weakly individualized. Frances St. Clair, whom Victor marries, is an aristocratic New York widow, seventeen years old, and, in Victor's words "the most lovely, modest, weeping, melancholy, blue-eyed, fair-haired, and mysterious creature you ever beheld" (190). Her marriage was arranged by her father despite her increasing misgivings concerning the motives of her prospective husband and father, but it was short-lived: Her husband died of accidental poisoning during their wedding banquet, which led her father-in-law to conclude that Frances was a murderess. Consequently, the bereaved man pursues the traumatized young woman, driven by animosity but with no apparent plan for retribution, as she travels to the springs of Virginia in an effort to regain her health. Her journey brings her into contact with people outside of her normal New York social circle (including Victor's mother), just as college has placed the men in contact with social peers from different sections, and like Victor, she has lost many of her sectional prejudices while visiting other sections. Frances seems to be an excellent match for Victor: She is aristocratic, educated, an accomplished musician, profoundly moral, and a good conversationalist—when she is not fainting in fear or shame.

Beverley's intended wife, Virginia Bell Chevillere, is Victor's cousin, educated at the female seminary at Salem, North Carolina (2: 47), so, like Beverley, she has not left her native region. Beverley initially notices that she is "'all that a cousin of my dearest friend should be—lovely, intelligent, and interesting'" (2: 76). He offers readers no further specifics on these characteristics, and his initial appraisal leads to some concern: She seems at first to be less than serious about Beverley (2: 76). Like Ned Hazard in *Swallow Barn*, she is playful and willing to poke fun at the pretensions of her suitor. Perhaps she is simply too carefree—enjoying her life as a belle too openly—because she has not experienced much of life.[1] Nevertheless, she shows herself as a suitable plantation wife when she must nurse Beverley through a case of the fever (2: 6).

All of the principal characters in the novel represent the long-settled states of the Atlantic coast; the Kentuckian of the title, Montgomery Damon, provides a striking contrast and very little more. His role in the plot is minimal. Curtis Carroll Davis, Caruthers' biographer, argues that the Kentuckian drover is neither more nor less than one of the western figures who had been appearing in novels as comic relief since 1802 (118); this makes his commentary on city life a humorous sidebar. Damon's lighthearted presence is a welcome change from the ever-so-earnest Victor and Beverley; moreover, he softens the didacticism of the novel. This diversion undoubtedly appealed to Caruthers' original readers, many of whom probably had found appealing such frontier figures as Davy Crockett.

The story develops as Victor and Augustus travel to New York with Montgomery Damon and Beverley travels to South Carolina. Victor, Augustus, and Beverley are making their journeys to become more familiar with other parts of the country and, by doing so, to lose whatever sectional prejudices they still have. Their journeys, therefore, seem to be the last stage in an education that will place them among the leading men of their com-

"An Ardent Desire": Kentuckian in New-York

munities and states. Their travels, then, are comparable in objective to Ned Hazard's education, although the process by which Caruthers' characters become more cosmopolitan is more self-conscious and purposeful than Ned's semi-chivalric wanderings. Before the South Carolinians are far into the journey, however, Victor meets Frances St. Clair. She is fleeing from a man she considers to be a serious threat to herself and to anyone (such as Victor) who befriends her, the father of her late husband. This leads to her efforts to evade Victor's courtship by fainting, abruptly changing the subject of conversation, or in extreme circumstances, leaving Baltimore and Philadelphia unexpectedly to avoid having to explain her circumstances to him.

The first of Frances's sudden departures occurs in Baltimore, where the travelers pause for a few days on their way northward. Victor escorts her on a walk in the town, and the two pause to admire the recently completed Washington Monument. While Victor praises the monument as a unifying icon in the community and nation, Frances's father-in-law suddenly appears on the scene. Frances declines Victor's offer to confront the older man on her behalf, and the two young people return to their hotel quickly. The next morning, Victor learns that she has left without any leave-taking except a cryptic note.

Irresistibly drawn to Frances, Victor refuses to give up his courtship when he arrives in New York, although by this time he is no longer in close or regular contact with her. The two have connections in the same social circles, and he sees her at parties and outings. Nevertheless, his determination to court her does not entirely overtake his determination to learn about New York; for example, when an epidemic sends many of the gentry scurrying out of the city, including Frances and the Hazelhursts, Victor is sufficiently interested in Northern disease and medicine to remain in town through the duration of the plague.[2] When his efforts to woo Frances conventionally in New York City fail, however, he follows her up the Hudson to her home, where he announces his presence to her by playing a flute outside her window and then introduces himself to her parents. This display of dedication and persistence leads Frances to write a long letter in which she finally explains that her marriage was arranged to resolve a long-standing difference between two families and to consolidate their estates. The death of her husband was the result of careless storage of a corrosive sublimate. Still, she believes that her father-in-law will continue to stalk her until his death or hers, and for her to allow Victor's courtship under the circumstances might endanger the South Carolinian. She asks that they end their relationship, but Victor refuses to do so. In the end, Frances agrees to marry him, influenced in part by the news that Isabel Hazlehurst has agreed to marry Augustus Lamar.

At the same time, Beverley Randolph has been in South Carolina, courting Virginia Bell Chevillere, Victor's cousin and the ward of Victor's mother. Beverley has found Virginia Bell even more attractive than the miniature portrait of her that Victor showed him during college, but she is standoff-ish at first because she is inexperienced. Nevertheless, she nurses Beverley back to health through a bout of what seems to be malaria, and seeing him thus vulnerable—and having a specific role to play in his treatment and recovery—she becomes more receptive to his courtship. Any doubts on her part seem to dissipate when Beverley proves himself even-handed, just, and courageous in dealing with the threat of a slave uprising. Before the Virginian's illness, an African American overseer at Belville, the Chevillere plantation, has unjustly whipped a slave, and the slaves are on the verge of uprising when Beverley returns to the plantation after visiting Savannah. The Virginian stops the uprising by promising to have the matter investigated and justice done. During Beverley's illness, Mrs. Chevillere does investigate, and she has the overseer whipped. The punished overseer retaliates by attempting to burn the buildings where Beverley and the Chevillere women are sleeping, but a loyal slave assists Beverley in saving himself and the women. After this incident, Virginia agrees to marry Beverley, thus setting the stage for Beverley to write Victor a letter in which he discusses the old Virginia (the state) and the young Virginia (Virginia Bell).

In this letter, he reports that he can see from his home that the eastern part of his native state (the Old Virginia) is in decline, with houses dilapidated and fields overgrown. Poor roads keep travelers away and protect the state from becoming the object of outsiders' pity. In the western (and more recently settled) part of the state, however, near the college that he, Victor, and Augustus attended, people are happy and prosperous, enjoying a social order that is more democratic and a population more self-sufficient than their counterparts in the eastern part of the state (the old Virginia). He predicted that a new order, similar to that of the western part of the state, would prevail throughout the state in time—and, of course, he is wedded to this new Virginia through inheritance of land as he is wedded to the young Virginia through marriage ritual. The new order is ushered in at the Randolph home between Christmas and the New Year, when the newlywed Randolphs entertain the newlywed Chevilleres and Lamars. Caruthers did not suggest in detail what the future held for any of the characters, but the robust pleasure of the occasion suggests that the celebration of intersectional bonds is a satisfactory ending.

None of the marriages in the novel, however, can be linked to any character trait of the principals; that is, none of the characters expresses explicit admiration for any particular characteristic of the beloved. On the contrary, the attraction that they feel for each other is immediate, mystical, and based on innate or predestined attraction rather than any evaluation of the beloved's character or suitability as a partner. When Victor first sees Frances in an inn, she is "still so enveloped in her traveling dress and veil as to be but partially seen" ([Caruthers]1: 15), and from the earlier description offered by a boatman, readers realize she is "so enveloped in a large

"*An Ardent Desire*": Kentuckian in New-York

black mantel and traveling hat and veil that but little of her form or features could be seen, except a pair of brilliant blue eyes" (1: 9). Each of the main characters is physically attractive, well-mannered, and morally upright. None of them ever explains, however, or otherwise reveals why they are attracted to each other. The bond is the mystical attraction that strikes at first meeting. These marriages take place for no other reason than to bind the characters together—and the sections that they represent—and to fulfill their destinies—and that of the Union. Before marrying, the characters must recognize their predestined attraction to each other and allow it to overpower any reservations that they feel—but they need not rationalize that attraction. During courtship, it is apparent (as we have seen) that Beverley depends upon Virginia Bell's care to recover his health, and one can easily argue that Frances depends upon Victor in a similar way. In return, Victor and Virginia Bell, who might otherwise be seen as idle young aristocrats, take on specific roles with respect to their beloveds. Except for the obvious parallels in the plot, Caruthers does not emphasize this dependency; he may have regarded it as sufficiently evident to anyone sharing his cultural knowledge. Nevertheless, it is evident that *The Kentuckian in New-York* is not simply about the courtship and marriage of some attractive and genteel young people; Caruthers saw their relationships as a means of reminding readers that the Union—states destined to achieve peace and prosperity together, like his characters—should be celebrated, preserved, and perfected. Were this not the case, he might have simplified his work by eliminating Damon and Augustus, who contribute little to the plot. But these two characters expand the range of relationships and courtship. Augustus's wooing of Isabel is far less exciting than the parallel courtship of Victor and Frances, suggesting that intersectional relationships (with all that term implies) can be quite ordinary and need not always require Victor's dogged persistence. Damon's courtship takes place, for the most part, off of the pages. It exists apparently only so the West and middle states can be brought together and all of the regions thereby united at the end of the work.

Any reading of *The Kentuckian in New-York* is somewhat conjectural because Caruthers' circumstances and views cannot be discovered in detail; the information concerning his life is minimal, and we cannot determine the extent to which national politics occupied his thoughts.[3] His family circumstances are somewhat recoverable, and they may suggest how he may have perceived the states as bound by inexplicable affections and dependencies. His ancestors had come to America early in the eighteenth century and scattered from Georgia to Canada and from the Atlantic to the Mississippi (Davis 1–3), living, in other words, in many of the areas with which his first novel was concerned. His father, William Caruthers, had settled in Rockbridge County, Virginia, where he was a successful farmer and merchant with business interests as far away as Columbus, Ohio (Davis

40   *Will the Circle be Unbroken?*

6–7). Caruthers himself, before writing *Kentuckian*, had grow up in Virginia, completed his medical education in Philadelphia, courted and married his wife in Savannah, and moved to New York City in an attempt to regain solvency. He had taken something from each region, and *The Kentuckian in New-York* suggests that he believed that the nation derived strength from regional diversity. The novel expands the familial paradigm to include courtship in an effort to promote this concept.

The *Kentuckian in New-York* also relies on the organic model of society on which the familial paradigm of Yazawa's formulation rests. This model, which Yazawa has identified as early as the works of John Winthrop and his contemporaries, posited that everyone in society had a divinely predetermined station and role. In the ideal society, all would recognize and accept their roles and would respect the roles of others. In *The Kentuckian in New-York,* the regions also have different identities. The Easterners need Damon's humorous speech to point out their foibles, and the nation needs people like Damon, who have no use for polite society and its trappings, to lead the way into the wilderness. At the same time, Damon needs his friends from the East to introduce him to the culture and pastimes that will follow him into the wilderness in time, such as the theater and city rituals. As much as Damon and Augustus enjoy each other's company, neither will become much like the other, if either does so, his value to the other—and to the community—will be diminished. As we shall see, Caruthers uses Frances to argue as well that differences between sections and sectional loyalties indicate vitality in the nation and need not be considered dangerous so long as they are kept in balance by recognition of mutual dependencies.

Caruthers' travels, wide-ranging though they were, took place in a family network. In 1821, at around the age of nineteen, Caruthers left Lexington to go to Philadelphia and enroll in medical school (Davis 42). This long journey did not carry him far from family, however; his mother's brother, Reverend Archibald Alexander, had served as pastor at the Third Presbyterian Church in Philadelphia for years, and he still returned there regularly from Princeton, New Jersey, to preach and to serve Virginian students at the medical school (Davis 41). While studying in Philadelphia, Caruthers met Louisa Catherine Gibson, a young woman from Savannah, Georgia, and in June 1823, shortly after his graduation from medical school, he traveled to Savannah and married her (Davis 48–49). The couple initially made their home in Lexington, but in the next six years, Caruthers incurred debts of over $6000. Struggling to become solvent, he borrowed money from his brother John, allowed John to pay his bills, and finally authorized John to sell his property to pay off new debts (Davis 50, 80–81). There is no record of how either brother regarded William's dependency, but in 1829, William moved his family to New York City.

After arriving in New York, Caruthers and his family boarded for a time with his Aunt Martha and her husband, Reverend Benjamin Holt Rice.

"An Ardent Desire": Kentuckian in New-York   41

Rice, too, sought to help Caruthers establish solvency, but the young physician earned more respect than income (Davis 83, 87). When his financial situation deteriorated further, he had to call upon his brother-in-law, Richard Turner Gibson, to come to New York and negotiate with creditors on his behalf (Davis 88, 89). By late 1835, the novelist and his family returned to Lexington, and by 1837, they had moved to Savannah, where Caruthers would remain until his death (Davis 196, 279).

By the time he was composing *Kentuckian,* then, William Caruthers had become dependent upon members of his family. As his circumstances had grown more desperate, he had called on them repeatedly for help. While practicing medicine might have been more attractive socially than being a farmer or merchant, it was not necessarily remunerative. When we consider Caruthers' 1829 debt of six thousand dollars in light of the five hundred dollars a year that physicians considered a satisfactory income at that time, the degree of the author's dependency on his family becomes clearer (Davis 87). For Caruthers, then, family had to be indissoluble; vital dependencies among members made permanent the ties among relatives of all degrees. Just as Caruthers' family ties extended throughout the nation, his first novel suggests that he saw similar ties of dependency binding the states in a permanent Union. Again, the organic model of society and the familial paradigm can serve as key to his family relations as well as his perception of the Union.

While a similar perception might come about easily for those who, like Victor, Augustus, and Beverley, travel to gain knowledge and overcome prejudice, Caruthers seems to have believed that improved relations among sections required that the unaligned middle states play a special role. For that reason, the novel begins with Victor, Augustus, and Frances traveling between Harper's Ferry and Baltimore on their way to New York City. It is important to recognize that the journey of the "southerns" to the North begins on a road that does not run north and south but east and west through Virginia and Maryland, two middle states.[4] The first part of their journey allows Caruthers to represent Harper's Ferry and Baltimore and to suggest much about the middle states' role and Caruthers' view of the states and the Union.

While Harper's Ferry is best known today as the setting of John Brown's raid and an important escalation in sectional tension, the events that would promote that notoriety were, at the time when Caruthers was writing, a quarter-century in the future. Nevertheless, the town was not unknown: It lay on an important route from north to south (Fischer and Kelly 61). In addition, it was the location of a Federal armory and sufficiently well known that engravers offered prints of the area. These prints hinted that this area, located at the junction of a river that divided North from South and another that divided East from West, combined the best that the country had to offer. Two 1833 prints, for example, show no signs of the armory, the best known man-made feature and perhaps the most distinctive feature of the area; on the contrary, one shows a decidedly pastoral scene, and the other presents a strongly agrarian view (Conway 1, 3). Harper's Ferry could also be represented as a place where the industrialism of the North coexisted with the agrarianism of the South. As Caruthers describes its appearance in *The Kentuckian in New-York*, "The black bituminous smoke from the hundred smithies of the United States' armory, had just begun to rise above the towering crags that seemed, at this early period, to battle with the vapours which are here sent up in thick volumes from the contest of rocks and rivers beneath" (1: 4).

The bituminous smoke from industry—a feature associated with the North—blends with the natural beauty of the place—a feature associated with the South. If such apparent opposites as nature and industry could be reconciled, the sections, despite their differences, were not irreconcilable. In Virginia—a middle state in Caruthers' formulation—the industrial town of Harper's Ferry and its surrounding area provided evidence that the reconciliation of opposites could occur. Moreover, roads, ferries, and canals met at Harper's Ferry, and they made possible the movement of produce and manufactured goods from one section to another so that all of the states were strengthened.

The middle states' role, however, was not simply to serve as a commercial link, but to aid the spiritual union of the states. This becomes clear when Caruthers' travelers reach Baltimore and Victor and Frances have their first outing together. With an entire city from which to choose, they walk to the Washington Monument. This monument, one of the earliest erected to Washington, was attractive to many visitors to the city in the early 1830s, and a travel author, chiefly concerned with pointing out unique features of various cities, states, and regions might have seized the opportunity to describe the monument and site in minute detail. Caruthers does not do so; instead, he allows Victor to rhapsodize on the significance of the monument:

> 'This is a noble monument to the great and good father of our Republic; and worthy of the high-minded and public-spirited people of Baltimore,' said Chevillere. 'Give me such evidence as this of their veneration for his memory, and none of your new-fangled nonsense about enshrining him in the hearts of his countrymen. Let him be enshrined in the hearts of his countrymen as individuals; but let cities, communities, and states enshrine him in marble. These speak to the eyes; and hundreds, and thousands will stand here, amid these beautiful shades, and think of him with profound veneration, who would never otherwise look into any other kind of history. The effect of such works as these is admirable; not only in showing veneration for the great dead, but also upon the living, in purifying the heart and ennobling its impulses. . . . A few years hence, the far West will be brought to her doors; and she will grow up to be a mighty city. Standing on the middle ground, between the angry sectionists of the North

"An Ardent Desire": Kentuckian in New-York

and South, she will present a haven in which the rivals may meet, and learn to estimate each other's good qualities, and bury or forget those errors which are inseparable from humanity . . .' (54).

The visit to the monument allows Caruthers to comment on the special role that he envisioned the middle states would play in resolving sectional tension. While that role may have fallen to them by virtue of geography, success in it depended upon the character of their people and on their ability to identify and collectively commemorate the heritage common to all of the states—as the people of Baltimore had done by erecting a monument to the immortal Washington. With such neutral zones defined and with reminders of shared values and history in place, diverse—even opposing—forces could coexist in the Union as did nature and industrialization at Harper's Ferry. Similarly, differences among people could be balanced to serve common purposes, such as the construction of a Washington Monument and the veneration of national heroes. That done, these common experiences would provide the basis for a broader sense of community. The middle states would benefit because they would become trade and commercial centers (as well as cultural centers) serving the other states.

While Victor and Frances are visiting the Washington Monument, Sandford, Frances's father-in-law, arrives on the scene. By introducing him here, in this setting, when Victor has just alluded to sectional conflict during his first outing with Frances, Caruthers links the difficulties attending the intersectional relationship between Frances and Victor to the tensions existing between the sections. Sandford, of course, is acting on the mistaken perception that Frances has murdered his son, and Frances's fear weakens her even as it leads her to isolate herself from everyone except her stepfather, who seeks to help her escape from her father-in-law. Before marrying Frances, Victor must overcome the isolation that she has maintained to protect herself against old Sandford, who acts on the basis of misinformation and distrust and is also associated with the greed and secretiveness that William R. Taylor found characteristic of the Yankee figure. The same kind of ill-informed prejudice concerning the sections and their people, when it appears in a letter from Beverley, draws a rebuke from Victor. It is the same ignorant prejudice that led Mark Littleton to Swallow Barn and that Ned overcame through his knight-errantry.

The question, then, is how can the barriers that separate these young people best be removed? A specific process is not necessary; as Caruthers follows two of his four young couples rather closely on their way to intersectional marriages, it becomes clear that these unions are a matter of the people involved acting initially upon indefinable but irresistible and natural attraction. Attraction is one thing; marriage is quite another. Both Victor and Beverley are attracted to their future brides at first sight. That first look reveals only a little, as we have already seen in the case of Victor and Frances. Likewise, Beverley has fallen in love with Virginia Bell after seeing

44   *Will the Circle be Unbroken?*

a miniature long before actually meeting her. And when he meets her, he believes that the miniature was an unsatisfactory likeness (2: 75). These imperfect glimpses, though, are enough to "fully rouse the slumbering energies of a lately emancipated college Quixote" (2: 9), and those energies make it possible for the couple to survive the intense and sometimes threatening experiences that they share: "'brilliant dreams, airy castles, 'hairbreadth 'scapes,' and miraculous deliverances,—cruel fathers, and perverse guardians, and stolen interviews, and lover's vows and tokens'" (2: 10).

Such a glimpse is conspicuously absent during Frances's first encounter with the younger Mr. Sandford, her first husband. Although young Sandford rescues her from serious injury in a riding accident, he gallops away before anyone can thank him, much less get a look at him. When he appears at her boarding school two days later, he makes "only an evanescent impression" because his courtesy arises from selfishness instead of genuine concern (2: 146). He seeks self-consciously to create an impression, and it is clear that he makes one, particularly on the young girls of the school. On the other hand, Frances never feels any emotion toward him; she finds nothing to dislike about him, but she finds no basis for liking him, either, despite his service to her and her family and his attentiveness. The mystical attraction is never present, and in the end, she decides that she cannot marry him and puts aside this decision only when she believes her father to be on his deathbed (2: 156–157, 2: 160–162). Readers learn later that Sandford and his father were all the while engaged in a scheme to gain partial control of a tract of land belonging to Frances's late uncle. Their attempts to construct a basis for the marriage fail, perhaps because they are entirely calculating and centered on the benefits that they will obtain from the marriage rather than the spiritual bond that must unite the partners. That is, they lack the spirit and energy unleashed when a relationship is destined to occur—a spirit and energy that seem closely related to the public spirit that the ideal ruler-father aroused in the traditional familial paradigm (Yazawa 23–26).

The energy arising from the early glimpses must be sufficient to keep the lovers together, even after they have seen each other's vulnerability. It takes only a little time for Victor to see Frances's weakness; in fact, he hears her crying even before he meets her (1: 8), and shortly after he meets her, he learns that she becomes faint even when a group of rude young men complain about their food at an inn. Equally early, however, Victor begins demonstrating his devotion to Frances: He is quick to escort her out of the room when she feels "a deathlike sickness" (1:15). He becomes more curious about what has made her so frail, his curiosity excited by his imagination, and his imagination energized by his first glance at her (1:36–39). Although Frances has accepted misery and melancholia as her lot, Victor is not put off but continues his courtship slowly, despite Frances's protests and the cryptic warnings of her father-in-law.

"An Ardent Desire": Kentuckian in New-York 45

Still, there appears to be no rational explanation for Victor's attraction to Frances. Caruthers, however, allows Augustus Lamar to say a few words on the subject to Victor, thereby underlining the mystery of this relationship: "'Lovers are truly a singular set of mortals—here is a young lady (and a Yankee, too, perhaps) of some dozen hours' acquaintance, and with whom you have never exchanged a dozen words; and yet you are already entrusted with profound secrets, which excite you in the most painful manner'" (1: 39). The relations that lead to permanent commitments, then, are not rational, at least in the early stages. Victor observes that such emotional attachments are deprecated because "it has become too much the custom to treat very young affairs of the heart with contempt" (1:175). Notwithstanding this custom, however, he argues that he has never seen "a couple who married, whether young or old, upon the strength of a first and mutual passion, who were not contented, prosperous, and happy" (1:175). Those who marry on any other basis cannot be truly happy: A happy relationship cannot be based upon calculation (1:176). Moreover, marriages are, ideally, a means of balancing extremes in human character so that the descendants of a particular couple reflect "the grand compromise of nature" (1:176). If this is true of people, the familial paradigm holds it to be true also of states, sections, or parties—any faction, regardless of differences.

Meanwhile, in South Carolina, Beverley becomes ill and Virginia Bell must nurse him back to health. While Caruthers did not represent in detail the course of his illness, Beverley is seriously ill, and in delirium he reveals his feelings for Virginia. Not only is he physically vulnerable enough to suffer a relapse, but he is emotionally vulnerable. Despite seeing him utterly dependent, Virginia continues to nurse him through his initial illness and his relapse, exhibiting the same devotion that Victor shows in remaining with Frances. In taking on the role of nurse, she is transformed from a carefree belle to a woman of substance. Her mother, after all, might have provided the medical care as Lucretia Meriwether would have at Swallow Barn. But Virginia is transformed by the experience, learning that another person, one for whom she cares, depends upon her for his well-being. It can be argued that in this nurturing care, she accepts the role for which she (and in the minds of many of Caruthers' readers, all women) had been born. Accepting this role and not seeking to prolong the intense excitement of bellehood, she can find happiness in marriage and avoid the aimless spinsterhood of a Prudence Meriwether or Catherine Hazard.

So far, then, the partners are drawn together by emotion, not rational calculation. They reflect, in other words, the view of marriage that Jan Lewis has associated with the early nineteenth century and the rejection of eighteenth-century rationalism. Lewis has also pointed out that the shift from reason to emotion was pervasive, emerging early in the nineteenth century as a necessary component of religious experience as well as family life (48). The openness that came with a willingness to acknowledge and display emotion also made possible free expression between partners in marriage, offered relief from external tensions, and allowed the partners to develop their character and personalities (170–172). Still, emotionalism had to be moderated, taking the form of Victor's rather stilted effusion at the Washington Monument as well as the ritualistic nature of the courtships in which partners are introduced by older relatives and friends and relationships progress in slow stages. This ritualistic maneuvering manages the growth of emotion and the maturation of the parties, as we see in the relationship between Virginia Bell and Beverley.

Despite her name, Virginia Bell has attracted little attention from scholars and critics, although she is near the focal point of the novel as Beverley's beloved and Victor's kinswoman. She appears only in Beverley's letters—indicating how impressions of the beloved may change from the initial emotional infatuation. Beverley initially notices that she is "'all that a cousin of my dearest friend should be—lovely, intelligent, and interesting'" (1: 76). He offers no specifics on how she is interesting or how she displays intelligence, and his initial appraisal leads him to express some concern: "'She smiles too innocently, and too calmly, and too openly, and has lost too much of that blushing mood in which she first received me; and I have thought several times that the little arch gipsy was laughing at me'" (1: 76). Because she is enjoying her unstructured life as a belle too openly, Beverley is not sure that she will be a good wife. Nevertheless, she performs the role of a plantation wife when she nurses him through his fever and he becomes first dependent upon and then indebted to her (2: 6). To this point, Beverley has called her Bell; henceforth, he calls her Virginia. He also comments that the nature of his affection for her has changed as he has become more aware of her character—her predestined role and its associated interdependencies—during his illness (2: 7).

Virginia, then, may well epitomize the Southern female myth. That is, she may represent Bel Tracy and Lucretia in a single character. At first, she is, like Bel, playful and something of a tease, but this is simply a matter of having the passion and vigor appropriate for her status as a young, unmarried woman. Unlike Bel, however, Virginia Bell shows distinct signs of becoming a plantation matron—like Lucretia—and every bit as retiring, self-sacrificing, hard-working, and efficient as she can be. If readers had only Victor and Frances on whom to base conclusions, they might conclude that successful marriages came about entirely through some mysterious process and that the parties to those matches had little to do but persevere until any external obstacles were removed. Given Beverley and Virginia Bell, however, it becomes clear that those matches may demand some real, concrete abilities to selflessly attend to the needs of others—in addition to maturity—on the parts of the principals. Otherwise, the very qualities that initially attracted might become unwelcome. Compromise is necessary, and it may be compromise of identity (as it seems to be in Virginia Bell's

"An Ardent Desire": Kentuckian in New-York

willingness to accept and attend to Beverley's dependency on her), but it is also a part of natural maturation that serves the interests of all parties involved.[5] Passion must be complemented with specific abilities; it may motivate and provide a basis for lasting relations, but it is not necessarily sufficient in itself.

While the characters may mature somewhat over the course of the novel, Caruthers never permits readers to lose sight of their sectional identities. Indeed, when he introduces sectionalism as a factor in the relationship between Victor and Frances, he suggests that sectional identity is natural and healthy. Victor, learning that Frances has traveled among the springs of Virginia, asks her to tell him her impressions of the places she has visited. She responds that her illness prevented her from forming any useful response. She can attest to the natural beauty of the springs, and she praises the kindness of the people, but she cannot draw effective comparisons between the springs and her native Hudson River valley. By having her attribute this limitation to illness, Caruthers suggests that sectional differences are not superficial; on the contrary, they are essential and become apparent only to those who are healthy. This implication gains strength when we recognize that Frances's home in New York is in many ways similar to Victor's home in South Carolina: Both are manorial estates in pleasant settings. Both are remote from cities, and both are populated by wealthy white people who are surrounded by servants. Beverley's home, although less grand, also sounds much like these two. Victor's mother, Mrs. Chevillere, reluctantly agrees to move to Beverley's home after he and Virginia are married. In doing so, she agrees to leave her home and native culture behind in the interest of the future. The change in her lifestyle may be minor, but the difference between the South Carolina sandhills and Virginia piedmont is dramatic. Moreover, Mrs. Chevillere perceived the change as a major one, but being healthy, she can recognize and accept differences.

Caruthers leaves it to Beverley to point out subtle differences between sections; that is, the gentleman from the middle state of Virginia, self-consciously anti-Yankee, is the character whose observations lead to a sense of the significant differences among the sections. Beverley sees distinctions between the middle states and Southern states in climate, economic prosperity, and slavery. His observations, coupled with Victor's impressions of New York, offer insight into sectional differences. For example, modern commentators, from Parrington to the present, have concentrated on the discussion of slavery between Victor and Beverley. Suffice it to say that Beverley finds fault with the slave system of South Carolina, where slaveholders remain, for the most part, aloof from their slaves and leave supervision of the workforce to overseers, some of whom are slaves themselves. While Beverley disapproves of slavery in general, he accepts more readily the Virginian system, in which the workforces on plantations are smaller and operate under more direct supervision of the slaveholders.

48   *Will the Circle be Unbroken?*

His critique, then, is similar to the comparison between New York and South Carolina years earlier in Crevecoeur's *Letters of an American Farmer*. In examining this part of the novel, however, the modern commentators have overlooked Victor's references to the servants he sees in New York. He does not specify that these servants are slaves, but they are clearly, black or white, a class apart. From the ease with which Victor's servant, Cato, converses with the Brumleys' coachman in Baltimore, it seems quite reasonable to infer that at least some of the New York servants are black. They differ from those in Virginia and South Carolina in that Victor never represents them in agricultural work. He suggests, however, that they are on relatively close terms with those they serve. This discussion, however, may have been less important to Caruthers' contemporary readers than it is today.

A more telling difference has to do with climate and health. Beverley is struck by the unhealthful climate of eastern South Carolina in summer and reports that it forces the gentry to leave their homes and form temporary settlements in an effort to avoid illness. In doing so, he acknowledges what Caruthers the physician must have regarded as conventional wisdom: The southern climate was less healthful than that of the north (McMillen 11). Still, Victor finds that New York also has plagues and to readers, the plague that Victor observes in New York seems more disruptive and devastating than the one that Beverley survives in South Carolina. Neither Victor nor Beverley can explain the causes of the diseases in the regions they visit, but they can both point to treatment and effects. Arthur, their classmate, is a New York physician, but he seems unable to do much more than wait for the plague to run its course in the patients he treats. Meanwhile, the wealthy can reduce their risk by escaping to the homes of friends outside of the city. In the South, treatment is less professionalized; Beverley is treated by Virginia rather than a physician. Her medical knowledge may not be as extensive as Arthur's; still, Beverley gets well in the end, a testimony, perhaps, to the value of affection over reason in medical treatment. While wealthy white Southerners, like their New York City counterparts, leave their customary homes to avoid illness, their migration is a routine seasonal departure that protects them from foreseeable epidemics, and if they become ill, their families care for them. Neither section, however, can escape epidemic disease.

Despite the evident happiness at the end of the *Kentuckian,* questions remain. What does the future in Virginia hold for Beverley and Virginia Bell? Where will Victor and Frances make their home—in New York, near her parents? In South Carolina, where he owns a plantation? In Virginia, where there may arise a new social order especially congenial to a man of Victor's progressive views? After marriage, how will the intersectional newlyweds deal with whatever differences arise between them as a result of their different experiences and world views? In a nation of people acutely aware of differences, these questions may have rendered Caruthers' opti-

"An Ardent Desire": Kentuckian in New-York

mistic ending somewhat less than satisfactory. But Caruthers' formulation of differences reconciled by recognition of shared dependency and passion requires no further development: So long as that recognition is present, the partners and the regions that they represent can remain together. The Chevilleres, Randolphs, and Lamars have recognized and acted on their attraction, and because that attraction is appropriate in the terms of the novel, they have the basis to resolve amicably whatever differences arise between them. Here again, however, Caruthers had modified the traditional familial paradigm. The problems of the Union, while connected to the relationship between the states and the central government, also were connected to relations among states and regions. Consequently, the traditional paradigm, focused as it was on relations between father-ruler and subordinates, was not entirely adequate to represent the issues of the early 1830s. Caruthers invoked courtship and marriage, which are also family processes, in order to draw on the paradigm that had served for centuries. Moreover, no ruler-father appeared to be available as leaders such as Jackson, Calhoun, and Clay fell short of the standard set by Washington. With no leader to inspire public spirit, the people would have to find it for themselves, in the process calling on persistence as well as shared memories and recognition of interdependency. But tensions would continue, and resolution appeared more difficult.

CHAPTER FOUR

Authority and Affection:
Cavaliers of Virginia

Caruthers' second-published novel, *The Cavaliers of Virginia,* appeared some six months after *The Kentuckian in New-York.* Unlike its precursor, *Cavaliers* is not a direct commentary on sectionalism, but it suggests the error in Louis Rubin's argument that "the literature of the nineteenth-century South is superficial and shallow, designed to appeal to an audience that did not want its own values and its social arrangements held up to critical scrutiny" (Rubin 30). The work can hardly be considered an indictment of specifically Southern values or institutions; on the contrary, it invokes the familial paradigm that had prevailed during the seventeenth century in which the work is set. Still, it uses a historical setting to examine schematically a contemporary issue—the basis for authority and the relationship between leaders and those whom they led—with recognition of the complexity of the matter. To do this, *Cavaliers of Virginia* presents an unflattering portrayal of a governor who closely resembles Andrew Jackson. That portrait resembles the image of the president promoted by anti-Jacksonian publications of the 1830s, attacking his authority and leadership style, issues that related to the president's handling of numerous issues and ultimately related to the distribution of power between states and the central government. Caruthers does not reject the traditional familial paradigm with its view of the faithful leader and affectionate subjects; he uses it implicitly to attack Andrew Jackson as an unacceptable leader.

The writing of *Cavaliers* cannot be dated with precision, but the representation of a royal governor who has significant qualities in common with Jackson suggests that it must have been composed between 1828 and 1834, the years when Jackson's policy and presidential style were becoming clear enough to be controversial. Curtis Carroll Davis argues that *Cavaliers* is about the struggle against three different kinds of oppression: the battle against the tyrannical minority, the battle of a nation against external oppressors, and the battle against people who would claim for themselves

52   *Will the Circle be Unbroken?*

all privileges in society (140). In all of these struggles during the early 1830s, authority and the structure of society were entangled, and in all of the manifestations of these issues, Andrew Jackson was implicated.

The central figures of Caruthers' novel include two characters based (at least loosely) on historical personages from seventeenth-century Virginia—Nathaniel Bacon, the leader of what Caruthers represents as a popular rebellion, and Bacon's adversary, Governor William Berkley. There are also a number of important fictional figures, including the Recluse, a gigantic Puritan soldier who comes to Bacon's aid in moments of crisis; Frank Beverly, Berkley's arrogant nephew; and the aristocratic family of Gideon and Emily Fairfax and their daughter, Virginia. All of these characters have parts to play in all of the struggles that Davis identifies, and kinship is the framework in which their struggles are enacted in the novel. The central conflict, however, is between Governor Berkley and Nathaniel Bacon, and Caruthers devotes roughly equal attention to the two sources of conflict between the two men: Berkley's conduct in office and his conduct with respect to his family. The intertwining of the courtship plot linking Bacon with Virginia Fairfax and the governor's official conduct has led some modern critics of *Cavaliers* to argue that the work is "essentially a romantic fantasy woven about the figure of Nathaniel Bacon, the eponymous leader in 1676 of Bacon's Rebellion . . . a champion of individual liberty [and] . . . a defender of the rights of the Virginia colonists against enemies foreign and domestic" (Ridgely 45). Others have dismissed it as no more than a melodramatic story that takes liberties with historical fact (Hubbell 501). For Davis, the work is "Caruthers' most vivid and thoroughgoing interpretation of the American democratic ideal" (Davis 141). To regard *Cavaliers* as a trivial assembly of Gothic and historical elements, however, is to overlook the novel's relationship to the historical context in which it was written and published.

Because of its historical setting, the novel makes few (if any) explicit references to the events and people of the period in which it was composed; it lacks even the passing references that appear in *Swallow Barn* and *The Kentuckian in New-York*. At the beginning of the work, the people of seventeenth-century Jamestown are preparing to celebrate the anniversary of the Restoration under leadership of their popular governor, Sir William Berkley. A band of Roundheads, however, have plans of their own to disrupt the celebration and forcibly overthrow Berkley. In addition to the threat from the Puritans, a nearby band of Native Americans has begun attacking settlers and travelers in view of the city of Jamestown. Of all of this, Berkley and his inner circle of cavaliers seem unaware, but Nathaniel Bacon, the ward of Gideon Fairfax, is well aware of the dangers. As commander of a militia company, he is a proven fighter against the Native Americans, and he has at his command the military resources to defend the governor when the Puritans strike during the Restoration Ball. When the

Authority and Affection: Cavaliers of Virginia 53

attack comes, Bacon's militia company holds off the mob until other citizens have rallied to the governor's assistance.

While this performance earns Bacon an honorable wound and public recognition, it does not overcome his questionable origins as a five- or six-year-old orphan who arrived mysteriously at Jamestown fifteen years before the time of the novel. Gideon Fairfax, the generous cavalier who took him in, has periodically received funds for Bacon's maintenance from a mysterious source, but no one has been able to discover the young man's pedigree. As a result, he is treated with scorn by Frank Beverly, the governor's nephew and ward. Beverly, with the governor's full support, expects to marry Fairfax's daughter, Virginia, but she and Bacon have fallen in love over years of close association. Gideon Fairfax does not seem inclined to intervene with his daughter on Beverly's behalf and proposes to leave the choice of a husband to Virginia, but he dies after a hunting accident with the matter unsettled. Seeing an opportunity (and perhaps a need) to intervene, the governor tells Virginia's mother that he and Fairfax had agreed that Virginia would marry Frank Beverly, but Mrs. Fairfax refuses to force her daughter to marry anyone. With her consent, Bacon and Virginia plan to marry, but their secret ceremony on a stormy night is disrupted when the mysterious Recluse arrives and announces that the two are children of the same mother—Mrs. Fairfax. She emphatically denies this, but moments afterward, the disruption turns to chaos when Beverly and the governor arrive, having been warned of the wedding plans by a servant. Virginia swoons; Bacon, heartbroken, gallops away into the night.

His wild ride brings him to a camp of Native Americans led by a woman named Weyanokee. She has ties to Bacon because he once rescued her from captivity with another band and placed her for safety in the Fairfax's home. Weyanokee is enamored of Bacon, but the death of one of her kinsmen in a fight against Englishmen has taught her that her culture cannot coexist with that of the English. She hopes to marry Bacon and keep him in her native environment, but as he recovers from his delirium and fatigue, he learns that other bands are beginning raids that will eventually lead them to Jamestown. He rides back to the city in hopes of saving the colony with prompt military action.

When he arrives, he finds that his attempt to marry Virginia has made him *persona non grata* with Governor Berkley and Frank Beverly. More to the point, the governor has thus far refused to take action against the Native Americans, even though they have by now taken prisoner Mrs. Fairfax, his own kinswoman, during a raid on an outlying estate. Under public pressure, he agrees to issue a commission for Bacon and a force of militia to suppress the uprising, and Bacon sets out with his force, expecting that a courier will follow with his commission. Berkley, however, does not sign the commissions; instead, he leads an expedition in pursuit of Bacon. The two forces pursue the Chickahominies up the peninsula

54 *Will the Circle be Unbroken?*

between the York and James Rivers to the site of present-day Richmond, where Bacon launches a successful attack against them before turning to face Berkley. Berkley, on the other hand, has turned back toward Jamestown where other forces loyal to him are gathering. Bacon leaves his forces and sails back toward Jamestown, but boats manned by the governor's followers force his boat aground and capture him. Berkley has Bacon taken to Accomac, across the Chesapeake, where the governor believes the young man can be tried, condemned, and executed without interference from his followers. During the trial, however, Bacon learns that Virginia is present at Accomac and that she is not yet married to Frank. From this point, the governor's scheme unravels.

After he has been condemned, Bacon is assisted by an old servant woman who helps him escape. She also tells him that his mother is not Mrs. Fairfax but another genteel Puritan lady. Armed with this knowledge and reinforced by the Recluse, Bacon pursues Berkley across the bay to Jamestown, where his own forces are just arriving. They lay siege to the city and thwart Berkley's efforts to escape by land. He escapes by water to Accomac, and the novel ends as Virginia and Bacon, now married, watch the Chickahominies begin the long trek to the west, where they can presumably maintain their culture without interference. They see Weyanokee and ask her to remain with them, but she declares her loyalty to her people and continues her journey.

Contemporary reviewers gave *The Cavaliers of Virginia* more notice and more praise than either *The Kentuckian in New-York* or *Knights of the Golden Horse-Shoe,* Caruthers' third novel. *Knickerbocker* praised the work for its use of American materials as well as its patriotism, pointing out that Bacon's Rebellion was the first step toward "'that greater revolution, from which we date our national existence'" (quoted in Davis 175). The reviewers saw the work as revolving around the battle between Roundheads and Cavaliers, but admired the presentation of Bacon's torture at the hands of the Chickahominies, the mysterious Recluse, and Bacon's companion, Brian O'Reilly, who is little more than a comic drunken Irishman. The *New-York Mirror* also had high praise for the work, finding the material always excellent if not developed to fullest advantage (Davis 176). Other publications praised the characterizations of Weyanokee and the governor, while still others joined in the praise of Caruthers' use of American materials and the accuracy of his treatment. In all, eighteen periodicals published reviews of *Cavaliers,* eleven praising it, two showing less enthusiasm but no condemnation, and five reflecting outright hostility toward the work (Davis 174, 176–179, 180). This range of responses indicates that reviewers may have found in Caruthers' second novel elements that they could enjoy but more material than they could digest in timely reviews.

Modern commentators, with the exception of Curtis Carroll Davis, have generally minimized their treatment of *Cavaliers.* Jay Hubbell found it

Authority and Affection: Cavaliers of Virginia 55

lacking in historical accuracy and dismissed it with brief notice (501). He is correct in pointing out that Caruthers' historical characters and events are not much like the models on which they were drawn—if we assume that those models were the historical Bacon and Berkley. William R. Taylor acknowledges that Caruthers had made the Virginia colony an emblem of the United States and had pitted Bacon, whom Taylor sees as neither Cavalier nor Roundhead, against Berkley, a Cavalier who represents the worst excesses of European aristocracy, thereby criticizing the Cavalier and Yankee mentalities of his own day (192–194). This overlooks, however, the emphasis that Caruthers places on establishing Bacon's Cavalier pedigree. J. V. Ridgely, however, sees the use of Bacon, a Cavalier, to serve as champion of individual liberty as unhistorical, but he dismisses the book as an inconsequential mixture of historical and Gothic romances (Ridgely 45). Ritchie Watson argues that Caruthers intended to write about national unity and manifest destiny in a romance. He views Bacon as extending the Puritan tradition and fusing it with the cavalier tradition to examine the conflict between the practical middle-class ethic and the aristocratic code. While the modern commentators have made some effort to place the work in its historical context, they have concentrated on the industrialization, commercialization, and democratization occurring during the 1830s. This overlooks the emerging political tensions that could be represented through similarities between Jackson and Berkley; if we are to have some recognition of what Bacon represents, it is important to recognize in some detail just what he opposes, and that recognition must be founded on a sense of Andrew Jackson's image at the time when Caruthers wrote the novel.

For some voters, Jackson was the lesser of two evils when he won the Presidential elections of 1828 and 1832—a man elected because of his opponents' weaknesses rather than his own specific strengths. In addition, he brought to the presidency a background very different from those of his six predecessors in office. They came from families that were, compared to Jackson's, well-to-do, and they were generally better educated and more experienced in politics and statecraft than was Jackson. All had served in a variety of national offices before election to the Presidency. Jackson's rise from a Carolinian log cabin to the White House was a path that no previous president had taken, and it was not one that necessarily inspired great confidence. It led through the Tennessee frontier to victory over the British at New Orleans, which, as John William Ward has pointed out, raised American morale and national self-esteem from a morass to a new pinnacle (4–6). This victory also elevated Jackson to the status of a national hero and associated him permanently with military victory (Remini 106). Yet while this military success may have been an important factor in Jackson's national reputation and rise to the presidency, it was also a matter of controversy. Jackson's detractors examined history and found numerous examples of military men who became tyrants when given civil authority.

56   *Will the Circle be Unbroken?*

Although Jackson's supporters used his military record as a basis for comparison with Washington, his detractors were well aware that General Jackson's respect for civilian authority had been inconsistent (Ward 188–189). In the afterglow of the victory at New Orleans, for example, he had refused to rescind martial law, arrested a Federal judge for freeing a prisoner who had been held under martial law, and ultimately paid a fine of $1000 when tried for contempt of the judge's court. The judge he had arrested wrote that "'the only question was whether the Law should bend to the General or the General to the Law'"; this does not seem to have been a question at all in Jackson's mind (Remini 109–110). Later, Jackson was arraigned by Congress for seizing Florida and establishing a provisional government there in 1818, when his mission, according to some, had been nothing more than the pursuit of the Seminole Indians (Remini 117–118, 122, 125–128). Based on these instances, Jackson's adversaries—and some of his less enthusiastic supporters—feared that he might place his own will above the Constitution or the will of the majority (Ward 188). Notwithstanding these concerns, his popular and electoral margins of victory in 1828 were among the largest that any candidate had received to that date.

Like Caruthers' Berkley, Jackson began his political career as a beloved figure. A similar parallel may be drawn between Berkley's exile at Accomac before the time of the novel and Jackson's defeat in the 1824 presidential election. This defeat temporarily removed Jackson from power, but it improved his position in the 1828 election, when some of the votes cast in his support were given to him by people who believed he had been unfairly denied the Presidency when the 1824 election went to House of Representatives. These votes, in some cases, expressed less support for Jackson than opposition to Adams, the beneficiary of political deal-making in the House of Representatives in the 1824 election. The reference in *The Cavaliers of Virginia* to Berkley's exile does little to advance Caruthers' plot, but it does raise another point of comparison between the governor and Jackson. This invocation of a national event hardly a decade past would not be lost on Caruthers' original audience.

An important feature of Jackson's administration—and one that intensified the fears of his opponents—was his use of the veto: He vetoed more Congressional bills than all of the previous presidents combined. *The Federalist* had identified the power of the veto with the British monarchy and had sought to assure readers that presidents would only use it to protect the presidency and the Constitution. That is, it was an instrument of checks and balances, not one that the chief executive would use to substitute his will for that of the legislative branch. Jackson, however, was quite willing to veto measures with which he disagreed, "making the President the *legislative* equal of roughly one-sixth of congress" (Pessen 323, italics in original), and he argued that he, unlike the legislators, had been elected to represent all of the people—not only those of a particular district or state.

Authority and Affection: Cavaliers of Virginia   57

Jackson's vetoes led his detractors to fear that the President might be as autocratic as Caruthers' Berkley. His handling of relations with Native Americans was a case in point.

In considering *The Cavaliers of Virginia,* it is important to note that Caruthers did not need to individualize his Native American characters or involve them in the plot. He could have examined generalized issues of authority by presenting them as an abstract force against which the principal figures operate. After all, Bacon's Rebellion has often been interpreted as a conflict between Berkley and Bacon in which protection from Native American raiders was catalytic. In these interpretations, the raiders are unidentified agents who serve only to set in motion the actions of the historical drama. (Wyatt-Brown's reading is a case in point (79–82), as is Mapp's (146–154).) Caruthers, however, makes the Native Americans far more concrete and individualized, particularly those of the Chickahominy band, and even more particularly Weyanokee, the woman who serves Virginia Fairfax early in the novel but later becomes Queen of the Chickahominies. Modern scholars have argued that "the Red Man, people . . . felt [in Caruthers' time], was America's only genuine claim to an antiquity of its own and, as such, was its most valuable claim to romance" (Davis 164), and they have set the matter aside after examining the accuracy or inaccuracy of the author's representation. Both of these arguments overlook that for many Americans of the early nineteenth century, the indigenous people, their claims to land, and their place in the nation were real and present considerations. This was particularly true along the southern frontier whence Jackson had come.

Even before New Orleans, Jackson had built a regional reputation in military expeditions against the southern tribes, and after that victory, his command of the southern district of the United States Army involved him with the Creeks, Cherokees, Chickasaws, and Choctaws (Remini 111). His 1818 expedition in Florida was related to Seminole raids into United States territory (Remini 117). His reputation, then, was in part the result of his management of tension with the southern tribes. Still, his achievements in this area had to do with handling isolated problems. He had not made much progress toward resolving the tension permanently.

In fairness to Jackson, he was not, before his presidency, a maker of policy in this area, and Federal policy since the Jefferson administration had evolved in the direction of removing the tribes to the west of the Mississippi. Jackson generally supported this policy, although he believed that individual Native Americans who could adopt white cultural norms, become what he called "industrious citizens," and accept the sovereignty of the states in which they lived could remain where they were. On the other hand, those who wished to retain their native cultures and allegiances could not be protected when they were surrounded by white people; they would have to move (Remini 114). Still, very little had been done to

58   *Will the Circle be Unbroken?*

implement this policy as late as the composition of *The Cavaliers of Virginia*. As general and president, Jackson, like Berkley, took over a potential problem that had gone unaddressed for the most part. When the peaceful Chickahominies in *The Cavaliers of Virginia* are forced to move west, Caruthers is showing the human dimension of a policy that was important at the time when he composed the novel. He personalizes this abstract policy by showing in specific terms the dilemma of those who faced the choice of giving up their cultural identity or their homes.

But policy with respect to the Native Americans was not simply an issue that pitted one race against the other; it was also an issue in which there arose the question of the central government's authority. Since the early days of colonization, when Captain John Smith had identified Powhatan as an emperor, the tribes had been regarded as independent nations, and the Constitution and tradition dictated that relations with independent nations had to be managed through treaties. While the Constitution gave treaty-making authority only to the central government and not to the states, there were tribal bands that lived within the boundaries of a single state. This gave rise to specific problems in several southern states, and those problems, in turn, came to national attention at the same time as the Nullification Crisis (Ellis 113)—and during the period when Caruthers must have been finishing *The Cavaliers of Virginia*.

The Cherokee and Creek nations claimed extensive land holdings in Georgia, Alabama, Tennessee, and North Carolina, and their claims rested on their sovereignty as independent nations. The states, hoping to seize the land, argued that the tribes were dependent tenants subject to state laws. Georgia took the lead in pressing the issue because the state had earlier given up western land claims in response to a federal agreement to extinguish tribal land titles as soon as possible (Ellis 26). There were still Cherokees living in northeastern Georgia, however, when gold was discovered in that area in the 1820s, and the state government took renewed interest in getting them out. The legislature passed acts that invalidated all laws that the Cherokees had adopted for themselves, divided their land and provided for its sale, denied them the right to testify against white men, and prohibited any effort to prevent them from leaving the state (Ellis 28). The Cherokees, in hope of retaining sovereignty, enlisted William Wirt to bring their case before the Supreme Court (Ellis 29).

Wirt's first step was to file a bill of equity with the Supreme Court, arguing that the Cherokees were a sovereign power whose treaty rights had been violated. The governor of Georgia, however, argued that the Court had no authority in the matter. Consequently, when the case was heard, no one represented Georgia (Ellis 29). Nevertheless, two of the three opinions in the case found the Cherokee claim to sovereignty invalid; Chief Justice John Marshall's majority opinion rejected the case because the issues were political and not legal, and a concurring opinion held that the Cherokees

Authority and Affection: Cavaliers of Virginia

were not a nation (Ellis 30). During the same period in 1830, however, the Court granted a writ of error so that the case of a Cherokee named Corn Tassels could be heard by Federal courts. Corn Tassels was accused of murdering another Cherokee on tribal land; consequently, his case was a tribal matter—*if* the Cherokees were a sovereign nation. Despite the Supreme Court's writ, however, Corn Tassels was executed, and the governor and legislature vowed that they would use force, if necessary, to see that state criminal laws were carried out (Ellis 29). During the period when South Carolinians were questioning the authority of the Federal legislature, then, Georgians were questioning the authority of the Federal judiciary in their responses to these cases.

In 1830, the Georgia legislature passed a law that prohibited white men from living on Native American lands without the permission of the state. The people most affected were missionaries who had gone to the Cherokee territory to work with the Native Americans and advise them as to how they might resist the state, and most of these missionaries, when arrested, accepted pardons in return for their promises to leave the state. But two of the missionaries thus arrested, Samuel Worcester and Elizer Butler, accepted their sentences of four years at hard labor and appealed to the Supreme Court with Wirt as their counsel (Ellis 30).

The case went to the Court in early 1832, and it followed a pattern similar to that of the Corn Tassels matter, with Georgia rejecting the Court's authority and refusing to send counsel. In this case, however, the Court agreed that the Cherokees were a nation and that the state's laws did not apply in Cherokee territory. Worcester and Butler, accordingly, were to be freed. A special messenger set out for Georgia to deliver the ruling, but the Court adjourned its session before it could learn and act on the state's response to the order. It was unclear what the Judiciary Act of 1789 would allow the Court to do to enforce its rulings, and President Jackson's position with respect to the case was somewhat ambiguous. He had not taken a position with respect to the issues in the case. On the contrary, he couched the matter in personal terms: He had no objection to Chief Justice John Marshall handing down a decision, but Marshall would have to find ways of enforcing the Court's will (Ellis 31). Would the president use Federal force to compel compliance with the Federal court ruling despite popular opposition in the state, or would he recognize the authority of the state?

The Worcester case and the tariff crisis arising at the same time appeared similar enough to attract attention. In both instances, a branch of the federal government was at odds with a state. Nationalists recognized the similarities and argued that both cases called for federal intervention (Ellis 114). The Nullifiers agreed on these similarities, but they believed that Jackson would handle the cases differently. They doubted that he would enforce the *Worcester* rulings; on the other hand, they expected that he would enforce the tariff because of his personal animosity toward Calhoun

60   *Will the Circle be Unbroken?*

and the Nullifiers who had not supported him in 1832 (Ellis 113). The matters, in other words, might be resolved on the basis of Jackson's personality rather than principle. Moderate Georgians, hoping to avoid conflict, argued that Congress, as an elected body answerable to the electorate and presumably representing the will of the majority, had authority to pass tariff acts—and, presumably, force bills to enforce them. The Supreme Court justices, on the other hand, were not accountable to the electorate (or, for that matter, the presidents who appointed them) and thus could not claim the same authority to intervene in the affairs of individual states (Ellis 115). This assessment approximated Jackson's; Caruthers, as we will see, may have agreed with the president's majoritarian principles while fearing Jackson as unprincipled and self-serving.

By 1833, when the Court reconvened, *Worcester* had become an embarrassment for Georgians and Jackson alike, and both sides looked for a non-confrontational way of resolving the matter without increasing the tension over states' rights bound up in the Nullification controversy. As a solution, they finally hit upon a pardon from Governor Wilson Lumpkin, a plan endorsed by Martin Van Buren and his New York allies of the Albany Regency (Ellis 116): In return for the pardon, the missionaries would drop their case before the Supreme Court (Ellis 118). Despite some last-minute fumbling, Lumpkin issued the pardon, Worcester and Butler were released, and the issue was defused.

The paucity of unpublished Caruthers writings does not permit us to say with any certainty what William Alexander Caruthers knew or thought about the Nullification Crisis or the Cherokee cases against Georgia.[1] Nevertheless, it is entirely reasonable to assume that he was well aware of both matters. Between 1829 and 1835, he lived in New York, where he had the benefit of regular news from other parts of the country , and given Van Buren's position and status in the state as well as the divisions within the Albany Regency, nullification was a widely discussed topic.

He had also been married to Louisa Gibson of Savannah, Georgia since 1823, and at least one of her brothers came to New York from Georgia on at least one occasion during the Nullification Crisis (Davis xxi, 88); during this visit, Caruthers undoubtedly heard accounts of what was going on in Georgia and South Carolina, including the Worcester case as well as southern responses to the tariff and nullification. In other words, Caruthers knew what was going on in national affairs, and his knowledge figured in the development of *The Cavaliers of Virginia*. The issues that he raised in the novel, moreover, were of national importance.

If these contemporary matters were in Caruthers' mind as he wrote, why did he set *The Cavaliers of Virginia* in the historical past and during Bacon's Rebellion? *Swallow Barn* and *The Kentuckian in New-York* both were set in the immediate past—the past that lay within the memory of his original audience. In *The Cavaliers of Virginia,* however, Caruthers set his

Authority and Affection: Cavaliers of Virginia 61

work in the past beyond memory of the living. A century and a half elapsed between the death of the historical Nathaniel Bacon and the publication of Caruthers' book featuring a protagonist of that name. During that time, only two other writers had put the story of Bacon's Rebellion into print (Davis 141–142). The only serious treatment to that time, and the one likely to have sparked Caruthers to write, was Stephen Mitchell's essay, "The Insurgent, or, A Tale of Early Times" in the first and only number of a periodical called *The Spirit of the Old Dominion* (Davis 142). Consequently, there is little chance that Caruthers' readers would have noticed or been much concerned with the novel's departures from the historical record. This leaves open the question of what Caruthers had to gain by setting a story over a century and a half in the past and in the colonial past instead of the Revolutionary past that had already proven popular through the works of James Fenimore Cooper.

In considering *Swallow Barn*, we have seen that Kennedy suggested indirectly that Revolutionary War loyalties persisted as part of family identity at least as late as the early part of the nineteenth century—the immediate past in which the novel is set. While that Revolutionary past was not directly involved in Kennedy's novel, his reference to the Revolutionary loyalties of the Hazards and Tracys suggests that this epoch remained an important element in the consciousness of Americans in the Jacksonian years: Jefferson and Adams, the last surviving signers of the Declaration of Independence, had been dead less than a decade, and only a half century had passed since Cornwallis's surrender at Yorktown. People who had been alive during the Revolution were still alive when Kennedy wrote *Swallow Barn* and Caruthers wrote *The Kentuckian in New-York* and *The Cavaliers of Virginia*, and if those people were not necessarily alive in large numbers, there were others—Robert E. Lee could serve as one prominent example—who had heard tales of the war from parents, relatives, or neighbors who had been directly involved. Moreover, less than twenty years had passed since the War of 1812 had renewed the struggle between Britain and the United States, and Jackson had been the principal hero of that war. Americans may have held strongly individualized views of the struggle for independence and its significance, and these views might have colored their readings of Caruthers' novel if the novel had focused on the conflict. Bacon's Rebellion, like the Revolution, offered many of the possibilities that Caruthers wanted to examine: "thrilling declamations, the logical defence of natural and primitive rights . . . , the seeming intuitive wisdom that burst so suddenly upon the world at the very exigency which called it into action . . . , citizens of the colony now [arriving] at the infant capital, resolved to take upon themselves as much power as was necessary for the defence of life, freedom, and property" (51–52).

In addition, the matter of authority and its limits had become heated in the early 1830s, as we have seen, and the names of the Revolutionary generation were invoked on both sides of such controversies. The Revolution had meant the end of hereditary monarchical authority in the United States, and Melvin Yazawa has argued that this meant the end of the familial paradigm. Others, however, have pointed out that the paradigm continued, particularly in the South (Bardaglio xi). Moreover, one of the central questions in the United States in the 1830s was whether monarchical power might still exist in the hands of a central government that had grown too strong and fallen into the hands of a former general who would have few objections to holding such unchecked power. Using Bacon's Rebellion as a setting allowed Caruthers to examine issues that had contemporary resonance without directly calling up the contemporary controversies. He could draw characters and events in terms that allowed comparison with those occurring around his readers, but he could avoid alluding to the immediate tensions. It may be that he hoped to show how an earlier generation had overcome adversity and achieved great ends, thereby bringing to life an era that had passed and, by doing so, informing and inspiring readers (Osborne 294–295). As we shall see, the problems of the novel relate closely to the issue of authority, and the happy outcome may suggest that the people of the nineteenth century could at least hope for the complete (if not altogether peaceable) resolution of their differences. Caruthers links Bacon's Rebellion with the Revolution in several places, and *The Cavaliers of Virginia* suggests that some social and political upheavals (but not all) have positive long term effects.

The two principal plots of *Cavaliers*—Bacon's Rebellion and the courtship of Bacon and Virginia Fairfax—both turn on the issue of authority. Who is empowered to make decisions? On what basis does that power rest? How should the power best be employed? Questions like these were familiar to Americans who lived in an era when the question of Federal authority was still largely unresolved.

Governor William Berkley represents authority in the novel; he is, after all, the highest ranking royal authority in Virginia, and Caruthers often refers to him in terms that make clear that he holds "the vice-regal chair" (Caruthers 4). Despite references to the governor's council and the burgesses, only Berkley has the authority to act as indicated when the colonists demand that he give Bacon a commission to pursue marauders who have already attacked the colony. His authority, in terms of the novel, is legitimate; it is his use of that authority and failure to recognize its limits that creates the tensions in the work. Berkley is, by Caruthers' repeated title, an *old* knight, but age does not keep him from an active life. In all of this, Berkley resembles Andrew Jackson, who was, at times, called "the Old Hero."

Berkley's position in the colony seems to reflect the confidence of king and colonists alike, just as Jackson's election seemed to some the triumph of democratic ideals; nevertheless, there are troubles ahead for the gover-

Authority and Affection: Cavaliers of Virginia

nor, as readers learn early in *The Cavaliers of Virginia*. We have already observed that Puritans, opponents of the governor and his fellow Cavaliers, have entered the colony in numbers sufficient to promote an insurrection. Similarly, the Native Americans, after years of peace, are restive. While the Puritan uprising represents an attack against the governor's person as well as his position, Caruthers does not allow Berkley to become directly involved in that conflict except as a tactician during the mob action. When the time comes to deal with the insurrection by punishing the leaders, an unnamed officer conducts the inquiries and metes out judgments. With respect to the uprising of the Native Americans, Caruthers is especially deft in having Berkley appear to be taking action: The governor meets with a committee of colonists and agrees that he will, the next day, sign the commissions they have requested—but when the next day comes, he does not keep his promise. It is especially important that this occurs even after Berkley's own country retreat has been attacked and burned. This allows Caruthers to show Berkley as an authority who is remote from those he governs and unresponsive to serious threats to their security—even after his own property has been destroyed. He is detached from the real problems of the colony, but he is quick to defend his authority. Instead of setting out to pursue the Native Americans, Berkley enters the field to suppress Bacon's activities. He is, at best, able to put forth the appearance of looking after the interests of his people, but in the final analysis, he serves only his own interests.

With widespread support, Bacon undertakes the campaign that Berkley should have (by popular will) pursued against the marauding bands. In doing so, he does, in effect, what many of Caruthers' contemporaries believed the Federal government should have done, and he behaves as a faithful ruler-father, looking after the interests of the people of Virginia. It is important to realize that he never intends to overthrow Berkley or seize power for himself. His interest is in the protection of the colony, and in this selfless regard for the commonwealth, he shows the faithfulness of the ideal ruler-father. While he expects trouble from the autocrat, his expectation is not so strong as to keep him from setting out with his army and then returning to Jamestown; the exigencies of the colony, on the other hand, require that he do so. Only after Berkley and his forces set out in pursuit does Bacon even consider how best to defend himself against the unfaithful governor. In a sense, then, Bacon may be taken to represent the ideal ruler-father of the familial paradigm: He takes the authority to act because he is doing the public interest, but to take the reins of government would usurp a position not rightfully his. His authority is not legal; he has no commission. But his action is morally right because it protects those who have been jeopardized by a faithless ruler. Bacon is distressed at the eager thoroughness with which his soldiers demolish a Chickahominy village during his absence, but he does not punish his subordinates. They are, after all, acting on behalf of the people whom the governor has ignored. Bacon's patriarchal attentiveness to the interests of the people is slightly different from simple majoritarianism. The former assumes that the leader has a broader perspective than others and considers the general good rather than what will ensure his continuation in power. The latter grants the leader authority but demands that he act upon the will of the people, no matter how misdirected. Under this view, Congress and the President both represented the popular will (on different scales) and their acts could not be set aside by a state.

But Berkley is not simply a governor. He is the head of a family, and in that role, he opposes the marriage of Bacon and Virginia Fairfax. This pits him, to some extent, against nature because many of Caruthers' contemporaries regarded marriage as a natural state of life for adult human beings. While the couples in *Kentuckian* were drawn together by mystical forces, though, Bacon and Virginia have been drawn to each other gradually through long association. Berkley, however, wishes to overrule the natural attraction so that Virginia marries Frank Beverly and thereby combines the Fairfax and Berkley estates. Berkley's deficiencies as governor, then, prove to be very similar to his deficiencies as a patriarch. His behavior as head of a household is as detached and unresponsive as is his behavior as governor.

We have seen that Berkley is detached from colonial affairs, remaining ignorant of the Puritan plans for an uprising and taking no action with respect to attacks on colonists. Similarly, he gives too little weight to people within his family. While hunting after the ball and Puritan insurrection, he talks with Gideon Fairfax and, perhaps, shows his true colors. He initially complains that Bacon may be presuming upon Fairfax's kindness by remaining close to Virginia, but Fairfax is quick to remind him that Bacon was instrumental in preserving the governor during the insurrection. The governor, apparently, is willing to overlook facts that do not support his own interpretation of Bacon's character. Fairfax indicates, too, that *he* (and not Sir William) exercises vigilance and authority over the goings on in his own household and can see no fault in Bacon's conduct. While Fairfax's arguments seem compelling, they do not really address Sir William's interest: the marriage of Frank Beverly to Virginia Fairfax. As Sir William explains, "'Lady Berkley has often of late mentioned her apprehensions to me, that there is a growing and mutual attachment between your ward and your daughter. Frank has observed the same thing . . .'" (150). In other words, Berkley does not claim to have seen these things for himself; his information comes from relatives, and the absence of direct observation makes him seem remote from what is actually happening with young relatives whose lives he would like to direct. He claims to act on Frank's wishes and Lady Berkley's concerns, although he later proves to have his own objective in the marriage.

Even if Berkley were fully informed, his view of marriage would draw attention. He has difficulty, he says, in discussing Frank and Virginia, "with

Authority and Affection: Cavaliers of Virginia

all the coolness and deliberation which ought to attend the negotiation of an alliance between the kinsman of his majesty's representative in the Colony, and the daughter of his nearest relative—the heiress probably of both their fortune" (148).

This is not, in Sir William's mind, anything close to a companionate marriage. It is an alliance, a contract, a business, and Frank's proposal is a formal tender of his hand and fortune (149). This view seems consistent with the idea that marriage was primarily a contract, an idea that had been a part of American culture (if not law) for some time. (Michael Grossberg indicates that this definition had deep roots in English tradition and colonial practice (19); Linda Kerber indicates that only in New England had this view taken hold before the Revolution (159)). On the other hand, Supreme Court Justice Joseph Story expressed an important nineteenth-century view when he held that marriage was "'something more than a mere contract. It is rather to be deemed an institution of society founded upon the consent and contract of the parties'" (quoted in Grossberg 21). Such a view may appear, particularly to modern readers, to squeeze the emotional content out of marriage, and it might have been comfortable to the Revolutionary generation for precisely that reason. It would have been less satisfactory to a generation (like Caruthers') that emphasized the affection and emotional content of marriage (Lewis 36, 126, 188). Given this emphasis, it seems unlikely that Caruthers' contemporaries would have had much sympathy with Berkley's attempt to make the proposed marriage a business negotiation.

While some readers of Caruthers' day may well have expected that parents or guardians would conduct some businesslike negotiations concerning what they would give the new couple as a start in married life, this would not have led them to be more kindly disposed toward Berkley. The purpose of these negotiations that they expected was much different from Berkley's. When the governor explains his plan to his kinswoman, Emily Fairfax, his real purpose emerges clearly: it is a strategic arrangement for the disposal of the Berkley and Fairfax fortunes that will add to the honor and dignity of both families, and only peripherally does it relate to the happiness—or even the wishes—of Frank and Virginia (200). The focus is not on giving the couple a start in married life, but on achieving the ends that Sir William considers important. This seems consistent with William Taylor's formulation of the Yankee as a schemer serving primarily his own interests. While Taylor saw the governor as a cavalier and hence oppositional to the Yankee, this reading overlooks that Caruthers had set his novel in the colonial period and associated Berkley with the crown as a member of what Kennedy called the Court party—the party in favor of executive privilege. Berkley, because of the historical setting, cannot be cavalier or Yankee because there is no way for Caruthers to present a clearly identifiable Yankee figure for comparison. On the other hand, the governor can be devoted to the empowerment of the executive, and he can be an unsympathetic figure as a result. Before the end of the first volume of *The*

66   *Will the Circle be Unbroken?*

Cavaliers of Virginia, Berkley has proven that he cannot quite be trusted; on the contrary, he inspires, perhaps, the sort of skepticism that Andrew Jackson inspired among the anti-Jacksonians who would later become Whigs.

Does Berkley usurp power in courtship as he does in governmental affairs? The answer is that he does to a point. He is a kinsman and guardian of Frank Beverly and an uncle of Virginia Fairfax. As an uncle, he could be expected to take an important role in the lives of both his niece and nephew; historians of the Southern family have pointed repeatedly to the importance of uncles and aunts in the family constellation. Moreover, Gideon Fairfax, whom Caruthers presents as a deservedly beloved father and member of the community, seems to have no objections to taking part in the planning of his daughter's future. But Frank has asked the governor to propose on his behalf, and this is not exactly what Fairfax had expected. This procedure may have been somewhat unusual in Caruthers' time. For example, Jane Censer's North Carolinians often began and sometimes ended engagements without their parents (or, presumably, uncles or aunts) knowing (78–79), and Catherine Clinton's findings indicate that Northerners, likewise, would have found this indirect proposal unusual; they, too, began engagements unassisted (63). Caruthers' readers, then, may have seen something amiss in the role that Berkley is willing to take in this courtship. However readers regarded Frank's indirect proposal, Fairfax's response is clear: "'But as far as I am concerned, I give my hearty consent to the proposed union, and you may so assure Frank from me, and tell him that he has nothing more to do but to appear as every way worthy in the eyes of Virginia as he does in mine'" (149). This response calls unfavorable attention to Berkley's role; Fairfax gives his assent, perhaps recognizing some of the same benefits that motivate the governor, but he does not regard that assent as a sufficient basis for the marriage. Fairfax, as father of the bride-elect, has the authority to dictate or at least intervene in Virginia's marriage plans; otherwise, any discussion with the governor of her marriage would be futile. But Fairfax says that Frank must win Virginia himself, and he imposes the condition that neither Virginia nor Frank knows about the agreement between their elders until they have decided on their own to marry (200). His actions suggest his belief that marriages must have a basis beyond rational considerations—and beyond the evident comfortable familiarity that Bacon and Virginia have developed over the years. He also believes that young women can judge prospective partners for themselves. On another level, Caruthers may again delight in giving a young woman the name Virginia, in this case as a warning: Any politician who wishes the support of the Old Dominion must, like Bacon and unlike Berkley and Beverly, prove himself worthy—presumably by comparison with the likes of Washington, Jefferson, Madison, and Monroe.

Virginia Fairfax has ample basis on which to judge Bacon in this regard; after all, he has grown up, for most of his life, in her parents' home,

Authority and Affection: Cavaliers of Virginia 67

and the constant exposure of these two young people to each other has led them to fall in love. As the Recluse puts it, the basis for this affection is common virtue:

> 'Thou hast been associating for some years with a youth of little more than thine own age. He is noble and gifted with every manly and generous attribute; well instructed too for his time and country. To thee I will give credit for corresponding qualities suitable to thy own sex, and I have no doubt that thou possessest them. Thinkest thou that two such persons could grow up together constantly within the influence of each other's expanding personal attractions, besides the nobler ones of mind and heart, without feeling more towards each other than two ordinary mortals of the same sex?' (45)

Reading this against Caruthers' intersectional marriages in *The Kentuckian in New-York*, then, it appears that the basis for a successful marriage or union must include the opportunity for the principals to know each other fairly well. The long association between Bacon and Virginia meets the test; however, brief but intense acquaintance, as occurs with Victor and Frances and Beverley and Virginia, can also suffice because the partners recognize their interdependencies quickly in times of intense difficulty. These acquaintances, whether long or brief and intense, allow the couples to know each other beyond the formal exchanges of courtship and to separate empty flirtation from sincere courtship; in this requirement, it is likely that Caruthers' readers would have acceded (Stowe 73). Given this acquaintance and an initial attraction, a relationship may evolve naturally, like that of Bacon and Virginia, but the mechanism of this evolution never emerges in Caruthers' writing and the evolution of permanent ties rests upon the same kind of inexplicable affinity that binds the couples in *The Kentuckian in New-York*.

The Fairfaxes do not seem concerned at all about their daughter's long, close acquaintance with Bacon, even though his parentage is uncertain. Gideon is satisfied that there is "'nothing more than fraternal affection'" between the young people, but the governor's response is particularly important: "'It is very difficult, Fairfax, for the parties themselves to draw an exact line, where the one kind of affection ends, and the other begins; the gradation from mere brotherly regard to love is so very imperceptible, that the very persons in whom it takes place are often unconscious of it, until accident or warning from others forces it upon their apprehension'" (147).

Thus the governor suggests that the difference between fraternal and romantic love is a matter of degree and difficult to discern. This is an important point in Caruthers' use of the familial paradigm. While the paradigm seems to work effectively in representing the relationship of ruler-father to subordinates in Berkley and Bacon, it proves less effective in considering relations among subordinate peers—the states. Caruthers' strategy of having Bacon and Virginia raised in the same household brushes away any distinction that might be raised as to whether the Union of the states was fraternal—an involuntary relationship based initially on common origins and experience and destined to become more distant as the parties' circumstances changed—or marital—a voluntary relationship based on initial irrational attraction and intended to become stronger over time with the recognition of mutual dependency and development of shared experience. That is, if the states were sisters, they were all equal and subordinate to the head of the household—the central government or its head—and might become dependent upon each other and the central government in new ways as time went on. If the Union was like a marriage, however, the voluntary nature and the permanency of the relationship should minimize concerns over the unequal distribution of power in such unions.

The Cavaliers of Virginia, then, is a complex work that may have confounded readers. Like Swallow Barn, it makes an extended allusion to two contemporary issues: Jackson's presidency and relations with Native Americans. Because Caruthers' references to such current matters as Indian removal, unlike those in Swallow Barn, are extended and integral to the plot, they are not so striking in calling on readers to consider these issues in light of the novel's metaphors. Consequently, The Cavaliers of Virginia can be read as a relatively insubstantial romance. Nevertheless, the similarities between Jackson, the Old Hero, and Berkley, the Old Knight, are undeniably present, and there is no question that governmental dealings with Native Americans were a concern for Americans during the 1830s. Having used this technique to relate the novel to contemporary issues, Caruthers lays out a critique that presents the Jackson-like governor as a divisive force in the polity and the family, an obstacle to the spirit of unity that leads to prosperity. As in The Kentuckian in New-York, Caruthers used courtship as a metaphor to express the relationships among factions within the Union: that is, the Union was a construction based upon attractions and dependencies that were not entirely rational. To interfere with such a relationship presumably made a Berkley or a Jackson more reprehensible than one who simply usurped political power and showed disregard of the popular will or the Constitution. In Cavaliers, too, Caruthers indicated that marriage might not be the only suitable metaphor for the Union: The states might be represented as siblings without sacrificing the affectionate ties and mutual support that served all of the parties.

Caruthers was not done. An addendum to Cavaliers indicated that another work, to be called Knights of the Horse-Shoe, would follow shortly. In fact, however, six years would pass before this work appeared. In the interim, the political climate would change with Jackson's departure from office and Van Buren's election. John Pendleton Kennedy would continue to articulate a nationalist view in his novels, and Nathaniel Beverley Tucker would emerge as a strident proponent of sectionalism. Their novels would continue to portray families under stress.

CHAPTER FIVE

Whigs and Covert Missions:
Horse-Shoe Robinson

While the Nullification Crisis aroused antipathy towards Andrew Jackson, it does not seem to have weakened him significantly. Opposed by Henry Clay and William Wirt when he sought re-election in 1832, Jackson still won handily with 55 percent of the popular vote and an electoral college margin of 219 to 56. Moreover, this margin was not significantly different from the 1828 election, when, as a relatively unknown political quantity, he had won 56 percent of the popular vote against John Quincy Adams and carried the electoral college by a margin of 178 to 83. This victory, however, did little to quiet the opposition that had begun to take shape during Jackson's first administration. On the contrary, it may have provided the impetus for the development of modern political organization: If Jacksonian power could not be broken through traditional caucuses and campaigns, some new approach—such as Jackson and Van Buren were developing to reach newly enfranchised lower-class voters—would be necessary.

Much of the Jacksonian Democratic political rhetoric of the times cast the president and his supporters as the champions of the poor and the middle class, and some anti-Jacksonian Whigs adopted this rhetoric to cast their adversaries as social levellers, Jacobins, and radical agrarians. Whig newspapers, such as the New York *American,* portrayed Jackson as a hero to the less respectable elements of the population and a threat to the more respectable, and Democrats found such representations useful in casting the Whigs as elitist opponents of the lower- and middle-class voters whose votes they hoped to secure (Pessen 205). While Edward Pessen points out that there were some observers who saw the parties as more similar than different, he also acknowledges that the rhetoric was strident and acrimonious and that it invoked class distinctions (207). In any event, after the election of 1832, it must have been clear to Jackson's opponents, Whigs and uncommitted, that they had to get the votes of rural yeomen and urban workers in order to win elections.

70   *Will the Circle be Unbroken?*

While John Pendleton Kennedy had supported Jackson in 1828, by 1832 he turned toward the developing Whig coalition as the best hope for the national future that he envisioned, and his second novel, *Horse-Shoe Robinson, A Tale of the Tory Ascendency,* tells the story of the Revolutionary War in South Carolina and embodies metaphorically his belief that the salvation of the Union required unification behind the Whigs—a position that he would argue more explicitly three years later in *Defence of the Whigs.* In his tale of the Tory ascendency, Kennedy shows families divided by political differences and intrigues, and he indicates that in struggles for principles (such as the Revolution), people—particularly women—would be required to step out of their ordinary roles. At the end of the novel, Whig principles win out because they appeal to and unify people of different social classes. Moreover, the families that are *not* divided—those that cling to Whig principles despite personal risks and sacrifices—seem to be more likely than the others to prosper. Kennedy does not invoke the traditional familial paradigm although the issues of the paternal authority, courtship, and sibling relations do arise. In raising these issues, Kennedy shows characters taking on roles not customarily available to them, thereby suggesting a need for flexibility and dedication to the common good.

Before examining *Horse-Shoe Robinson,* however, it is important to recognize that Kennedy claimed to have based the novel loosely on the Revolutionary War record of an actual veteran named James Robertson. Just how Kennedy came by the story is unclear, but at least three accounts have survived. Kennedy's account, in the introduction to his novel, holds that the author heard the story under exciting circumstances: While traveling in western South Carolina, he was passed on the road by a boy about ten years old. A short time later, he found that the child had been thrown from his horse and had dislocated a shoulder, and the narrator helped him home. The boy's father called for a doctor and also for a blacksmith named Galbraith "Horse-Shoe" Robinson, who had taken his nickname from his trade. (The nickname of the historical James Robertson seems to have come from his residence at a bend in a river. (Dickson 36)) The blacksmith arrived first and reduced the dislocation, then spent the remainder of the evening regaling the author with stories of his experiences in the war (Kennedy 5–7, 9–10). The local account in the South Carolina Piedmont is slightly different: It holds that Kennedy heard of James Robertson while staying at an inn in the upcountry in the early 1830s and then sought out the veteran to hear the story as the basis for a possible novel (Dickson 36). Kennedy's journal, perhaps the most credible source, offers a third account that suggests that the author heard *something* about Robertson/Robinson while traveling in South Carolina in 1818, but he had the story fleshed out in Washington D.C. in 1830 by Warren R. Davis, a South Carolinian whom he had met at that time (Kennedy, 1830).

The common thread in all of these accounts is the lapse between the time when Kennedy heard the story and the time when he began to write it in

Whigs and Covert Missions: Horse-Shoe Robinson 71

December 1832 (Kennedy 1832). Some of the delay may be accounted for, as Charles Bohner has proposed, by Kennedy's enjoyment of historical research and insistence on historical accuracy (Bohner 94–95, 101, 103). This interpretation effectively synthesizes the three accounts because it suggests that Kennedy heard the story from Robertson in 1818 and had it corroborated (and, perhaps, expanded) by Warren Davis in 1830. By the same token, it is not inconsistent with any of the accounts to suggest that the delay may relate to Kennedy's understanding and interpretation of the significance of the Revolution.

Fictional works set during the American Revolution had begun to appear in the early 1820s, capitalizing on growing interest in that period. After all, the approaching fiftieth anniversary of the Declaration of Independence had increased public interest in the Revolution and promoted the success of James Fenimore Cooper's Revolutionary War romances, such as *The Spy.* Kennedy, given his literary bent, could not have overlooked the popularity of Cooper's works, and as an aspiring writer in the 1820s, he may have hoped to draw on the market that these works were creating. But even if he knew the story of James Robertson and recognized its commercial potential immediately, he may have had no clear idea of how to use it until the political parties began to emerge in the 1830s and Kennedy began to interpret the emergence of American political structures.

Defence of the Whigs was the culmination of that interpretive process. In that work, Kennedy treats American politics as part of a recurring struggle dating back to England in the days before Cromwell's commonwealth. In this struggle, those who supported the prerogative of the executive—the Tories or Court party in Kennedy's formulation—opposed those who upheld the privilege of the people to direct the executive through the legislature—that is, the Whigs or Country party. For Kennedy, the American Revolution was only one of a series of upheavals in which this conflict was acted out, and he was willing to call upon Americans to return to the principles of the Revolutionary Whigs by supporting the Whigs of the 1830s. As we saw in considering *Cavaliers of Virginia,* Jackson's use of the veto pitted the executive branch against legislature and judiciary. There is little question that the president had become a Tory in Kennedy's formulation[1] (and too little is known of Caruthers's views to know whether he shared Kennedy's formulation, but his Berkley does have pronounced Tory tendencies.)

Jackson's war on the Second Bank of the United States was the last straw for Kennedy. On 10 December 1833, as counsel for the Union Bank of Baltimore, Kennedy told the president of the bank that he regarded Jackson's actions with respect to the Bank of the United States "usurpations" and expressed his dislike of the administration. The bank president, a Mr. Ellicott, cautioned him that "opinions on the subject so freely expressed were calculated to do great harm to the Union Bank (which was . . . the financial agent of the [government])" and could lead to withdrawal of government deposits. Kennedy, however, regarded this as infringement of "free expression

72   *Will the Circle be Unbroken?*

of sentiments." A similarly heated exchange took place on the next day, Wednesday, 11 December 1833. Because Kennedy completed the first volume of *Horse-Shoe Robinson* on Tuesday, 10 December and began the second volume on Sunday, 15 December, the conclusion of his account of the 10 December incident is particularly suggestive:

> I replied to Mr. E. that this was the first administration (Jackson's) that had ever sought to interfere with the free expression of sentiments of any citizen, on government affairs. I therefore repeated my utter repugnance of Jackson and his cabinet and spoke very freely of the servility of his followers . . . I concluded by [saying] that I thought the time was come when every man who valued constitutional liberty should unite in an unsparing assault upon Jackson and his party until (if possible) they were broken down. That as to the president, he deserved impeachment. I record this conversation because I consider it the first advance of a design of the U.S. Bank as a government functionary to initiate the rule of its patron, Genl Jackson by affecting a completed subserviency to his views in proscribing all freedom of expression amongst them in its service. I shall resist this authority whenever it is devoted to myself and if the thing is expressed to me again, I shall expose their servility. (Kennedy Journal, 1833)

Suffice it to say that Kennedy supported the Whigs vocally from then on. His reluctance to support Henry Clay (and, presumably, Clay's supporting Whigs) while he was completing *Swallow Barn* had become subsumed in his hatred for Jackson. What is even more important in terms of the present project is that this hatred had to do with Jackson's expansion of executive privilege, that is, with acts that he had taken without Congressional approval, and the incident occurred in the midst of the composition of *Horse-Shoe Robinson*.

As we have seen, Jacksonians portrayed the Whig party as made up of planters, mill owners, merchants, and mainline Protestant clergy—relatively wealthy men who were bent on preserving their own power and privilege while denying opportunity to others (Feller 188). Jacksonians portrayed themselves and their fellow Democrats as simple, honest, hardworking people—farmers, craftsmen, and workers in the factories that had begun to spring up. While the Jacksonian Democrats concentrated on self-determination and liberty for the individual, the Whigs called for discipline and cooperation. Kennedy, by the time he began writing *Horse-Shoe Robinson,* was experienced in politics, and he undoubtedly recognized the importance of winning votes from an increasingly diverse electorate and attracting to the Whig movement the previously disenfranchised poor and the middle class. This awareness shows in the Whig characters of *Horse-Shoe Robinson*, who represent the yeoman class as well as the gentry.

Horse-Shoe Robinson, the novel's title character, is a strapping veteran in his mid-thirties. He comes from the Waxhaws district along the boundary between North and South Carolina, which readers of the 1830s would have recognized as the birthplace of Andrew Jackson and the location of

Whigs and Covert Missions: Horse-Shoe Robinson

his violent encounter with a British officer whose boots he refused to black (Remini 8). By invoking the Waxhaws, Kennedy casts Robinson, who remains faithful to Whig principles, as an implicit indictment of Jackson, who struck out at the Royalists and expressed Whig principles during the Revolution but betrayed them by attempting to expand executive power and privilege.[2] To Kennedy, who had supported the Old Hero in 1828, the sense of this betrayal by Jackson must have been especially acute, at least acute enough to be a factor in presenting a heroic Whig figure from the community where Jackson was born and raised.

In any case, Robinson's courage and cunning have earned him assignment to serve with Major Arthur Butler, a wealthy officer from eastern South Carolina. Their mission at the time of the plot in 1780 is to assist in mobilizing and organizing resistance to Cornwallis's advance northward through the Carolinian upcountry into Virginia. When Butler is captured by the British, however, this mission becomes impracticable. Robinson assists Mildred Lindsay, the young Virginian woman who is secretly married to Butler, in making a long journey through North Carolina in time to rescue the major before the battle of Kings Mountain in October 1780.

Over the entire proceedings, a shadow is cast by Philip Lindsay, Mildred's father. Philip is a man of retiring habits who has sought to retreat to a world of abstractions only to be drawn into the conflict by Tyrrel, an undercover British officer seeking to organize Tory supporters in the mountains of Virginia. Although he is not a committed Royalist, Philip disapproves of the rebellion as a challenge to established authority, and he does not wish his daughter to associate with Butler or other Whigs. As she makes her journey, however, she meets a number of good Whigs of the lower classes, honest yeomen and their families who are willing to risk much for their cause. She faces constant danger, however, because some of the rural poor of South Carolina have been taken in by the blandishments of the British, and they are all too willing to assist in capturing Robinson and his fellow travelers. Philip finally places love for his daughter ahead of politics and pursues Mildred to Kings Mountain. Although he suffers a mortal wound during the battle, he survives long enough to forgive her for seeing Butler despite parental objections and to give his blessing to her marriage. All in all, Kennedy was able to pack his second novel with tension and characters that American reviewers and readers found attractive.

Horse-Shoe Robinson was an immediate success. The first printing sold out within three months and earned the author $1200—a substantial figure in the 1830s. George Putnam, the publisher, then struck an agreement for a second printing, paying Kennedy $500 more. The foreign market results were less satisfying. *Swallow Barn* had been pirated in England, apparently leading Kennedy to believe that the mother country might be a strong market for his fiction; consequently, he arranged for the legitimate publication of *Horse-Shoe Robinson* there. Unfortunately, the novel

74   *Will the Circle be Unbroken?*

included passages that could be read as strongly anti-British, and British sales were poor. Kennedy, however, read the novel differently. He did not see it as the story of a war between the British and Americans, separate nations, but as a tale of a clash between two groups of Anglo-Saxon descendants who held different theories of government. This is entirely in keeping with the familial paradigm, which had represented the North American colonies as children of Great Britain. It is also consistent with Kennedy's belief in the progression of generations. He believed that he had treated the Tories and Whigs of Horse-Shoe Robinson as people engaged in a civil war being fought over fundamental principles of government. Moreover, the ruthlessness of the war was not a reflection on any combatant; the title character, during combat, is every bit as violent as any Royalist in the work. The author's actions in offering the novel to a British audience, however, suggest the validity of the reading proposed here, one that is not anti-British but pro-Whig and anti-Tory. Kennedy would hardly have sought British publication of a novel that he thought expressed anti-British sentiments.

Modern commentators have found *Horse-Shoe Robinson* to be a problem novel. Jay Broadus Hubbell gave it only brief treatment, although he pointed out that Robinson was a splendid character: "Courageous, honest, resourceful, athletic, the blacksmith scout and protector of his friends is more alive than any other character that Kennedy created" (492). William R. Taylor concentrated his attention on Butler and Robinson, arguing that through them, Kennedy was juxtaposing the cavalier (Butler) with the "new man" (Robinson) to produce an appealing dialectic (172). In doing so, Taylor points out that the differences between Robinson and Butler are actually superficial; Robinson, for example, is a better soldier than Butler, but only to the extent that the blacksmith fights a grim, somewhat ruthless battle for survival while the planter clings to the values of European chivalry (176–177). J.V. Ridgely places Robinson in the tradition of frontier scouts that had begun a few years before Kennedy's novel with Cooper's Leatherstocking, the advance guard of civilization moving into the wilderness. While these characters often appear as squires to knightly leaders, Ridgely holds that Kennedy's blacksmith scout was something more: Possessing "knowledge of the terrain, contempt for sham, [and] physical superiority, [all scouts] serve as a rein on the gentry's impetuousity and occasional pomposity," but Horse-Shoe Robinson is "an exemplar of the spirit of rebellion against unfairly imposed authority" (Ridgely 155–156). Ritchie Watson, examining the cavalier figure in Southern literature, saw the blacksmith soldier as "a kind of compromise between the extremes of aristocratic chivalry, on one hand, and uncivilized frontier brutality on the other" (92). The cavalier figure typified by Butler cannot prevail against the British; he represents one extreme on a continuum of chivalry while Wat Adair, the amoral and bloodthirsty woodsman who betrays Robinson

Whigs and Covert Missions: Horse-Shoe Robinson

and Butler to the British, represents the other. Horse-Shoe Robinson is the middle ground (93).

All of these modern readings posit that Kennedy was writing to participate as a Southerner in a conversation between sections—the emerging conflict that would end in civil war. As we saw in examining *Swallow Barn,* however, Kennedy perceived the nation as a single interest rather than a confederation of states that had potentially conflicting interests. Kennedy's politics thus render implausible a reading that has him advocating a narrowly Southern view. With this in mind, two other modern readings appear closer to the mark. While acknowledging that *Horse-Shoe Robinson* was the first important novel dealing with the Revolution in the South and praising Kennedy's accurate representation of that war, William Osborne held that the author's purpose had been to inform and inspire readers to respect the accomplishments of their forebears and strive to emulate them (295). Osborne also argued that Kennedy represented the war—accurately, according to the histories available in the 1820s and 1830s—as one in which the members of families and communities were pitted against each other (291). Donald Ringe, examining *Horse-Shoe Robinson* with other Revolutionary romances, argued that Kennedy, like other successful writers in this genre, represented the war as a civil conflict that pitted neighbors against each other for no clear reason and ultimately disrupted the social order (355, 357–358). That is, Kennedy does not show readers why Wat Adair should be a Tory while Robinson fights for the Whigs, but the latter's role in the war seems likely to assure him of recognition in peacetime. And women, far from remaining in their domestic spheres, play heroic parts in the adventures of Robinson and Butler. It was also a war, in the successful romances, in which the young opposed the old and laid the foundation for a natural aristocracy based on virtue and talent (Ringe 362, 363). These readings seek to place *Horse-Shoe Robinson* (along with the works of Cooper and Simms) in an historical context, but they overlook that such works as *The Spy* were written in the early 1820s, in a political climate far more placid than that of 1832–1833, when Kennedy was writing *Horse-Shoe Robinson.* Given Kennedy's view of the Monroe and John Quincy Adams years, this distinction is too important to overlook.

Kennedy expressed his view of American history in *Defence of the Whigs.* Although Kennedy wrote *Defence* years after *Horse-Shoe Robinson,* his journal entries for the earlier period indicate that the basic outline of his interpretation was taking shape at that time; this is especially clear in the passage quoted earlier concerning his conversations concerning the administration's removal of federal deposits from the Bank of the United States. In that passage, he condemned Jackson for expansion of executive privilege. Kennedy did not see the Revolution as a struggle against an external oppressor but as conflict between a Court party that supported executive prerogative (such as Jackson sought to expand) and a Country party that

76   Will the Circle be Unbroken?

was suspicious of that prerogative (320, 322, 325–326). The Revolution, he argued, had ended with Whig principles unanimously accepted in the United States. While he acknowledged that there had been tension between Federalists and Democrats, Kennedy pointed out that the balance of power between the parties had been fairly even in the years before 1815, and the adherents of both positions had been men of principle who were willing to sacrifice personal advancement for the common good (Kennedy 326). He wrote that these felicitous circumstances had prevailed until 1815, when the nomination of James Monroe for President had mobilized Federalists who resented the decline of their party—and their personal opportunities— during the Jefferson and Madison administrations (332). According to Kennedy, these Federalists had sought to advance Andrew Jackson as their nominee, but the Virginian Democrats had been too strong, and the Jacksonians' efforts had been unsuccessful until 1824 (332–333)—after the first wave of Revolutionary romances—when Jackson had lost the election in the House of Representatives. Kennedy held that this had added to Jackson's strength because some moderates believed that the outcome of the election was a result of intrigue rather than the popular will; this additional support contributed to Jackson's election in 1828 (338).

Kennedy argued that Jackson, at the time of his election, had espoused the fundamental tenets of Whiggery: support for the American System and limited executive power (342). As a military officer, however, Jackson was accustomed to unquestioned authority, and during his first term, he turned against his basic Whig principles, placing members of the legislature in executive offices, invoking questionable executive powers, and using the veto to block measures with which he was not in agreement (344–345). Jackson's conduct in his first term called the hitherto quiescent Whigs to renew their activity. In 1835, with Jackson acting strongly against the Bank of the United States (which Kennedy supported), the Marylander believed that the time had come for a return to Whig Revolutionary principles, and he had begun to speak out in support of the Whigs in public speeches (Kennedy Journal). That *Horse-Shoe Robinson* emerges from the same vein seems quite clear: After all, the novel does not refer to those who support independence as patriots or Continentals, but as Whigs. As we will see, the novel points out the necessity of support for the Whigs and predicts dire consequences for those who take other actions.

Commentators on *Horse-Shoe Robinson* have struggled with the question of principal characters, and to some extent, of central plot. Undeniably, Kennedy gave great attention to Arthur Butler and Mildred Lindsay Butler, and he at first referred to the work as "the story of Mildred Lindsay" in his journal. Still, Robinson and Mary Musgrove have struck some readers as far more colorful figures than the aristocratic couple, and this has led those readers to identify the Carolinian yeoman and miller's daughter as the protagonists of the work. These readers find the conclusion

Whigs and Covert Missions: Horse-Shoe Robinson

of the work unsatisfactory because Kennedy almost completely abandons his yeoman figures in favor of the aristocratic Butlers. Those who focus on Arthur Butler as protagonist, however, have difficulty in accounting for the major's ineptness and prissiness. He is, after all, unable to free himself from captivity without assistance from Robinson. Moreover, much of the novel revolves around Mildred's journey through North Carolina; that is, it revolves around a woman doing something far more extraordinary than holding political views that are at odds with those of her father. Most discussions of the novel leave out the other figures who populate Kennedy's pages. A reading focusing on familial relations and tensions involves more of the characters and does much to overcome these incomplete readings.

Kennedy's military Whigs in the novel are, for the most part, acting covertly and without much apparent coordination, just as the political Whigs of the 1820s had done and those of the 1830s were doing. Major Butler and Horse-Shoe Robinson are on a covert mission to assist in organizing resistance to the Royalists in the Carolinas. That resistance, for the most part, takes the shape of guerrilla operations by men such as Francis Marion, who makes a brief appearance in the novel, because the Royalists have seized Charleston and gradually expanded their control into the western regions of South Carolina. Similarly, Mildred Lindsay must carry on her relationship with Arthur Butler covertly. The Whigs are also, for much of the novel, unorganized, as suggested by the Whig troops who gather to confront the Royalists at Kings Mountain. That is, while there seem to be assembled bodies of Whig troops scattered throughout the South, the Whig commanders do not stand on a hierarchy of command, as do the British. They operate cooperatively, responding to circumstances.

Kennedy deploys plainly visible structure and hierarchy of the British forces and their Tory supporters against the rigidity that Democrats sought to associate with the anti-Jacksonian Whigs. The Tories are attached to executive power, hierarchy, and order, even when (in the case of the guerrillas) no one seems to have control over the group. Their leaders, no matter how inept, insist on precedence and on such rituals as roll calls, even when they cannot command effectively in combat or see to the daily needs of their troops. In some cases, their action is delayed because they must ascertain first whether they have authority to act in order to protect themselves from higher echelons. Kennedy's Whigs, however, do not possess this inflexibility. As the Whig forces gather in the upcountry before the battle of Kings Mountain, their leaders readily work out command arrangements because they share the common and overriding objective of defeating the British (505). Moreover, the behavior of these Whig irregulars contrasts dramatically with that of Hugh Habersham's Tory irregulars, who seem unable to keep straight who is in command, and they actually injure each other about as badly as they injure their enemies. Their antics would be comic—except for their drunkenness, their tendency to unprovoked violence, and their willingness to steal during military operations. Whig authority, it seems, is mild but effective; in a cooperative, egalitarian environment, there may be a need for leadership, but there is little need for authority. Among the Royalists, however, authority seems necessary to control the bloodthirsty and amoral crowd, but only Cornwallis—a figure far removed in every way from most of the action—seems to have the authority to act without obtaining permission elsewhere.

There are several families in *Horse-Shoe Robinson* that deserve fairly detailed consideration. It is important to recognize at the beginning, however, that these families represent three specific social classes. The Lindsays represent the Virginian aristocracy. Philip, the politically moderate and personally retiring head of the family, has the wherewithal to withdraw from the pressures of business and society to a secluded home where he may enjoy a contemplative life. This is a far cry from the Tory Adair family in South Carolina. While they, too, live in a remote mountain region, Wat Adair and his partner, Michael Lynch, seem to pursue haphazardly several occupations, milling, hunting, and farming among them. Despite this range of activities, they seem to remain impoverished. The Whig Musgroves and Ramsays, on the other hand, are yeoman stock, the former a miller and the latter apparently a moderately prosperous farmer, but both are far less well-to-do than the Lindsays. Not only are these two stable families models of yeoman virtue, but they are model Whigs, and Kennedy uses them to suggest that Whigs are not the enemy of the working class but are successful yeomen and workers themselves.

While the Lindsays represent the aristocratic class that the Democrats tried to associate with the Whigs, Kennedy does not hold them up as exemplars. Their problems are evident and individualistic. To begin with, Philip has mild Royalist leanings; he has been drawn into the war rather reluctantly on the side of the Royalists. His father, Kennedy points out, was secretary to the governor of Virginia, and Philip combined his own generous patrimony with his wife's inheritance to become one of the wealthiest men in Virginia (81). But he has taken little part in the controversies of his own times; on the contrary, he has moved to Dove Cote, a site near the western frontier that is ideal for retirement, contemplation, and meditation (95). His actions with respect to the war indicate a desire to evade circumstances: he has conveyed his land to Mildred to protect it from confiscation. Some of Kennedy's readers must have recognized this strategy as an acceptable way of protecting assets in times of economic turmoil (Lebsock 57–67), but Lindsay's action seems cowardly in the course of the plot because readers already know that Mildred and her brother, Henry, have taken strong stands in support of the Whigs, and Mildred is daily making sacrifices out of loyalty to Whig principles.

Moreover, Philip's association with British officers is not an act of commitment. Isolated though it may be, Dove Cote is in a militarily strategic

Whigs and Covert Missions: Horse-Shoe Robinson

location because it lies near a major road that joins the Northern and Southern colonies. Tories and British officers visit Lindsay often and attempt to involve him in the effort to suppress the rebellion; while Philip finds this attention flattering, he still resists when Tyrrel, a British officer working undercover, asks him to mobilize other gentlemen in his area to support the Tories (Kennedy 85, 100). The reasons he offers for his refusal all have to do with the preservation of his status or his life. Philip thus contrasts with Arthur Butler, who explicitly places his life and estate at risk by supporting the Whigs, and Phillip's cowardice continues when he accompanies Tyrrel on a recruiting mission despite his misgivings. Thus, Phillip is hardly the devout Tory that some commentators have sought to make him; on the contrary, he may be bent on protecting his interests, or he may be no more than a weak-willed and withdrawing man.

Just as Phillip has tried to withdraw from the turbulence of his times, he has tried to withdraw from his children. Other fathers—Allen Musgrove and David Ramsay—interact more effectively with their sons and daughters. Lindsay opposes his son Harry's involvement with the local Whig militia, but he makes no particular effort to interfere with it, and Harry remains an active militiaman. Similarly, Lindsay gives Mildred explicit guidance with respect to Arthur Butler: She is not to see him or communicate with him. But Phillip knows nothing of the secret communications channels that she and Butler have established, and she is able to maintain contact and the secrecy of her marriage until she decides that her father must know. Phillip does not seem to react to evidence that one of his children is simply ignoring his wishes; both Harry and Mildred do as they see fit. Phillip's irresolute behavior keeps them from respecting his authority, and while there is evidence that the Lindsays love each other, the war divides them so that they can no longer function cooperatively. Phillip's wishes govern his children's actions only when he is present.

Phillip's detachment has a political dimension in his reluctance to join the Tories as well as a familial dimension in his distance from his own children. Thus, Kennedy could use Phillip to make a point about the political currents of the early 1830s. We have seen that Jackson's expressed willingness to use Federal force against a state led Southern states to express sympathy for South Carolina. Many Southerners, however, found themselves in awkward positions as a result. On one hand, the tariffs of the American System seemed likely to deprive Southerners of imported goods at the same time that the proposed internal improvements seemed likely to strengthen the North more than the South. Many Southerners believed that the real sympathies of the Whigs were with Northern manufacturers, particularly when the Whig candidate was a consummate New Englander such as John Quincy Adams—whose father had opposed Thomas Jefferson, the beau ideal of many Southerners, and who himself had opposed Jackson and narrowly defeated him. In 1828, then the South had rallied to Jackson, and just before the climax of the Nullification Crisis, the South, for the most part, had rallied to Jackson again, expecting that he, a fellow Southerner, would aggressively pursue the tariff reforms they sought. That did not happen, and by the end of 1833, Southerners were considering remaining independent of the emerging parties. They hoped to lead the South to support whatever candidate seemed most likely to promote distinctively Southern interests. We have seen that Kennedy himself went through a period of disenchantment around the time he was writing *Swallow Barn* and that he became angry and active during the writing of *Horse-Shoe Robinson.*

But Kennedy had not lost faith or interest in politics or the political process. His disenchantment had to do with the personal ambition of politicians and the meanness of the debate over important issues, but he would recognize and accept changes in political practice, too. He must have recognized that the Democrats were rapidly becoming better organized than the Whigs—he was, after all, an active Whig organizer in Baltimore—and that they would seek to make strong bids for Southern votes that could weaken the Whigs in 1836. When Kennedy presents Phillip as well-meaning and ineffectual, he is urging those who had become disenchanted to avoid withdrawal. In light of this, to lament modern trends, as Frank does in *Swallow Barn,* and withdraw from change seems a less acceptable course than renewed activism of the sort that led Kennedy back into the Maryland House of Delegates and eventually the national cabinet (as Secretary of the Navy) in the years after *Horse-Shoe Robinson.*

The Lindsay family contrasts with that of Mary Musgrove, whose parents send her alone to visit their relatives, the Adairs, who live as much as thirty miles away. Indeed, young Mary has traveled to Camden, an even greater distance from her home, although it is not clear that she made the latter journey alone. The Adairs may be lower class, unruly, and seedy, and the roads between the Adairs' home and the Musgroves' mill may be traveled by Tory marauders, but the Musgroves repose sufficient confidence in their daughter to allow her to travel alone. There is reason for their confidence, too: It takes Arthur Butler only brief conversation with her to ascertain that she is a remarkably observant and insightful young woman. Within a few minutes after getting a good look at him, for example, she notices a locket and concludes that the Adairs' visitor is a gentleman and not, perhaps, the cattle grazer he claims to be.

The Musgroves can easily afford their confidence in their daughter; she is the product of an orderly, stable home that stands in stark contrast to their relatives, the Adairs. Her parents are anything but irresolute. In fact, Allen Musgrove, the patriarchal miller, seems at first an overly stern evangelical who appears to pay as much attention to his Bible and prayer book as to events around him. He is a devout Presbyterian whose description sounds almost like that of a Biblical prophet, and he seems inclined to avoid the political issues of the war. Still, he does not seek, like Philip

Whigs and Covert Missions: Horse-Shoe Robinson 81

Lindsay, to avoid the conflict; he sees that it has a moral dimension, and for this reason he makes himself available to assist the Whigs. He has been persecuted for his religious beliefs, and so he prays for a government that will grant freedom of conscience—not specifically a victory for Whigs or Tories. First and foremost, Musgrove is portrayed as a man of principle who recognizes the moral rightness of the Whig cause and is willing to lend his assistance, which turns out to be moral as well as practical. Through Allen Musgrove, Kennedy gives the Whigs an appealing exemplar of patriarchal authority in a yeoman figure, and he associates the Whigs with tolerance as well as staunch morality. He is a kindly man whose Whig leanings become clear only after he has assisted Arthur Butler on a personal level, extending kindness to the captive officer without making any explicit judgment on the major's cause. He is also quick to offer what consolation he can to the Ramsays when their son John is killed. He is at all times an upright and hard-working man who shares a comfortable home with his family. He supports this further with David Ramsay, father of Mary's fiancé, John Ramsay. David's role in the action is more limited than that of Allen Musgrove, but he loses his first-born son, his house, and his barn to the Tories and still remains faithful to the Whig cause.

Both of these men stand in contrast to Wat Adair, the woodsman who tries to betray Butler and Robinson to the Tories. The initial description of his home conveys disorderliness and squalor, far from the quiet of Lindsay's Dove Cote or the industry and order of Musgrove's mill. It is possible to argue that Wat Adair never appears to function as a father; while Phillip Lindsay, Allen Musgrove, and David Ramsay all at least interact pleasantly with their children, Wat seems to ignore his. If we recall the generational model of *Swallow Barn*, in which Ned and Rip are groomed by their parents or surrogates for their future roles, Wat's lack of attention to his children takes on a greater significance: It suggests that he has no ties to the future. Even Phillip, who seems out of touch with his children on an operational level, at least provides materially for them, and he tries to fill a fatherly role in their lives even if they do not follow his guidance. Wat's concern is with immediate gain, and his loyalty is to the bag of gold that the British have given him to deliver Robinson and Butler into their hands.

Similarly, his loyalty to other members of the family seems weak. Mrs. Crosby (apparently his mother-in-law), an elderly woman, believes that Wat and his family value the room that she occupies in their home more than they value her. The woodsman's isolation, in her mind at least, has permeated and served as a model for his entire family, and it is not difficult to see how she might reach such a conclusion. Wat's wife, Peggy, when Robinson and Butler arrive, complains that her husband is too generous with hospitality; certainly she is not guilty of excessive kindness with respect to her visiting niece, Mary Musgrove. Indeed, Mary seems to be a servant at first because in her first appearance in the novel, she is working

82   *Will the Circle be Unbroken?*

alone in the kitchen and the Adairs order her around in ways that seem unusual for a visiting kinswoman.

The children of the Adair household, likewise, are chiefly notable for their inattention to what is going on around them: Although they live in a remote area and must see strangers infrequently, the arrival of Butler and Robinson does not attract their attention. They are also notable for their unruliness: One of the boys has shot away a lock of his sister's hair and speaks impudently to his father during dinner. These children do nothing to advance the plot, but they contribute to the characterization of the Adairs, and, by extension, the unruly Tory militiamen. The only parental nurturing act that readers see in the Adair household involves the couple's infant son. When he cries, Peggy Adair picks him up and nurses him "without scruple at the presence of her visitors" (Kennedy 145). Sally McMillen has indicated that breast-feeding was regarded as beneficial for women and infants alike during the period when Kennedy was writing and that the incidence of wet-nursing would have been higher had the act been stigmatized (111–134). In other words, there was little reason, if any, for Kennedy's readers to see Peggy's act as unusual or inappropriate, but the author, in a few short words, manages to make it seem exhibitionistic or animalistic rather than nurturing.

The Adairs represent, in some way, the antithesis of the Whig virtues which are best typified in the Musgroves. Kennedy leaves unclear just how the Adairs reached their state of degeneracy. His contemporary, Beverley Tucker, might well have attributed their state to an innate shiftlessness and lack of direction. Kennedy suggests that Adair does several types of work rather than one, but this was not unusual on the frontier. By establishing the kinship ties between the Adairs with the Musgroves, however, Kennedy indicates that the condition of the former is neither innate nor externally imposed on them. Kennedy had seen in Baltimore that wealth could be acquired by those who wished to do so; his own family and his own success indicated that Americans could hope to improve their material condition. Moreover, as a Whig, he must have wished to indicate that Whigs represented those who sought to rise from poverty—the Musgroves and Ramsays—while the Democrats promoted complacency of the sort represented by the Adairs.

The families of *Horse-Shoe Robinson*, then, create very different impressions. The Musgroves and Ramsays are industrious, affectionate, and economically comfortable, and their support of the Whigs is not fanatical, it rests upon principle. The Tory Adairs are shiftless, detached, and impoverished, and their commitment to the Tories—or any other party—depends upon cash for service rendered rather than principle. The Butlers, Arthur and Mildred, are much like the Whig families, but they are imperiled because of the rift in the Lindsay family. Moreover, Phillip Lindsay's indecisiveness and lack of commitment threaten his family's well-being. His friendship with Tories and opposition to Whigs sets a barrier between him

Whigs and Covert Missions: Horse-Shoe Robinson   *83*

and his children and, by extension, between him and the future. These families allow Kennedy to underscore the importance of commitment, which Philip lacks, as well as to associate the Whigs with a prosperous, resilient, and attractive middle class.

The times in which these families live, of course, are unusual. The characters confront two issues: Will the mission of Butler and Robinson be completed so that the Whigs can win a victory in the South, and will Mildred be reunited with Butler? These issues are intertwined through the characters of Mildred and Butler, of course, but Kennedy links the personal and national plots by pointing out early that private grief and public misfortune are mingled in time of crisis (Kennedy 39). On the most superficial level, he reminds readers often that a British victory will mean that Arthur forfeits his life and his property, and it may trap Mildred into a marriage with Tyrrel, who is chiefly interested in possession of her father's estate and in Mildred as a possession rather than a partner. In the other families, Mary Musgrove and John Ramsay have postponed marriage pending the end of the war, and although John is killed, the cause that led him to his death provides for Mary's future: Because she shares his commitment to the cause, she becomes acquainted with Robinson and the Butlers. After John's death, she moves to Dove Cote as a servant to Mildred Butler on the basis of their shared commitment and experience. Wat Adair is killed by a rabid wolf; Kennedy tells readers nothing about the effect of his death on his family, but perhaps it made little difference. The Adairs' poverty and squalor could be little less appealing than they appear early in the novel.

This intertwining of public and private matters may have been a matter of Kennedy's invention, a set of devices set in place so that the novel could carry a political meaning metaphorically. James "Horse-Shoe" Robertson, when questioned by an interviewer after the novel had been published, attested that the story Kennedy told was true, except for the parts involving women, which he claimed to "disremember." While historical romances did feature imperiled characters being rescued by their lovers, the imperiled woman rescued by her beloved—as is the case in *Kentuckian in New-York* and *Cavaliers of Virginia*—seems to have been more common than the imperiled man—particularly the imperiled military officer—rescued by his wife, as is the case in *Horse-Shoe Robinson*. In assigning Mildred and Mary prominent roles in the rescue of Arthur Butler, then, Kennedy must have recognized that he was stepping outside of the existing literary and social conventions. The prominence of these two heroic women is striking, too, because Kennedy had demonstrated in *Swallow Barn* that he could write a successful novel in which women were on the periphery of the central action. In other words, he could have chosen to write a book in which there were no important female characters and soldierly men carried the action. In addition, the frontier yeoman type represented by Horse-Shoe Robinson as well as Montgomery Damon in *Kentuckian in New-York* was part of a genre that did not require much emphasis on the female charac-

84   *Will the Circle be Unbroken?*

ters. Thus, if one argues that *Horse-Shoe Robinson* revolves around the title character's efforts to rescue Arthur Butler and complete his mission, there remains a question of why an experienced soldier such as Robinson would follow his commander's orders to travel to Dove Cote, in Virginia, instead of to a military headquarters in South Carolina after escaping from the Tories. This is especially true when we consider that the soldier, Robinson, is a skilled woodsman and ruthless fighter who, unassisted, could probably rescue Butler alone or complete the mission. Still, Kennedy has Robinson travel back to Dove Cote and then details his return to South Carolina with Mildred and her brother, Henry. Similarly, in carrying out the rescue, there is not much need for Mary Musgrove. Other male characters, such as Christopher Musgrove and Andrew Ramsay, are young enough to travel without arousing much suspicion among the Tories, and they could do much of what Mary does. But instead of giving the male figures larger roles, Kennedy created a female character who proved to be as appealing as the title character in the minds of the reviewers and modern commentators.

Why would an author make these choices? A possible answer is that Kennedy wished to associate the Whigs with virtuous women who were willing to step out of their normal roles in time of crisis. Much of what Mary and Mildred do is aimed at protecting their families from the depredations of the Tories in dangerous times. While women in Kennedy's time (as in the Revolutionary period) were denied direct participation in political action, Mary Beth Norton has pointed out that by the time of Kennedy's birth in 1790, "it seemed as though republican theorists believed that the fate of the republic rested squarely, perhaps solely, upon the shoulders of its womenfolk" (Norton 243). This republican motherhood, as it has come to be known, "altered the female domain in which most women had always lived out their lives [and] justified women's absorption and participation in the civic culture" (Kerber 284). While neither of the principal female characters in *Horse-Shoe Robinson* is shown as a mother raising her sons to be virtuous, both are willing to support the cause for which their men are fighting, even when doing so requires that they step out of traditional female roles.

The childlessness of Kennedy's heroines does not quite mean that they cannot function as republican mothers: Mildred appears several times in a maternal role with respect to her brother, Henry. Henry and Mildred seem to be about the same age, and Kennedy tells readers that Phillip Lindsay was not much concerned about his son's ability to make his way in the world (Kennedy 104). This seems to be an indication of Phillip's detachment from his family rather than Henry's ability; there is little reason to believe that the slightly immature, enthusiastic Henry can fend for himself. In fact, in his earliest appearance he is returning from hunting with a deer that will find its way to the Dove Cote dining room, but the deer was actually killed by Stephen Foster, a yeoman neighbor. Henry's idea of war seems

Whigs and Covert Missions: Horse-Shoe Robinson   *85*

to involve wearing a uniform and blowing a bugle, but Mildred acts out a maternal role, which is appropriate because their mother is dead. She insists that Henry study military arts, and she occasionally has him demonstrate or report on the progress of his martial education. In this way, Kennedy has a secretly married childless woman play the educational role that historians associate with the republican mother (Kerber (228) and Norton (247) discuss women's educational roles; examples of women performing this role are found in another useful, but unpublished, source: St. George Tucker's 1812 essay praising Virginian women (Hare 31)). It is also important to recognize that Mildred's teaching role directly supports the Whig military effort.

But the dangerous times of the Tory ascendency call for women to step out of their normal roles as wives, mothers, and domestic mistresses. Peggy Adair does not do this; the Whig women do. In taking his leave of Mildred, Arthur asks that she notify him, through the headquarters of General Horatio Gates, of any information she can gather concerning Tyrrel's covert activities (Kennedy 126). She is thus made an informer and a direct participant in Whig military activities, and she participates willingly. By the same token, Mary alertly recognizes that Arthur and Robinson are not what they seem to be, and she gives them warning of Wat Adair's plans to betray them to the Tories (Kennedy 157–159, 612–163). This act constitutes treason because it gives aid and comfort to the Tories' enemies, and it requires that Mary put aside "maidenly scruples" by entering Butler's room, but she warns Butler and Robinson because she hopes that her direct action on behalf of fellow Whigs will please John Ramsay (Kennedy 161).

While both of these acts involve the characters in danger and are to that extent extraordinary, neither requires the woman involved to step far out of her normal routine or role. They are arguably tasks that women might take on in the interest of assisting the men in their lives, and they suggest the interdependency that we identified in *The Kentuckian in New-York.* But Kennedy has his heroines do far more than this. Mildred must make a long, harrowing journey through North Carolina, and Mary must become an active co-conspirator in the efforts to free Arthur Butler. Mildred is in danger throughout her journey; as Kennedy points out, she is unused to riding long distances, and he repeatedly calls attention to her exhaustion as the journey progresses (See, for example, Kennedy 390, 399, 414). Similarly, although she is reluctant to confront Tyrrel directly, she is quite willing to approach Cornwallis, a figure of far greater authority (Kennedy 481–483). By undertaking an arduous journey and confronting one who occupies a position of far greater power than she, Mildred steps outside of a purely female role to address the exigencies of the times.

As we have already seen with respect to her effort to protect Butler and Robinson from Wat Adair's betrayal, Mary's activities also require her to set aside maidenly scruples. She sets aside more than this, however, as she becomes increasingly active in support of Butler's rescue. After Butler's capture, she initially follows the instructions that Robinson gives her (Kennedy 256–257). Before much time passes, however, she seems to develop some military acumen. When the time comes to free Butler from his captivity at Musgrove's mill, Mary is the one who actually develops the plan and successfully promotes it to Robinson and John Ramsay (Kennedy 417–419). In the course of this action, when she finds John sleeping in the presence of the enemy, she chides him, thereby taking on the role of a military sergeant or officer of the guard—a role not open to women. John's defense—that he was dreaming of her—is one that might carry weight with a fiancée, but Mary, acting in her military role, does not accept it (Kennedy 418). In performing this role, Mary's earnestness contrasts with the playfulness of Mildred's engagement in Henry's military training. While Mildred does things that are outside of her normal range of activities, Mary actually takes on new roles as covert agent and military officer. Both take extraordinary actions because this is what the times demand; it may be that Mary's acceptance of new roles and resultant growth have drawn reviewers and modern commentators alike to find in her an especially appealing character. Moreover, to represent female characters taking on such traditionally masculine roles suggests that Kennedy did not view roles or functions as innate and immutable, but as socially constructed and flexible enough to adapt to changing circumstances.

The circumstances of war demand more than extraordinary action. We have already seen that Mary loses John Ramsay (and dies a spinster as a result) because of the war. Similarly, Mildred loses her father: During the battle of Kings Mountain, he is mortally wounded. Upon returning to Dove Cote with Tyrrel, he found a letter from Mildred explaining her secret marriage to Butler and this news depressed him, calling to his attention the depth of the rift between him and his children. This led him to go in pursuit of Mildred, hoping for reconciliation. At the end, he explicitly forgives both of his children for their Whig sympathies (Kennedy 544–545), and this forgiveness and acceptance pave the way for the Lindsay family to be reconstructed and the marriage of Arthur and Mildred to be fully legitimated—even though Phillip does not adopt his children's political views before his death.

But not all outcomes are so happy. When Mary loses a fiancé, the Ramsays lose their elder son. David Ramsay, John's father, places this in perspective by saying that no man could ask a better death than to die in the service of his country, and he expresses his new willingness for his younger son, Andrew, to enter the army, despite Mrs. Ramsay's objections. Andrew argues that John's death, the burning of their home, and the terrorizing of their mother justify him in fighting the Royalists, but Allen Musgrove, who is with the Ramsays at the time, urges him not to fight for vengeance but for justice (Kennedy 437–440). The sacrifices also fall on other subordinate characters, particularly the women who assist Mildred and her party as they journey southward. Mrs. Wingate, the wife of one of

Whigs and Covert Missions: Horse-Shoe Robinson 87

Francis Marion's rangers, loses her husband and her home in an incident that Mildred takes as evidence of the savagery of war (Kennedy 398, 403–405). Similarly, Rachel Markham, the widow of another of Marion's men, shelters the travelers (Kennedy 414–416). She is presented as remaining staunchly sympathetic to the Whigs, despite the loss of her husband in action against the British. As a result of her fidelity, the Whig commanders, particularly Marion, have sought to protect and assist her (Kennedy 415–416). In other words, the sacrifice that she has made in the service of the community ensures that the other survivors of the community will assist her, just as Mildred and Arthur assist Mary after John's death—and Kennedy's silence about any assistance offered to the Adairs after Wat's death becomes particularly suggestive. In a broader sense, Kennedy also makes the point that those who have shared in risk and sacrifice are bound by the experience and assist each other throughout their lives.

In *Horse-Shoe Robinson,* then, Kennedy demonstrated that the Whig values of cooperation and self-sacrifice were not limited to the upper class but could exist among the yeomanry as well. Moreover, these values could bind the virtuous members of all classes together. He also demonstrated that unusual times could call for unusual measures from all members of the community; if Mildred or Mary refuses to step out of her normal female role to assist the Whigs, the likelihood of Butler's rescue and the successful outcome of the campaign must be in doubt. By setting the novel in the South, where the Revolution approximated a civil war in its divisiveness and wanton destruction, Kennedy was also able to suggest that division within a community could lead to horrible consequences. Those consequences he had foreseen as early as December 1832, when he predicted in his journal that nullification would lead to secession and war (Kennedy). This consequence, he believed, would ensue if the states continued to assert their rights instead of recognizing and acting upon their common interests and interdependencies. His second novel, like his first, was aimed in part at averting that eventuality. Not all authors, however, saw division and war as entirely undesirable. As *Horse-Shoe Robinson* went to press, Beverley Tucker was measuring Andrew Jackson and his chosen successor, Martin Van Buren, against the standard of the faithful ruler-father that Caruthers had invoked in *The Cavaliers of Virginia,* and he found them wanting. If proper leaders did not emerge, Tucker would hold, the political system was a failure, and secession would be necessary, even if it led to war.

CHAPTER SIX
Birthright and Authority:
George Balcombe

While the novels that we have so far examined treated the course of human events as generally positive and the Union as an entity, these views were anathema to Nathaniel Beverley Tucker, who was, in the mid-1830s, becoming known as a staunch advocate of slavery, states' rights, and secession. So powerful has Tucker's reputation become in this regard that one might be tempted to seek evidence of these positions in *George Balcombe* or, finding little there, to dismiss the work almost entirely. But both of these approaches overlook the historical facts of Tucker's early literary career. While *George Balcombe* and Tucker's other well-known novel, the unabashedly political *Partisan Leader,* are treated separately here, the two works are most productively viewed as companion pieces that were probably completed at about the same time. *George Balcombe,* written during Jackson's last term, provides a model ruler-father in the title character, an example of the kind of leader the nation needed, and it high-lighted the most important qualities of this figure through the narrator, himself a ruler-father in training.

Robert Brugger, Tucker's biographer, indicates that *George Balcombe* "surely was conceived in the West [that is, in Missouri] and was probably begun there" before Tucker returned to Virginia in 1832 (121). The plot of the novel turns on the restoration of order and fortune in a family disrupted by usurpation of a will. This situation roughly parallels events that occupied much of Tucker's attention as a result of the will of his half-brother John Randolph and thus suggests that the bulk of the work must have been done after 1833—after Tucker had returned to Virginia. The novel features a complex plot that places the principal characters in a range of settings from the well established Virginia Tidewater to the Missouri frontier.

A young Virginian in reduced circumstances, William Napier, rides to Missouri in pursuit of a man named Montague, whom he suspects has usurped his Grandfather Raby's estate. Before he finds Montague, though,

89

he encounters George Balcombe, a displaced Virginian who has ties to the Raby household and takes the leading role in recovering the estate. Throughout the work, Balcombe displays the qualities of a faithful leader with respect to his affectionate subordinates, Napier, another young man named James Scott, and their families and friends. The work may be read as a gentle treatise on leadership that reacts in some respects to Andrew Jackson, whom Tucker had supported but with whom he had come to differ increasingly. Where Caruthers had attacked Jackson through the character of Governor Berkley, Tucker regarded Jackson as a fellow Southerner and slaveholder who might be brought back to the proper course with the gentle admonition offered by a positive model. The same admonition might provide the electorate a standard against which to measure candidates to succeed Jackson.

Tucker's second novel represents a counterpoint to this gentle admonition. *The Partisan Leader* was written some months after *George Balcombe,* during the early stages of the presidential campaign of 1836. It focuses on the experiences of the Trevor family of Virginia after the Southern states have seceded but before Virginia has followed them out of the Union. This extended family includes two aging brothers, Hugh, who has resisted secession, and Bernard, who favors it. As we shall see in the next chapter, this work aims directly at Martin Van Buren, whom Tucker detested. Both *George Balcombe* and *The Partisan Leader* reflect Tucker's increasing concern over Jacksonian democratization, which he associated with social disorder and mob rule. By writing two novels at about the same time, Tucker may have sought to move from general constructive criticism to a more specific critique and proposal for action as circumstances shifted.

By looking at these novels as works revolving around families, we can see similarities indicating that for Beverley Tucker, the family retained a central position in considerations of authority and subordination. While *The Partisan Leader* shows an extended family restructured by political controversy and secession—the twin consequences of continuing the present course toward nationalism and democratization—*George Balcombe* shows a family drawing together around a patriarchal figure who aids them in defining, coordinating, and securing their interests. It also shows a young man gaining the wealth and experience necessary to assume his rightful position of leadership in his family and community.

George Balcombe traces the efforts of William Napier to secure his inheritance, ensure the economic future of his mother and sisters, and marry his cousin Ann. Napier, a young Virginian, is descended from a distinguished line: His father had little wealth because his own father had sacrificed much of his estate in public service during the Revolution, but his mother came from the wealthy Raby family. Through his mother, William would have had a substantial inheritance from his grandfather, Charles Raby—if the latter's last will had not disappeared mysteriously (Tucker

Birthright and Authority: George Balcombe 91

1:32). Napier's inheritance from his father, on the other hand, consists of a memorandum reporting that a man named Montague holds Raby's last will, which bequeaths half of the Raby estate to Napier. The novel begins as Napier seeks to locate Montague along the Missouri frontier.

Napier has left his mother, his sisters, and his cousin Ann in poverty in Virginia, where no one seems inclined to acknowledge his place in the community or to assist him in reclaiming his birthright, so it is critical that he find Montague (Tucker 1:35, 45). If he can do this and retrieve the missing will, his mother and Ann (Raby's grand-daughter, the orphaned daughter of Napier's maternal aunt) will divide the remaining half of the Raby estate (1:88, 32). This represents a great windfall to Napier because he and Ann have loved each other since childhood and have expected to marry. Without this inheritance, however, their economic circumstances seem likely to preclude what Tucker represents as the natural evolution of their relationship (1:88–89)[1]: Napier's father, before dying, explained to him that marriage to Margaret Howard, a wealthy young woman from outside of the immediate community, would be a pleasanter means of upholding the honor of the family than the study of law or medicine that his son proposes (1:93). This course would also leave Ann free to marry Margaret Howard's brother, thereby further increasing the assets and the security of the Raby descendants (1:94). To restore the family fortune and make the marriage that he wishes to make, Napier must locate Montague and the last will. By doing so, he indicates Tucker's belief in marriage.

Montague, however, is a formidable adversary. He is the last of a respectable but impoverished family, and he owes his education and his start in life to Napier's grandfather, Charles Raby (Tucker 1:34). His conduct as a young man before the time of the novel, however, has been reprehensible: Montague seduced Mary Scott, the daughter of Raby's overseer, and then abandoned her to avoid jeopardizing his chance of receiving an inheritance from Raby (1:57). While he has financially assisted Mary's mother and brother, the provisions he has made have not been motivated by real contrition but calculated to buy his way into Mary's affections and ensure her cooperation in keeping secret his usurpation of the Raby estate (1:139–141). Although he professes that he has become an evangelical Christian and a reformed man since the misdeeds of his youth (1:140, 163), he is quite willing to spend time with some of the worst rogues in Missouri (1:217), to lie to almost anyone (1:205, 207, 248, 2:133), and to commit arson (and probably murder by arson as well) (2:159).

Montague's usurpation of the Raby birthright has disordered an extended family. Families that should have lived comfortably—the Napiers and the Scotts—are caught in poverty and lose their standing in the community. Young people who should have been planning to marry for affection— Napier and Ann, Jane Napier and Angus Douglas—are instead concerned with marrying for financial survival. People like Napier and Mary, who might otherwise have enjoyed at least the respect of their community are, because of Montague, almost outcasts. Montague has not simply taken the money and property that was left to Raby's daughters and eldest grandson; he has robbed the family members of their status and reduced them to dependency. Because he is utterly unscrupulous, he can only be opposed successfully by a figure of considerable moral force. Napier, who is described somewhat sketchily as the narrator of the novel, is too young and lacks the experience to confront him successfully. Fortunately, at the beginning of the first chapter, Napier meets George Balcombe.

Like Montague and Napier, Balcombe is a native Virginian and a gentleman; indeed, he suggests that he and Napier are related (Tucker 1:21) although it later develops that there are neither blood nor legal ties connecting them. This is a significant point: The relationships around which the action of the novel revolves are identified by the characters as familial even though they are not based on blood or legal ties, nor on rational choices, nor on mystical attraction. This extended family group, however, is bound by common interests.

Balcombe was orphaned early and, like Montague, was able to complete his education at the College of William and Mary only through the generosity of Charles Raby (Tucker 1:40). As a young man, Balcombe loved Mary Scott, and he would have married her except for the guilt that she felt after Montague seduced her (1:49, 63). Rather than pursuing wealth after graduation, Balcombe traveled around the world seeking his fortune; he has not become wealthy, but this may be due to his generosity (1:40). Although he is a capable and honorable man, esteemed by friends and adversaries alike, he converses and cooperates easily with people of all classes, which allows him to enlist the aid of lower-class frontiersmen when necessary (1:82, 84). Throughout the novel, he is punctilious in seeing that his efforts to bring about a proper settlement—just provisions for Mary Scott and her family and the restoration of the Raby estate to the rightful heirs—are carried out in an honorable way (See, for example, 1:150; 1:192). This is a striking contrast to Montague, who, according to Balcombe, "'would murder his own father and dishonour the memory of the mother that bore him'" (1:178). Balcombe is also a devoted family man with a wife and a child and an advocate of affectionate marriage (1:70–71).

The efforts to bring about a just resolution of this matter span the United States from the Virginian Tidewater to Missouri. Balcombe and Napier are joined by James Scott, Mary's younger brother and emissary, and they narrowly escape death and imprisonment several times as they pursue their elusive adversary. Montague has Balcombe and Scott kidnapped by unscrupulous frontier ruffians, but they escape with the assistance of a woodsman from western Virginia and his Native American allies. When one of Montague's ruffians is killed during the rescue, Montague has Balcombe charged with murder. Balcombe defends himself

Birthright and Authority: George Balcombe 93

successfully, but the trial requires that he remain in Missouri, and this allows Montague to return to Virginia unimpeded. When Balcombe and his party pursue, they must again outwit the accomplices whom Montague has dispatched to murder them. Finally, when Montague seeks to retrieve the will from Mary Scott, Major Swann (Edward Raby's plantation manager) intervenes and seizes the packet containing the document so that a court can determine the rightful owner. As Scott and Napier are taking the packet to court, Montague makes one last effort to waylay them and seize the papers, but Scott kills him in a fit of rage inspired by hearing how the villain dishonored his sister. The packet is lost briefly during the fight, but Keizer, the loyal frontiersman, locates it and returns it to Balcombe. In due course, letters arrive from Edward Raby, the supposed heir in England who has benefited from Montague's suppression of the true last will. Raby is mortified to learn that he has been cheated and has been a party to cheating others. Having received from Napier's great-grandfather the "rights *and duties* of head of the family," he is eager to set matters right financially and in familial relationships (2: 299, italics in original). This entails transferring land to Napier and Balcombe, although the latter returns to Missouri because he cannot afford to maintain the estate without accepting charity from Napier.

At the very end of the work—fifteen years after the end of the main action—the family has drawn closer and is about to reunite. Balcombe, a wealthy man after his father-in-law's death, is on his way back to Virginia with James Scott, who has married his daughter. Howard has married Napier's sister Laura, and Napier has married Ann. Even Howard's sister, Margaret, who had sworn never to marry unless she married Balcombe, has married a man from the West. To fulfill the last condition of Charles Raby's will, Napier has changed his name to William Napier Raby (2:310, 317–319).

Tucker's friends and relatives wrote to Tucker about the work, and their readings provide some indication of how Tucker's contemporaries may have read his works. Moreover, they suggest that Tucker's relatives were chiefly concerned with the families in the novel. For example, St. George Coalter, a nephew of the Tuckers, wrote to Beverley that Henry St. George Tucker, the author's brother, thought *George Balcombe* one of the best books of its kind that he had read. Coalter found the work gripping because of "the variety of incident, the diversity of character, and the varying scenes," but its real greatness, he thought, lay in "the bright portraits of human character, in its rarest and most difficult forms." The importance of Balcombe himself might be a flaw, Coalter believed, apparently because the hero struck him as implausibly virtuous. Similarly, Coalter worried that the book was "only faulty in the too plain tale of M. Scott's fall in bringing it too close in time, place, and circumstance." This last may be a reference to a Randolph/Tucker family scandal of the 1790s, in which Nancy

Randolph had an affair with her cousin (and brother-in-law) Richard Randolph after the death of his brother, Theodorick, with whom she was in love (Wyatt-Brown 221–222). Both Richard and Theodorick Randolph were half-brothers of Beverley Tucker. While the details of this affair differ significantly from those of the Mary Scott story, Coalter, the son of Beverley's sister, Ann Frances Tucker Coalter, may have feared that the inclusion of a sex scandal could recall to readers that the Tucker family had not been far removed from a similar occurrence. (His fears seem exaggerated because the novel was originally published anonymously.) Other relatives, giving their own impressions, gave more detailed readings and pointed out other concerns. Elizabeth Tucker Bryan, a niece, complained that Montague, the villain, professed to be a Christian while the otherwise admirable hero "might have been a moral Deist, a Jew, a Universalist" because he never "[recognized] our Saviour and religion without a Saviour such as we are told of in the Bible is a thing of nothing." For her, the possible correspondence to a family scandal was immaterial; she was chiefly concerned with the principal characters as representatives of different ethical foundations.

George Balcombe was popular enough that not all of Tucker's friends were able to obtain copies of the book. T. M. Robinson complained that he had found only two copies of *George Balcombe* in Philadelphia because the supplies of the work sent to that city had been sold immediately after their arrival. William C. Preston, a South Carolinian friend, suggested a reason for the book's popularity: In his estimation, *George Balcombe* differed from other American works of the period because it did not follow the models of Scott and Mulvern but went "forth with a free and confident step" rather than imitating English authors. Reviewers, including Edgar Allan Poe and William Gilmore Simms, praised the work as a strong representation of the frontier and regarded it as one of the best American novels (Hubbell 429). Apparently then, these contemporary readers saw *George Balcombe* as a novel about a distinctively American character in distinctively American settings. While Tucker reminded the readers throughout the text that his principal characters—good and evil—were Virginians, the contemporary readers seem to have seen them as Americans, or as Americans should be, with George Balcombe himself as the ideal ruler-father, a man of heroic character who could identify and organize the interests of his subordinates and lead them as they returned to their rightful place in the community.

More recent commentators have been less impressed. Jay B. Hubbell praised Tucker's representation of the frontier on the whole; however, he argued that *George Balcombe* was little more than an extended local color piece (429). William R. Taylor saw the point of the novel as promoting the relocation of the plantation aristocracy to the West and Southwest—even though the principal characters are all in Virginia at the end and they never

Birthright and Authority: George Balcombe

seem to transplant much of Virginian culture to Missouri. He saw Balcombe as a "new man," a "bastard hero" who was half Virginian gentleman and half frontiersman (152–153). J.V. Ridgely dismissed the work as a "drearily conventional narrative which is only partially redeemed by some genre pictures of the border territory" (43). Robert Brugger saw the work as part of Tucker's broad attempt to define Southern manners and values as distinctive and worthy of preservation. This is in keeping with Tucker's literary values and explains Balcombe's heroic stature as well as the novel's emphasis on the dire consequences of men's failure to defer to their natural betters (121, 123–124). Strikingly, these commentators make little mention of Balcombe's return to his inherited estate in Virginia at the end of the novel.

Many commentators, ante-bellum and modern, gloss over *George Balcombe* to address Tucker's second novel, *The Partisan Leader*. Little attention is paid to the circumstances surrounding the composition of these novels. Those circumstances are revealing, particularly when we consider that Tucker seems to have written both novels at approximately the same time during 1834 and 1835. In these years, an anti-Jacksonian (but not committed to the Whigs as Kennedy had been), he hoped to see the Democrats defeated. At the same time, he must have recognized that his brand of Whiggery, which emphasized state's rights, was far removed from that of staunchly nationalistic Whigs such as John Pendleton Kennedy. But like Kennedy and Caruthers, Tucker was concerned with the nature of authority and the ideal character of a leader. In *George Balcombe,* he addressed these matters in the title figure and his relationships with other family members.

We have observed that *George Balcombe* is a tale of the disruption and reconstruction within an extended family, a point that commentators have chosen to overlook. That family, in some respects bears resemblance to the family as Beverley Tucker had experienced it.[2] The relations between Charles Raby, his daughters, and his grandchildren are clear enough. It is equally important, if a bit more difficult, to recognize that Balcombe and Montague are also members of the Raby family: Both live with Raby and receive from him their education and early assistance in their careers. By providing this support, Raby assumes a paternal role that eighteenth-century Virginian parents took for granted. These parents set out to establish estates that were large enough to assure a satisfactory start in the world for their children, and they encouraged their children to maintain the gifts and bequests that they received (Lewis 117). Providing a son with financial assistance was part of locating him economically in the Jeffersonian Virginia of Beverley Tucker's youth, just as giving him a name was a means of locating him socially. By extending this assistance to Montague and Balcombe, then, Raby brings them into his family.

96   *Will the Circle be Unbroken?*

Beverley Tucker undoubtedly recognized that informal adoptions of this sort conferred a status within the family; after all, he was born into what is today called an extended family. His father, St. George Tucker, married Frances Bland Randolph, the widow of John Randolph, in 1778, and she brought to the marriage control of several estates as well as three sons—Richard, Theodorick, and John. Nathaniel Beverley was the youngest of the five children born to Frances and St. George Tucker (Brugger 4). After Frances's death, St. George Tucker married Leila Skipwith Carter, who was also a widow and brought to the marriage her own two children, both younger than Beverley. The year after their marriage, she gave birth to St. George Tucker, Junior (11). This brought the number of people having filial relationships with St. George Tucker to eight, ranging from Richard Randolph (who was 22 years old when his youngest step-brother was born), to the infant St. George, Junior. Sorting out degrees of kinship was complex—especially for young children; the Randolph children, for example, were siblings to each other, step-siblings to the Carter and Tucker-Carter children, and half-siblings to the Tucker-Randolph children. It appears, however, that the Tucker parents and children set aside degrees fairly readily (Wentworth 58; see also Smith 87, 97). In the mind of Beverley Tucker, then, Balcombe and Montague are members of the Raby family, bound by ties of affection of which we shall say more later. Thus, *George Balcombe* is a novel about occurrences within a family, and the family's future—like that of the Union—depends upon a leader who combines physical courage, a sense of personal honor, and the ability to discern the interests of his subordinates and mobilize those subordinates to act in concert. Balcombe is free of the autocratic insensitivity that Tucker saw in Jackson, and, to a more dangerous extent, in Van Buren.

Similarly, Mary Scott, although the daughter of a servant, has a claim to membership in the family, even though (according to Montague) Charles Raby had objections to a romantic relationship between her and Montague. To understand this, we need to recognize that some paid servants of a genteel family could assume some status within that family. Once again, Beverley Tucker's familial experience provides an illustrative example. The Tuckers hired John Coalter to tutor Beverley and his older brother, Henry St. George, but within weeks of Coalter's arrival at the Tucker home, he had become one of St. George Tucker's law students while continuing to serve as tutor (Hamilton 90). Coalter remained close to the Tuckers after completing his legal education, and Beverley's older sister, Ann Frances, became Coalter's second wife (Brugger 24). By the time of this marriage, Coalter was a successful lawyer, but he was living in Staunton, far from Williamsburg. This suggests that the relationship that led to the Tucker-Coalter marriage must have begun while Coalter was the tutor in the Tucker household. Granted, Coalter, as a law student, was preparing him-

Birthright and Authority: George Balcombe   97

self for better things, but the same may be said of Mary Scott, who seems to have been groomed for marriage to a gentleman.

The disorder in the extended Raby family also roughly parallels a disorder in the Tucker family that occurred during the period when Tucker must have been writing *George Balcombe.* In the novel, Montague's concealment of Charles Raby's true last will interferes with the orderly transfer of accumulated property to Raby's posterity. It is possible to better understand Tucker's use of this plot feature by considering briefly the testamentary issue concerning the novelist's father, St. George Tucker, and his half-brother, John Randolph.

Despite the eleven-year difference in their ages, Beverley and Randolph appear to have been close during their youth. Both had lost siblings to early deaths, and Brugger argues that they may have felt the "unconscious sense of specialness, of being 'chosen,' and perhaps of guilt over being spared [from early death]" (Brugger 11). In addition, it seems that John Randolph, the last survivor of his family, and Beverley, who appears to have felt consistently subordinated to his brother Henry, may have felt a particular closeness because neither of them seemed as able to find favor with St. George Tucker as Henry did. This shared experience may have proved a stronger bond than the blood ties between Beverley and Henry.

An 1808 episode reveals the bonds that bound Tucker, John Randolph, and St. George Tucker. While Beverley was studying law with John Coalter (by this time his brother-in-law), he met Coalter's younger sister Polly (Brugger 24, 33), and by 1807, he was eager to marry her. St. George Tucker, however, was not impressed by Beverley's protestations of the couple's love. He recognized that Beverley was not yet self-supporting, and in light of his own recent resignation of his professorship at William and Mary and the threats of war with Britain, he advised his son against the marriage (33–34). The following year, however, Beverley received from John Randolph 300 acres of farmland, 15 slaves, and farm animals. Given this change in Beverley's circumstances, St. George capitulated and agreed to the marriage, which took place in February 1809. By late 1810, however, Beverley had become entangled in an argument between John Randolph and Judith Randolph, Richard's widow; it was this tension, apparently, that led him to move from Randolph's plantation, Bizarre, and eventually to Missouri (43).

In 1833, Randolph had successfully urged his half-brother to return to Virginia, and the two men were together through the last months of Randolph's life. But Randolph's estate was in disorder. As Tucker described the matter to his father-in-law, Thomas A. Smith, back in Missouri,

> [Randolph] was certainly non compos when he made the last [will] that has been found. But there has been found a cancelled will without date, but, from circumstances not less than 12 years old, and those interested under that contend that it was cancelled when the other was made, and

98   *Will the Circle be Unbroken?*

> that [Randolph] being then insane it is to be set up. . . . There is moreover
> reason to believe that he has made a will long since either of these, and we
> certainly have not yet got the papers he had with him just before his death.
> The will be contested, and my knowledge of men and things here makes
> my presence indispensible [sic] for the collection of proofs (Tucker).

This passage makes clear that for Tucker, the problem of the Randolph will was more than the distribution of property. By omitting his Tucker relatives from his bequests and criticizing St. George in the will, Randolph was not simply depriving his kin of money and property to which they may have had some claim; he was also cutting himself off from the family and the cultural progression on which his own identity and success were founded. In doing so, he disrupted the link between past and present and between himself and the community at large. In writing to Smith, Tucker explained that he would remain in Virginia until the matter was settled. The accusations against St. George, he argued, were not only false, but Randolph "in his senses would have cut any man's throat for uttering [them]." To restore the proper order required that Beverley stay in Virginia, not because of his legal background but because he knew "more about the matter and the people hereabout than anybody else." While he stood to inherit between $10,000 and $50,000 if the will was set aside, he saw attending to the Randolph will as a "duty to the memory of [his] father and brother."

What is at stake in *George Balcombe,* likewise, is not simply money. We have already seen that lacking the Raby will, Napier is shunned by those in his native community who should recognize and assist him. Without the inheritance, the course of natural affection is blocked. Napier, at the beginning of the novel, is a lonely and somewhat bewildered young traveler; at the end, he has become a patriarch and a man of sufficient means to dispense charity and justice. In case readers overlooked the change in Napier, Tucker makes clear that the young man has a new name—a new identity—to go with his new position in the family and the community: William Napier Raby. He has become a man of authority within the family and by virtue of that, a model of civil authority. To understand this authority, we must examine Balcombe and Napier in greater detail.

It would be inconsistent with the order of the extended family for a young man such as Napier to accomplish his mission alone: At the beginning of the book, he is not aware of the dimensions of Montague's wrongdoing because he does not know Montague's background. He has no idea of how Montague came to be associated with his family, and he knows nothing of how Mary Scott came to be a reclusive woman. Thus, he is unsure of how to proceed, even to the point of uncertainty about the road that he is traveling. Fortuitous circumstances, however, place him in contact with the man who can appropriately take action, George Balcombe. At first, Napier thinks that Balcombe has a clownish appearance, but this reflects more upon the young man's hasty judgment than on the older

Birthright and Authority: George Balcombe

man's appearance (Tucker 1:3–4). To ensure that readers recognize Napier's rashness, Tucker introduces evidence that Napier misinterprets Balcombe's dogs' names as mispronunciations when they are actually literary names conferred by a man more widely read and traveled than he. Throughout the remainder of the novel, Tucker has Napier show similar lapses that would lead to failure if Balcombe were not on hand to guide him.

As we have noted, Napier sees Balcombe and forms an incorrect impression of him; this early episode suggests that the young man is not observant and lacks the experience to correctly interpret what he observes. On the contrary, Balcombe quickly recognizes Napier as a Virginian (on the basis of his saddle) on a journey (given the condition of his horse), and based on the young man's features, Balcombe believes that Napier is probably a member of a Tidewater family with which he has connections (Tucker 1:10–11). Indeed, the next morning, when Napier awakens later than he wishes, he is upset that he has delayed his journey until Balcombe points out that the weather is rainy and unsuitable for travel—a point that most travelers would notice immediately after arising, especially if rain was a likely problem (1:19). This young traveler is a man chiefly concerned with his own perceptions and his own wishes and, as a result, less attentive than he should be to the world around him. A leader with this shortcoming could not prove faithful to those he led; he would be unable to recognize and coordinate the interests of his subordinates.

By the same token, Napier does not know himself well. He does not see, at first, that his identity derives in part from his family; he claims that he is not concerned with his lineage beyond knowing who his father was— beyond knowing, that is, that he is of legitimate birth. At this point, Balcombe, for the first time of many, points out that Napier hardly knows his own mind: the young man really is concerned with his familial heritage, despite his advocacy of democratic notions aimed at diminishing the importance of aristocratic lineage (1:24). While the bulk of this passage early in the novel deals with Napier's view of his family, Tucker seizes it as an opportunity for his hero to offer an attack on Jacksonian thought:

> 'Then you do trace yourself beyond your father, as well you may. My dear sir, do not disparage yourself by adopting the cant of a political fanaticism. It is not for you to give into the humours of those who swell and rage at the word 'gentleman,' as if here as in England, it was one of the designations of an order in the state. What does it mean with us [that is, with Americans], but a man who scorns what is base, and detests what is brutal, and whose manners, either by nature or by training, conform to those sentiments? From this aristocracy, none are shut out but by their own fault . . . (1:23–24).

This may sound similar to Kennedy's view that Whiggery was open to people of all classes, but Tucker sets out to show that community is not a matter of partisan allegiance, but of recognizing and participating virtuously in an orderly society that necessarily includes various classes. At this point early in the novel, however, all of this is lost on Napier (1:24–25). For Tucker, however, there are orders of society into which men are born. This is clear in his treatment of John Keizer, a rough woodsman who assists Balcombe. Keizer is remarkably skilled as a fighter and hunter and, like Balcombe, he has strong skills in observation and reasoning. He is necessary to the defeat of Montague and the reconstruction of the Raby family, even though he is, according to Balcombe, thoroughly evil. These two men, in so many ways unlike each other, are nonetheless dependent on each other. Keizer can do covert and underhanded work for Balcombe and thereby protect Balcombe's reputation and status as a gentleman. At the same time, the woodsman's association with the gentleman immediately lends the former a legitimacy and eventually leads to his moral reformation.

Napier claims to have no interest in or knowledge of his own antecedents; his forgetting actually goes beyond that. His encounter with Balcombe in Missouri is not the first time that the two have met. On the contrary, Napier was taken to his grandfather's home before his second birthday and while there he was in regular contact with Balcombe, who lived there during vacations until Napier was about six years old. On one occasion, too, Balcombe saved Napier from drowning in a millpond, for which Napier and his cousin Ann, who was also in residence, rewarded him with the title "my George" (Tucker 1:69). Without dwelling on how likely Napier would be to remember or recognize a childhood acquaintance fifteen years after the fact, Balcombe remembers the younger man quite clearly. Napier's inability to remember shows him as a less capable man than Balcombe. It also shows his self-centeredness when we consider that it places him in contrast with the large number of people in Virginia who remember Balcombe despite his long absence.

Napier does not share Balcombe's view of a hierarchical society; on the contrary, he seems to have been an indulged child (Tucker 1:33). Balcombe, who quickly establishes a reputation for accurate observation and character assessment, attributes his egalitarian (and, presumably, Democratic) leanings to the younger man's background as "the pampered child of indulgence, the overweening inheritor in anticipation of unpurchased and unmerited affluence." Because Napier has lived in comfort and expectation of plenty, Balcombe says, the young man does not understand that the privileged are "the stewards of God's benevolence" (1:261). That is, he has not learned that wealth carries the duty of faithful stewardship. Those whom God favors with wealth and power receive as well the obligation to use their wherewithal to assist those who need assistance. Eliminating this would disrupt the natural order of society and overlook the inherent distinctions among people. Until he has learned to understand the role in society that accompanies his inheritance, Napier cannot come into his legacy as head of a prominent family. On numerous occasions, he exhibits an

Birthright and Authority: George Balcombe

inability to establish priorities: He wishes Balcombe to report on what has taken place, while the older man recognizes that preparing for the next day's events with a restful sleep may be far more important (See, for example 1:86, 213). He is, at times, immoderate enough to risk endangering himself (1:75), and his conversation with strangers risks jeopardizing his integrity. For example, when Balcombe's wife, Elizabeth, asks him what model she should use to train her daughter to be the wife of a good man, Napier offers a flattering (and arguably, quite accurate) response: Elizabeth herself can serve as her daughter's model (2:51). However, as Balcombe points out gently, this would rule out the academic education that Napier has already claimed to favor for young women (1:275, 277–278)[3]. All of these weaknesses make Napier appear imprudent. He appears to forget that even without his inheritance, he has a responsibility to his mother, sister, and cousin. They are virtually helpless without him and might become, like Mary Scott, dependent on the kindness of others. Still, he pursues chivalric action without any regard for this. Inexperienced swashbuckling cavalier he may be, but he overlooks the needs of those depending on him. He is, in a sense, far out of touch with the needs of his family as Jackson, in the Whig construction, was out of touch with the needs of the electorate.

With these shortcomings, it is no wonder that Napier fails miserably in his first attempt to function as head of the house in an important decision. Granted, the circumstances of this first momentous decision are difficult: Howard has written to ask that Napier, as Ann's guardian, permit him to court her (1:104). At this point, Napier is about to leave for Missouri, and he hopes to return with some means of marrying Ann himself. While the happiness of his parents' marriage for affection makes it reasonable for him to question whether marriage for financial reasons is desirable, his family's position is precarious, and the marriages between Howard and Ann and Margaret Howard and Napier seem most likely to serve the interests of Napier's entire family (1:97–98). Indecisive, he tries to leave the answer to Ann, but she balks, recognizing that he must make whatever decision will best serve the interests of all members of the family (1:106). As he haltingly tries to respond to her, his passion for her overcomes his reason—in Tucker's language, "the fervour of [his] manner more than [his] words, [makes] her at length perceive [his] meaning" (1:108). Ann is distraught and, by way of a note the next morning, expresses astonishment at his behavior: She tells him "'I owe it to myself *and all concerned* to insist that the subject of [the] conversation shall never be resumed" (1:109, italics added). Ann understands the dimensions of this decision, and she knows that by considering his own wishes without reference to the needs of the family, he has shattered her idealized image of him and made himself, for the time being, unsuitable as a potential husband.

To fully grasp the importance of Napier's shortcomings and what he must learn before he assumes his legacy and his position in the community, it is necessary to understand that Tucker is referring to the model of the family and the community that Yazawa has identified as the familial paradigm. As we have seen, Yazawa argues that this model of relationships derived from the notion of a divinely ordered pattern of inequality that existed to make people dependent upon each other, just as is evident in the relationship between Balcombe and Keizer. In this hierarchical society, each member contributed to the well-being of the whole and excessive self-interest was held in check (9, 10, 12), just as Balcombe gently restrains Napier from acts that do not take account of the interests of others. In the family and in the commonwealth, the superior members (parents and magistrates) served as God's agents in seeing to the welfare of His people (19), as Balcombe sees to the Rabys' interests without regard for his own. These rulers, like George Balcombe, owed those subordinate to them their faithfulness, a complex blend of humility, modesty, sincerity, self-denial, diligence, watchfulness, justice, benevolence, prudence, and constancy. Having more power, they had to do more good than their subordinates while enduring greater temptations (24). By doing this, they would inspire public spirit, which means in this construction the sense of dependency and connectedness that would lead people to strengthen, defend, preserve, and comfort each other (15). This spirit gradually extends throughout the Raby family and into the broader community, including the likes of Keizer and incidental figures who appear in the novel. In addition, the subordinates would be bound to their rulers with filial affection, a response that combined love and a fear of displeasing the parent or magistrate (21). The result of this continuing, organic relationship was that the family or commonwealth founded on such affection would prosper: It would be blessed with a moral reformation as well as health, happiness, peace, and prosperity. Without the restraints imposed by affection, jealousy, selfishness, and acrimonious confrontation would prevail (26). All of this depended not on the capitulation of the subordinates but on the character of ruler (27).

Beverley Tucker, far more than his devoutly democratic father, accepted hierarchy as necessary to the well-being of society. The politics of the period had been shaped by the personalities of prominent men: Jackson had been elected with no clear agenda, and some observers, like Tucker, could disagree with him on issues but regard him as more acceptable than other candidates. Tucker, then, was writing in a period when a devout states' rights Whig, particularly one who had supported Jackson in 1828, could see "King Andrew" as the source of bad policy, an autocratic ruler who put his good and that of his closest friends ahead of the general good, and one who might easily call upon force to compel obedience instead of inspiring public spirit to promote cooperation. And the same writer, rather than launching a barrage of invective, could offer a reasonably gentle fable to instruct his fellow Southerner in the White House. Thus it is that Napier can be read as possessing some of the deficiencies of Jackson: self-absorption, impulsiveness, and unpredictability. Fortunately, Napier has an excellent guide and model in George Balcombe. Throughout the novel,

Birthright and Authority: George Balcombe

Balcombe, through habits of minute observation and skillful inference, is able to define and order the needs of the extended family that forms around him—and Napier makes great strides in this direction during the course of the novel.

For example, Balcombe needs no introduction to William Napier; on the contrary, it is he who identifies Napier as a Virginian (1:10) and provides readers information on Napier's origins and mission (1:10, 20). This, of course, might be explained in literary terms: It avoids the necessity of having a narrator introduce himself and thereby raising at an early stage in the action the issue of the narrator's credibility. But while there may be strictly literary explanations for Balcombe's introduction of Napier, these do not satisfactorily account for the hero's behavior when Mary Scott's brother, James, arrives in Missouri seeking assistance. Tucker is quite explicit: Balcombe awakens Napier, shows him a letter from Mary, and explains to James that Napier must be part of their undertaking (1:131,150).

Throughout the novel, Balcombe usually makes introductions and informs characters of how their interests intertwine with those of other characters. We have seen that Balcombe identifies Napier quickly; he also introduces his protégé to a number of other figures in the work: James Scott, Colonel Robinson (Balcombe's own father-in-law), and Montague, to name a few. This might not be remarkable if Balcombe's introductions were limited to characters who were the social equals of Balcombe and Napier, but he also introduces characters such as John Keizer, the Virginia-born frontiersman who works for Balcombe in nefarious ways that demand unusual skills of observation and cunning. Tucker apparently did not mean for readers to overlook this relationships among men of different classes. After all, Montague attempts to employ some of the worst rogues in Missouri in his efforts to escape Balcombe and retain access to the Raby estate. Confronted by Keizer, Montague's rogues confess their misdeeds to save their lives. On the other hand, one of Keizer's Native American accomplices, knowing that Balcombe is on trial for his life, strides into the courtroom and admits to killing a ruffian, even though the ruffian is white and the confession may cost him his life. Undeniably, Napier, James Scott, and their families are bound to Balcombe by affectionate familial ties. The rest of the community around him seems bound to him, as well, with ties that are equally strong. While the other members do not comment on the reasons for their affection, Keizer may speak for them when he recognizes Balcombe's influence and character: "If such a poor fellow as I was put out of the way, there's plenty more just like me" he says, but Balcombe is a different matter (Tucker 65).

These ties allow Balcombe to balance the contending interests of James Scott and Napier at several points. He demonstrates early that he can simply command the young men (1:151), but he does not depend, as a tyrant would, on the use of power. Indeed, he permits his young subordinates considerable latitude. It would serve Napier's interests, as well as those of

104   Will the Circle be Unbroken?

Balcombe as pursuer of a suitable settlement, for Scott to allow them to read a letter in which Mary identifies the whereabouts of the missing will and explains how Montague, after meeting specified conditions, will be able to retrieve it with a token. Balcombe and Napier, however, determine that for Scott to give them access to the letter would be dishonorable, and they do not press him to do so (1:173–175). Later, however, they seek to convince him that he should give them the letter, and the young man becomes deeply offended. Balcombe and Napier, however, are not insistent (1:190–192). It is Balcombe who manages to prevent this incident from becoming a matter of prolonged contention between his two young friends by recognizing and prioritizing the contending interests of both. By doing so, he demonstrates on a personal level an ability that Jackson could be said to lack on the national level.

In assisting Napier, Balcombe must set aside his own interests for a considerable time. He becomes enmeshed in a situation that does not necessarily involve him directly. While his early hope is that he can resolve it in less than a week, the resolution actually takes far longer. He finds himself charged with murder and after his acquittal, he must travel across the country—all without expectation of gain. In addition, his life is often in danger because Montague seems to understand that Napier and Scott cannot oppose his villainy without Balcombe to guide them. Finally, when the will is located, Balcombe does not profit: he receives a legacy, but he cannot claim it immediately without again disordering the family by restructuring the relationship that he has developed with Napier and the rest of the Raby family.

Tucker uses Balcombe to demonstrate what progress the younger men are making by questioning them (Tucker 1:243). Gradually, Napier's answers suggest that he has learned some of Balcombe's habits of thought. His growth is especially evident, though, when Balcombe fights an abortive duel with Howard. The problem is that Napier's sister Jane believes that Balcombe has kept Napier from marrying Margaret. On this basis, she concludes that Margaret has been wronged and tells Howard that the fault is Balcombe's. Howard, taking this as a slur on his sister, challenges Balcombe, who manages to end the affair without injuring anyone, but Howard, now mortified, tries to kill himself (2:216, 225–237). Napier immediately recognizes his sister's role in this, just as he realizes that the events to come with respect to the will should allow Jane to marry her beloved Angus Douglas—something that would have been impossible otherwise (2:238–239). After reluctantly heeding his mother's admonition to go to Howard's plantation and assist in his care, Napier tells Jane that the affair was her fault, a result of her selfish disregard for others (2:247–248). Jane is fearful because she has offended her protector and believes he may leave her without a home (2:251). In other words, she recognizes his authority as patriarch; he is playing the role better than he did with Ann before leaving

Birthright and Authority: George Balcombe

for Missouri, and he is calling to her attention what he had to learn from that earlier encounter—the interdependency of family members.

Given Napier's growth, it is not difficult to understand why the local gentry, upon learning of his inheritance, look forward to giving him a place on the local court. They even hope that he will take, in time, the position as presiding judge in which his grandfather served (Tucker 2:284). Similarly, Tucker has other members of the community demonstrate their loyalty to Napier, particularly Swann (the manager) and the slaves (2:161–163, 284). In the end, the emergence of William Napier Raby does not simply reestablish the order within his extended family. It also, by virtue of the young gentleman's anticipated activity in government (and, undoubtedly, politics), reinforces the divinely ordained order of the community.

Before leaving *George Balcombe,* it is important to recognize that the novel's reordering is not the reshuffling of authority within a community. At the end of the novel, when Balcombe is returning to Virginia to take his place, the Raby authority has been divided between two men, both of whom are capable of leading in the family and the community. While there is no reason to fear much conflict or confrontation between Raby and Balcombe, the fact is that the house has been quietly, peaceably divided. The youth has grown, just as the colonial "child" of England grew, and is now ready to leave home. While Tucker believed that this departure—secession—was possible, he recognized some of its implications as he wrote *The Partisan Leader.*

CHAPTER SEVEN
The Family Restructured:
The Partisan Leader

Nathaniel Beverley Tucker's second novel, *The Partisan Leader* (1836), has attracted attention since 1862, when a New York publisher offered it as proof that Southerners had conspired for thirty years to secede. The novel revolves around the experiences of a family in an imagined civil war between Northern and Southern states; however, the argument for the author's prescience is weak. What Tucker shows in the novel is hardly a detailed prediction of secession and war, but rather an account of the disruption and reconstruction of an extended Virginian family as the Old Dominion teeters between remaining in the Union and joining a confederation of seceded Southern states. While *George Balcombe* reveals a great deal about Tucker's notion of social structure and authority, *The Partisan Leader* explicitly compares a specific leader—Van Buren—to a standard of faithful leadership portrayed in Bernard Trevor (and in George Balcombe) and reveals a great deal about Tucker's notions of the nature of the Union and the relationships among the states. Written just before the 1836 presidential campaign, it predicts that the Union will not survive if Van Buren succeeds Jackson. In the novel, this national disunion parallels a division within the Trevor family, and the results are mixed: One son, Hugh, is killed while fighting against the secessionists; another, Douglas, is captured while leading secessionist guerrillas. On the other hand, Hugh and Bernard, the brothers who head the opposing factions, are reconciled, and their families are more tightly bound through a cousin marriage. At the same time, Virginia secedes, but it appears that the state's entry into the Southern confederation will not be welcomed by North Carolinians. Thus, the novel presents a formulation in which families and the relations among the states could be restructured without necessarily incurring wholesale destruction. In addition, it suggests that the only satisfactory course for Virginia is founded on principle rather than pragmatism.

107

108   *Will the Circle be Unbroken?*

The central family in the novel, the Trevor family, comprises two branches. One is headed by Hugh Trevor, the older of two brothers and, until recently, a moderate Unionist. He is a prosperous man who has "long and honorably filled various important and dignified stations in the service of his native State . . . endowed with handsome talents, an amiable disposition, and all the accomplishments that can adorn a gentleman . . . as well as the most exemplary virtues" (Tucker 36). Hugh has a dozen children; two of them, Owen and Douglas, are West-Point-trained officers in the United States Army at the beginning of the plot. Even though Hugh has recently come to oppose Van Buren and to favor secession, his opposition has not become active.

Hugh's younger brother, Bernard, is in many respects his opposite. Hugh lives near Richmond, takes an active role in politics, and has held a variety of unspecified "important and dignified" government offices; Bernard lives near Roanoke, comments on political matters as an outsider, and has held no elected or appointed office. Where Hugh is successful, Bernard is something of a failure. Hugh provides handsomely for his twelve children; Bernard can barely provide appropriate education for his two daughters. But Bernard is quicker and more intuitive than Hugh, and he has long supported the secession of the Southern states as the only means of maintaining the state's sovereignty against a national government that continually encroaches upon the prerogatives of the states (44–47).

The novel begins at a time of turmoil. The year is 1849, and Jackson's successor, Martin Van Buren, has just won an unprecedented fourth term as President. The Southern states have seceded, and although Virginia still remains in the Union, the opposition to Van Buren in the state makes secession increasingly likely. The Old Dominion has already turned against Van Buren in the national election, and the upcoming state election will determine the state's future alignment. For the moment, however, Virginia is held in the Union as a result of the President's political chicanery and the deployment of United States troops dispatched to counties that are known to favor secession. While Hugh has thus far considered his first allegiance to be to the Union, the administration's recent efforts to interfere in elections and deny Virginians a free choice have led him to believe that Bernard's support for secession may have been well considered. As the situation has worsened, he has invited Bernard's daughter Delia to visit his family, and her visit coincides with the furlough of his son Douglas, a West Point-trained lieutenant of dragoons.

A close friendship between Douglas and Delia goes back to their childhoods, but the political differences between their fathers have combined with Douglas's absences from home on military duty to limit their time together in recent years. Delia, moreover, almost worships her father, and she is less admiring of her Uncle Hugh because of his reluctance to abandon the Union. Douglas is another matter for her, however. Although he is

The Family Restructured: The Partisan Leader 109

a Union army officer, he seems to manage fairly easily the apolitical stance of the professional soldier, and Delia finds him a thorough gentleman who treats her father and his political opinions with the utmost respect. Douglas is impressed by Delia's beauty arid intelligence. As a result, the two cousins are often in each other's company during the visit, but for a time, there is no romantic attachment between them.

Even social outings are overshadowed by the political tensions of the day, and Delia and Douglas find themselves in the company of a young man named Phillip Baker, a political climber whose career has stalled at the state level despite his father's cultivation of a friendship with President Van Buren. Young Baker believes that a relationship with Delia is a means to higher office because of her family connections: If Van Buren holds Virginia in the Union, he will undoubtedly reward the family of Hugh Trevor, whose well-known integrity reflects favorably upon an administration otherwise associated with dubious ethics. If, however, the state leaves the Union, the officials of the new government will consider Bernard Trevor a prime mover for their cause and will reward his son-in-law accordingly. In other words, Philip sees this marriage as a means of advancing himself, without reference to Delia's wishes or beliefs. He overlooks that Delia comes from a family of scrupulous integrity and that she finds him unattractive if not loathsome. When Baker finally recognizes this, he is unable to fully control his anger toward Delia and Douglas.

While a group of young people, including Delia, Douglas, and Baker, are on an outing at the falls of the James River, they receive word that the new confederacy has negotiated a free trade agreement with England. As a supporter of Van Buren, Baker speaks against the treaty and the Southern states in terms that are calculated to offend Delia through derogatory reference to her father. Although Van Buren is his commander-in-chief, Douglas steps in as his cousin's protector and obtains Baker's formal apology and written pledge that he will never seek her company again. Baker, however, complains to his father, who denounces Douglas to the President for failure to speak against the seceded states and their treaty with England in a public discussion. Van Buren, conscious that he needs the veneer of integrity that Hugh Trevor provides, does not wish to offend Douglas's father, but neither does he wish to lose the support of unquestioningly loyal and servile men such as the Bakers. He tries to learn from Douglas what actually took place, but the young officer is unwilling to risk involving Delia in a matter that might be made public. For the moment, only the names of Douglas Trevor and Phillip Baker have been involved in accounts of the incident, and only their behavior is subject to scrutiny and discussion. If Delia were named, her conduct might also become a subject of public comment, and Douglas is unwilling to allow this. As Bernard points out, too, women who become subjects of public discussion come to love notoriety, and they are then unfit as wives.

110   *Will the Circle be Unbroken?*

In the meantime, Douglas and Delia have gone to Bernard's plantation. Douglas has asked Bernard for permission to marry Delia, but Bernard has refused to allow his daughter to marry anyone in the United States Army. If Virginia secedes, he points out, Douglas might be torn between duty to state, duty to father, and duty to the Union, and to compound that dilemma by adding consideration for the emotions and loyalties of in-laws, Bernard says, would make almost impossible any decision based upon principle. Douglas has offered to resign, but Bernard has told his nephew that his support for the Southern cause must be motivated by principle rather than love for Delia. While Bernard hesitates to discuss politics with Douglas, fearing to alienate the young man from his father, Douglas still hears some political discussion from Bernard's wife and a South Carolinian friend, Mr. B___. Gradually, he decides to resign his commission rather than request a court of inquiry (as Van Buren proposes) or accept a court martial as an alternative. Van Buren, working closely with Baker and a shadowy man known only as the Minister, accepts the resignation, confident that he still maintains some control over the Trevor family through his preferential treatment of Douglas's older brother, Owen, whom he has promoted rapidly and out of order to the rank of colonel.

At about this time, elections are held for the Virginia state legislature and Van Buren's party has made arrangements to hold a majority through a combination of subterfuge and military intimidation in key counties. One of those counties is the one where Bernard Trevor lives, and Van Buren has sent a detachment of troops there to intimidate the anti-administration candidate and close the polls. Bernard, with some assistance from Douglas and a company of armed slaves and anti-administration voters, defeats this scheme and is elected to the legislature. Van Buren, however, has foreseen this possibility, and it provides him an excuse to arrest both Bernard and Douglas on charges of treason. By doing so, he will eliminate an influential opponent and ingratiate himself with the Bakers, who have supported him. But when Federal troops arrive at Bernard's plantation to make the arrest, they find that Bernard has prepared for their arrival by arming his slaves and setting up a scheme to capture the men who have come to make the arrest. The next morning, Bernard and his household leave Virginia for North Carolina, accompanied by Douglas and Mr. B___.

When the party arrives in North Carolina, Mr. B___ lays before Douglas a plan by which Virginia will be brought to her place in the Southern confederacy. All that is required, B___ says, is a leader with sound military judgment to command a corps of partisans. This corps will maneuver in such a way that the legislature will be able to escape the Federal troops around Richmond for long enough to vote the state out of the Union. The citizens of Virginia will then be free to throw out of the state any Union troops that do not leave after secession. Douglas, of course, is qualified to become that leader, and he accepts the mission with the condition that he

The Family Restructured: The Partisan Leader   *111*

be allowed to marry Delia before he assumes his new responsibilities. Mr. B___ performs the marriage, and Douglas joins the confederacy.

His command, headquartered in southwestern Virginia, is a band of yeoman farmers and frontiersmen. Combining Douglas's military sense of strategy with the frontiersmen's notion of tactics, they are able to force the Union troops opposing them back to their headquarters at Lynchburg. In an effort to defeat the partisans, whom Douglas commands under the *nom de guerre* of Captain Douglas, Van Buren sends Douglas's brother, Colonel Owen Trevor, to command the Lynchburg forces. Owen, who has risen beyond his military competence, receives and accepts as valid the disinformation given to a spy by Douglas and his men, and he sets out to defeat the partisans. When Owen and his regiments arrive on the scene, however, they march into a trap that Douglas has contrived for them. In the ensuing battle, Owen is captured and his forces are defeated. The remnants of his command flee back to Lynchburg pursued by Douglas's forces, and Owen's deputy determines that the only practical course of action is surrender. Before the surrender can occur, however, Owen escapes from his captors, returns to Lynchburg, has Douglas abducted and carried to Washington, and dies trying to lead his command out of the surrounded city. Douglas, in Union hands, arrives in Washington, where he is to be tried and sentenced to death by a special court presided over by Judge Baker. Although the Minister and Whiting, one of Douglas's army friends, conspire to help the young man escape, the novel ends with Hugh Trevor and Delia pleading for Douglas's life before President Van Buren.

Duff Green published 2000 copies of *The Partisan Leader* and distributed them as far north as Boston and as far south as New Orleans (Brugger 241, n.20; Green). Green believed that Tucker should have made slavery rather than the tariff the basis for secession in the novel, and this may have led the publisher to err in his distribution plans (Brugger 241, n.20); Abel Upshur, a friend of both Tucker and Green believed that *"The Partisan Leader* [was] killed or severely strained at least, by the bad management of the publisher." While Upshur had never expected that the work would find an audience in the North, he believed that Green failed to provide adequate numbers of copies to booksellers in the Southern cities. Upshur never made his charges against Green specific in his correspondence with Tucker, but a letter from Green to Tucker accounts for distribution of 1303 of the copies. Of that number, 339 copies (26 percent) were shipped to Boston and Philadelphia. Green had sent 446 copies (34 percent) to cities in Maryland and Virginia (although, given the political division between western and eastern Virginia. the 235 copies shipped to Charlestown, Virginia, might be added to the total shipped to Northern cities.) The rest of the copies, 518 (40 percent) went to Columbia, South Carolina; Augusta, Georgia; and New Orleans, Louisiana. Green shared with Tucker and Upshur the hope that the work would rally opposition to Van Buren and the Democrats and build support for a state's rights Whig. This distribution, however, placing over a quarter of the copies in cities where there was no national candidate opposing Van Buren, may have struck Upshur as unproductive.

These distribution problems may have diminished the effect of *The Partisan Leader* on events, but the reality is that the novel was poorly received. Reviews, in this case, provide little detailed insight as to how the contemporary audience read the work, but they leave little doubt that the novel was highly regarded only by those who shared the author's political views. The reviewer for the Richmond *Whig* agreed with Abel Upshur's review in *Southern Literary Messenger,* which held that the book was worthy because of its political message: If the government could not be reformed, the Union would have to be dissolved (Brugger 132). Outside of Richmond, some reviewers were horrified by the author's eager support for secession; others dismissed the work as badly written. Those who were close to Tucker had reservations about the work. Tucker's niece, Elizabeth Tucker Bryan, worried because the work drew "the character of [Martin Van Buren], attributing to him the blackest and most cold hearted conduct, making him a compound of ambition, selfishness, meanness, cruelty, and hypocrisy"—a characterization that might "excite a prejudice against the cause that [her uncle proposed] to serve [with the work]". St. George Coalter, his nephew, believed that the work was "a very bold conception," but "more commonplace [than *George Balcombe*] in its characterization"; as a political work, he regarded it as powerfully prophetic and fearful. A. S. Johnston, a South Carolina newspaper publisher, commented that the plan of the work was similar to one that he had considered himself, although he believed that the real personages who appeared in the pages would have aged more over a decade than Tucker's work showed. William Preston, who helped to arrange for publication of the work, praised the characters and the style of the work, but he found "inherent difficulties" in the plan of a work that was "at once fiction and prophecy and thus [opposed] a double difficulty to that belief or acquiescence in the narrative which is to be the foundation of the novelist's passion." That is, the acceptance of Tucker's prophecy required belief, but fiction demanded only suspension of disbelief. Apparently, then, these readers felt some discomfort with the blend of reality and prediction. Other readers must have felt similar discomfort; *The Partisan Leader* never enjoyed commercial success.

Modern commentators have found the work more intriguing, largely because it seems to have predicted secession a quarter century before it occurred. Vernon L. Parrington held that Tucker wrote to remind Virginians of the dangers of democracy—a reading that might apply equally to *George Balcombe*— but he is on weaker ground when he holds that the work was "an obvious attempt to dramatize the political philosophy of Calhoun" (34): Tucker considered nullification an illegal and weak measure compared with secession, and he considered Calhoun an over-ambitious

The Family Restructured: The Partisan Leader   *113*

and dangerous man (Brugger 84). Jay Hubbell was similarly intrigued by Tucker's efforts at prophecy, although he was quick to point out that "*The Partisan Leader* was in many respects wide of the mark" as a prediction of the Civil War, and he had little comment beyond an attempt to identify characters in the novel with historical personages (430–431). Introducing a new edition for the Southern Literary Classics series, C. Hugh Holman treated the novel as a campaign document from the 1836 election that would have little enduring interest except for its embodiment of the sentiments that empowered the secession movement: sectionalism, states' rights, abolitionism, the national bank, the tariff, the American System, judiciary authority, and the meaning of sovereignty (vii–ix). Of these issues, however, abolition, the national bank, and the American System are never mentioned in the novel. Among these modern commentators, only Holman points out that *The Partisan Leader* shares a hortatory voice with *George Balcombe* (xvi). As we have seen, the latter is a generalized treatise on the nature of authority and the danger of mob rule; *The Partisan Leader* is aimed at a specific president and his followers. J.V. Ridgley saw the work as a warning to Virginians that was driven by a political intent so strong that it led Tucker to lay aside narrative technique in a novel featuring a murky plot, a powerful political message, and a somewhat inaccurate prophecy of fratricidal war. Ridgely also points out that the resurrection of the work in New York in 1862 and Richmond in 1863 contributed greatly to the modern scholar's sense of the novel's importance (43–44). Finally, Robert Brugger, Tucker's modern biographer, holds that *The Partisan Leader,* like *George Balcombe,* was a sermon on nobility for Virginians who were watching the decline of public leadership, suggesting that people should defer to their natural betters and that they could influence the course of history (124–125). Interested in psychobiography, Brugger also suggests that Tucker created Hugh Trevor as a means of dismissing the success of his brother Henry while creating Bernard and Douglas Trevor as models of what the author wished to be (126).

A brief review of Tucker's antipathy for Van Buren helps to demonstrate why Tucker's political message became so overpowering. In reality, however, it is necessary to bear in mind that he saw his political efforts not as negative rear-guard actions against progress, but as positive efforts to preserve and improve society. This message was not lost on Tucker's contemporaries: One reader wrote to the author:

> Since I last wrote to you the Partisan has fallen into my hands—each volume cost me a whole night's sleep. I found the story deeply interesting, the political portraits well drawn, some of them admirably, and the train of events perfectly natural—in short, the whole is well adapted to the end aimed at by the author—but it will not do Master Bev.—bodies politic, like bodies natural, when they fall into decay, are never regenerated—the progress to dissolution may be retarded by wholesome reform; but the youthful vigor cannot be restored by any alternative. (F.P.)

Tucker himself saw his purpose in positive terms; that is, he was not simply striving to dissolve the Union, but to preserve the principles that Jefferson and Madison had expressed in the Kentucky and Virginia Resolutions of 1798, and he makes this connection between the novel and these Resolutions clear when Douglas argues that the Constitution means what the president, Congress, and the Federal courts say that it means—a position contrary to Bernard's view, Tucker's, and that of Jefferson and Madison in the Resolutions. In these latter interpretations, the Union is represented as the product of a compact among sovereign states. Within this compact, the states delegated to a central government specific powers to do what they could not do for themselves. In disputes concerning the powers of this central government, the final arbiters had to be the states; to allow the federal judiciary to determine whether the central government had exceeded its jurisdiction was self-defeating because it required that the government be willing to limit its own powers.

For Tucker, the voluntary nature of the Union was the basis for its strength, and the people of all states were best served when the central government was prohibited from infringing upon the powers of the states or the rights of the people. He opposed Van Buren because he associated him with the efforts to coerce compliance with the tariff acts during the Nullification Crisis. In reality, Van Buren had opposed Jackson's Force Bill and had been a moderating influence on the President throughout that crisis, but Tucker had hoped that the crisis would lead to a show of force by the administration and thus alarm people—not specifically Southerners—to the dangers of centralized power.[1] Opposing Van Buren was part of Tucker's immediate purpose, but it was not all that he hoped to achieve. Accordingly, in explaining the novel to his brother Henry, Tucker held that

> The book was written under a belief that the conservation of all that makes this Union valuable, and, by consequence, the Union itself, depends on the maintenance of principles of what constituted the old republican party of 98, which I would now denominate the States Right party. I believe that these and all other good things are jeopardized by a difference of opinion among those who cherish these principles, as to the proper means of securing their common object. There are those who believe it to be promoted by drawing closer and closer the coercive bond that unites the States. There are others who believe that there is a point beyond which this ligament cannot be safely strained, just as a blow too many bursts the hoop. I agree with the latter, and believe the former to be in error. My wish was to show the error, by prefiguring the results of the coercive policy.

Tucker wrote *The Partisan Leader* between February and April 1836, at a time when it was clear that Jackson would not seek a third term as President and that his Vice President, Martin Van Buren, would probably succeed him in office. By this time, the last of Tucker's tolerance for Jackson had vanished and he had written that the president had "thrown himself into the arms of the faction against which [Tucker, in 1828, had]

The Family Restructured: The Partisan Leader 115

supported him." The election of Van Buren, he predicted, would mean that the South passed "directly into a state of colonial vassalage worse than that from which the Revolution freed us."

Tucker distrusted Northerners in general, and he had supported Jackson, in part, because he believed that any Southerner in the White House would at least recognize Southern concerns (Holman 11). Van Buren's birth in Kinderhook, New York, then, probably provided Tucker adequate cause for opposing him. Given Tucker's highly developed sense of order and hierarchy in society, the son of the Virginian jurist probably regarded the New York tavernkeeper's son as an inferior man who should no more aspire to a position of leadership than should John Keizer, the frontiersman of *George Balcombe,* or Witt or Schwartz, Keizer's counterparts in *The Partisan Leader.* Even Van Buren's important role in moderating Jackson's position and averting a confrontation over nullification operated against him in Tucker's mind:

During the crisis, the Virginian "had said to General Jackson . . . that if a government of opinion was to be exchanged for a Government of force [he hoped] that the people might lose no time, in [resolving] the question 'Whether they can be governed by force."

Tucker was hardly alone in detesting Van Buren: As Arthur Schlesinger pointed out, "Beverley Tucker's novel, *The Partisan Leader,* . . . set forth the Van Buren stereotype in somewhat more literate terms (than other denunciations of the period]" (214). William Seward, another New Yorker, referred to Van Buren as "a crawling reptile, whose only claim was that he had inveigled the confidence of a credulous, blind, dotard, old man" (quoted in Schlesinger 214). Henry Clay observed that he respected Van Buren as a man but detested him as a magistrate (Schlesinger 49).

Van Buren had developed a reputation for equivocation and evasiveness. Politically, he had sought to avoid taking fixed positions that might rule out the possibility of compromise and coalition, and he had striven to avoid making his political opponents personal enemies (Schlesinger 49). In *The Partisan Leader,* Van Buren never appears outside of the private quarters in the White House, and he makes his political utterances in the presence of only one or two associates, thereby leaving himself a means of disclaiming his positions if they cease to be advantageous to him. This places him in contrast to Bernard and Douglas Trevor, who make their political pronouncements in both private and public venues. Moreover, Tucker shows Van Buren basing his actions on personal advantage for himself and his supporters; the Trevors choose their positions based on what will benefit Virginia—particularly when Bernard leaves behind his home and moves his family and slaves to South Carolina in order to support Virginian entry into the Southern confederation.

To the anti-Jacksonians who saw Jackson's retirement from public life as a great opportunity for his adversaries to regain the White House, Van

Buren seemed even more detestable. He was not simply Jackson's chosen successor as Democratic candidate; he was the man who had perhaps done more than any other to develop the modern political organization. He had strengthened the partisan press, aided in the development of city political machines and county party committees, and promoted nominating conventions. These efforts, as Schlesinger has pointed out, broadened the opportunity for voters to participate directly and effectively in the electoral process (50). To those like Tucker, who opposed extended white male suffrage, the broad participation that Van Buren had promoted could only place the nation in the control of the mob. In addition, the Democratic party newspapers, machines, and committees that Van Buren had helped to develop made it likely that he and his party could readily mobilize voters in sufficient numbers to capture the election of 1836.

To make matters worse, the anti-Jacksonians had drawn together under the Whig banner, but the Whigs did not select a national candidate. Against the Democratic organization, their best hope was to throw the election into the House of Representatives, and to that end, they nominated regional candidates. In the South and Southwest, Hugh Lawson White, a Tennessee senator who had been a friend of Jackson and a conservative Democrat, seemed likely to present Van Buren a strong challenge, even though some Southerners were put off by his opposition to nullification (Brugger 111). In the Northwest, the Whig candidate was William Henry Harrison, whose managers sought to keep him out of the spotlight so that he could capitalize on animosity for Jackson and Van Buren. In the Northeast, Daniel Webster was the Whig candidate (Schlesinger 210–212). Tucker, a former Jacksonian himself, supported White, and he made several speeches on behalf of the candidate who was, regardless of his political credentials, married to Lucy Tucker's aunt and appears as "Uncle Hugh" in Tucker's letters.

Jackson's retirement, the best opportunity to stop the progress of Jacksonian nationalism and democracy, then, seemed likely to be an opportunity lost for the Whigs, and Tucker wrote to his wife in December 1835 that he had nothing to do with politics because the attitude prevailing in Virginia paralyzed him. Van Buren would probably win the election, and the South would be forced to secede. The only hope, so far as Tucker was concerned, was to campaign against Van Buren, hope that voters would support his opponents, and prepare the South for the rift that must follow Van Buren's election. In writing a novel that counseled his state to abandon caution and leave the Union peacefully, Tucker was suggesting that the destruction of the Union was not necessarily the destruction of all of the ties that had unified the states. The loss of the patriarch did not necessarily separate the siblings. In applying the familial metaphor to this argument, Tucker must have been conscious of circumstances within his own family, specifically his own relationship with his older brother, Henry St. George Tucker.

The Family Restructured: The Partisan Leader   117

A number of commentators, contemporary as well as modern, have attempted to argue that Hugh Trevor and his brother Bernard are actually representations of Henry and Beverley Tucker. This line of interpretation is necessarily speculative, and it leaves open the question of how important the similarity between characters and their counterparts could have been to readers outside of that family or a circle of intimate friends. After all, the work was published pseudonymously, and many readers could not have associated it with the author. (Tucker had gone so far as to arrange publication through intermediaries in order to minimize the chance that his authorship would be recognized (Holman xvii–xvili.)) The similarities between the Trevors and the Tuckers might have been unimportant had it not been for Henry Tucker's conviction that his brother was the author and had used him as a model for a character that he did not regard as sympathetic. This conviction prompted an exchange of letters in which Henry angrily charged Beverley with representing him as an indecisive and weak man in the character of Hugh Trevor. Beverley, in a carefully worded response, replied, in effect, that he had not written *The Partisan Leader,* but Hugh was not intended to be a weak figure.

Beverley's response to Henry's query on this point offers insight that is useful in interpreting a novel that shows many signs of the author's haste and inattention to craft. We have seen, in our consideration of the relations among the Tucker and Randolph brothers, that Henry St. George Tucker, older son of St. George and Frances Bland Randolph Tucker, seems to have occupied a favored status in the household. From an early age, the Tucker brothers seemed to follow opposite courses. As Robert Brugger has summarized it, "Henry's mark was Beverley's target. Henry was cheerful when Beverley was glum, successful when Beverley strained not to fail, and in authority while Beverley was accountable to him" (Brugger 13).

This description sounds much like the novel's description of the Trevor brothers, perhaps because Brugger saw *The Partisan Leader* as the interpretive frame for Beverley Tucker's later life. Undeniably, though, Beverley and Henry Tucker had their differences. As a congressman in the early 1820s, Henry had supported an active role for the central government in internal improvements financed by tariff revenues (Brugger 55). When the tariff question and federal powers became central during the Nullification Crisis, Beverley opposed the tariff and viewed nullification as conceding the central government's power; secession, he argued, was the only course that maintained the state's sovereignty. Henry, on the other hand, opposed nullification because he saw it as a step towards conflict that would weaken or destroy all of the states. Perhaps recalling his father's role in the Annapolis Convention of 1786, Henry believed that the crisis might best be managed through a convention of the states aimed at clarifying the charter of the national government (85). On many political issues, the Tucker brothers were at odds; it does not stretch the point to say that their relationship schematically represented some of the major political divisions within the United States—and within any of the states. As with the Trevor brothers, however, these disagreements did not interfere with their regular, affectionate correspondence.

Henry heard rumors that Beverley was the author of *The Partisan Leader* and wrote "That my own brother would have published such a libel on me and so flattering a panegyric of himself, I ought not to believe. . . . [T]he former is so much my concern that I have come to the resolution of enquiring whether you are or are not the author." Beverley replied at length, arguing that he and his brother were bound perpetually as sons of their mother, and he would no more have injured Henry than he would his own small children—that is, family relationships superseded political differences. In this case, however, it is birth—a matrilineal connection—that determines who belongs irrevocably to the family: Beverley cannot wish Henry injury without setting aside their indisputable link through their mother. As a father—or as a ruler in Yazawa's formulation—he cannot wish ill on his children, and the paternal relationship is, in this respect, analogous to the relationship between siblings. In political terms, the affection that binds ruler-father to subject-children also binds the subject-children to each other as they recognize that they are similarly positioned in society and dependent upon each other (Yazawa 10, 12, 17–18).

Familial relationships, then, could not preclude differing and conflicting views within the family or the polity, but the question arose of how deeply those differences might cut into the relationship. Beverley regarded himself and his brother, he pointed out, as representatives of factions within a single political party rather than members of different parties. In other words, he saw their aims as similar: Both sought to preserve the "old republican principles of 98"—that is, the limitations on central power proposed by the Kentucky and Virginia Resolutions of 1798. The methods proposed by their respective factions, however, seemed mutually exclusive. Moreover, although Hugh was portrayed as politically wrongheaded, Beverley argued, he was a man of integrity, and Henry should take any similarities between himself and the character as complimentary. When Beverley sent a copy of this letter to his wife (who apparently had expressed concern over the potential rift between the brothers), he pointed out that he had never done or intended any harm to Henry. In the face of their differences over the four years since nullification, he had not violated "the tie of blood," despite Henry's disapproval of his positions (Brugger 85). Henry replied that he had not read *The Partisan Leader* in its entirety, but he disliked being associated with a character who was "a contemptible imbecile and parasite, who condescends to league himself 'with Rubic and others of the same kidney to bring down the pride of Virginia' and to humble her at the foot of a tyrant. . . . a doting old man whose impulse on reaching 'the presence' is to throw himself on his knees before the president." Whatever their differ-

The Family Restructured: The Partisan Leader   119

ences, the brothers continued to correspond as long as they both lived, and when Beverley lay dying, perhaps in the same bed where Henry had died several years earlier, Henry's family took care of him (Brugger 194).

While *The Partisan Leader* describes the disruption and reconstruction of familial relations within an extended family, it is important to recognize at the onset that the families in the work are not represented in the same detail—and not all characters seem to belong to families. Douglas Trevor is the central figure of the work, and he is also the link that connects Hugh's family with Bernard's and the personal plot with the political plot. Because Douglas is politically uncommitted but generally loyal to the Union at the beginning of the work, he occupies a position similar to the one that Tucker sees Virginia occupying in 1836 as well as in the fictitious 1849. The young officer faces a sequence of decisions. First, he must decide whether to resign his commission in the army. Although he wishes to do so to marry Delia, his uncle Bernard dissuades him because this reason may set aside principle for the sake of romance and lead to conflicts of loyalties for the couple. It is significant that in denying permission for Douglas's resignation and the marriage, Bernard explicitly leaves open the possibility of the marriage if Douglas resigns for appropriate reasons (Tucker 107–110). This requirement rules out a pragmatic decision to resign simply in order to marry Delia and requires that Douglas act on principle. Moreover, it makes Bernard something of a ruler-father. He denies permission for the marriage, but he uses the occasion to teach Douglas more about virtue. The situation is not strictly disciplinary because Bernard is not correcting Douglas after some wrongdoing, but as Yazawa points out, discipline under the familial paradigm was not only corrective, but educational (39, 47).

Moreover, Bernard expands the conditions for marriage that we have seen in previous novels. In Tucker's view, the mystical initial attraction on which Caruthers based marriages in *Kentuckian* is not necessary; the affection that binds Delia and Douglas evolves over an unspecified period, as does the affection of Bacon and Virginia Fairfax in *Cavaliers*. Despite their childhood association, the couple must gradually develop appreciation for each other. Much of this process, as Tucker's narrator explains, takes place out of the public eye and even away from other family members (107). The bond between the two is not entirely emotional; if it were, obstacles such as Douglas's commission could be overcome simply on the strength of the couple's passion for each other. That is, Douglas's passion would lead him to resign at once, and Delia's passion would lead her to accept this outcome, but if this occurred, the character traits that had attracted the two to each other would no longer exist, and their loyalties might be divided. When Douglas finally does resign, Delia raises this point and he must convince her that his resignation was a matter of principle—not simply love for her (129–130). When he first tells her of his resignation, Delia says that this is what she had feared; she had hoped he would remain in the army until he could honorably resign on the basis of his convictions. She is so fearful on this point that she even questions her father's role, saying "'O! can it be that my noble father has imposed dishonorable conditions, and that you have been weak enough to comply with them? O! Douglas! Is my love fated to destroy the very qualities that engaged it?" (129). Douglas must convince her that Bernard and Mr. B___ "have made no attack on [his] opinions or allegiance" and that the process leading to his resignation began with the incident at the falls of the James (130). As we shall see, however, the sword of principle is two-edged. It allows Douglas to resign, but it does not keep the interests of the Southern states from colliding.

Douglas's second decision, which does not follow directly from the first, is whether to support Virginia's secession and membership in the confederation of Southern states. Immediately after this decision, he marries Delia, again connecting the personal and political plots. The striking aspect of this decision is that it rests on principle; that is, Bernard and Mr. B___ explain the constitutional and moral arguments against the Union and Van Buren and in favor of secession. Douglas accepts their positions, although Tucker does not present the cases for those positions in detail (107, 189–191). After the party flees into North Carolina, however, Douglas encounters the pragmatic side of the secession question. In a tavern, a planter, a small farmer, and a drover converse about the future of North Carolina and Virginia. All agree that North Carolinians will suffer economically if Virginia secedes. The Virginian commerce that has been leaving Norfolk for the Carolinian free trade ports will return to the Virginian port city. The three North Carolinians make clear that they will not welcome Virginia into the confederation, but even the possibility of hostile reactions in other states does not deter Douglas from his support of secession and membership in the Southern confederation. As in the case of his resignation, Douglas rejects the pragmatic solution in the name of principle.

Douglas's life is shaped by four paternal figures: Hugh Trevor, his own father; Bernard, his uncle and a faithful ruler-father; Judge Baker, the father of Phillip Baker (with whom Douglas quarrels); and Martin Van Buren, the faithless ruler-father. Among these characters, only Van Buren and Bernard Trevor are finished products. That is to say that their political views and their social status seem to be fixed while those of Judge Baker and Hugh Trevor are in flux. Tucker apparently intended that Hugh and Baker be considered together; otherwise, there seems to be no simple explanation for his emphasis on comparing the principles of the two men: Baker explains to the President that Hugh's principles are so numerous that "it would take an expert mathematician to calculate the result of all the compound forces which act upon him, and to determine what course he might take" (Tucker 76). Baker, it turns out, is moved by only one principle, the president's pleasure (375–376).

Both Hugh and Baker are men in transition, seeking to change their political allegiance or social status. Tucker has Van Buren notice this in speaking to the Minister about Baker's appointment to be presiding judge

The Family Restructured: The Partisan Leader   121

of a special court. The president has secured Baker's support, and the Minister asks how: "'Has the golden ray of additional favors again caused its face to shine? . . . No new emoluments to him or his? . . . No new honors?" The answer is that Baker has been placed in a position from which he can only do the president's bidding and, for the first time, he will not receive additional favors for doing so. While the president does not specifically say that Baker's desire for position and the president's favor have drawn him into a trap, he does point out that Baker will have "the honor of doing additional duty, for the first time in his life, without additional compensation" (154). Moreover, readers know that Phillip Baker is the son of "a father, who, fifteen years before, had openly bartered his principles for office" and that Phillip himself is "determined never to exchange his place in the Legislature for any in the gift of the Court, unless some distinguished station should be offered to his acceptance" (71). The Bakers, then, are quite willing to set aside principle for political preferment; they hope to enhance their political power and social status through unprincipled service to the administration.

Hugh, of course, is a different matter. He seems to be well-placed socially, and he is undeniably wealthy. He is "a man in affluent circumstances, and [has] long and honorably filled various important and dignified stations in the service of his native State" (Tucker 36). Moreover, his principles have not been questioned, although he has been known to compromise. Since the election of Jackson in 1828, however, he has looked fearfully on the course of the country and expressed in his usual moderate terms his disapproval of this course. His belief that union, on any terms, would be better than disunion has led him to support Van Buren, but Van Buren's usurpation of state elections through political patronage has led him to believe that he must adopt, on principle, a new position favorable to Virginian secession (37–41). Still, Van Buren never seems to realize that he no longer enjoys Hugh's full support, nor does the elder brother seem to do anything specific to support the Virginian secession or the overthrow of Van Buren.

Both Hugh and Judge Baker have families, of course, and they interact with their families—Hugh directly in the text and Judge Baker indirectly. Their families are not shown in complete detail, either. Hugh has about a dozen children of whom only Owen, Douglas, Arthur, and Virginia appear in any detail. He also has a wife, but she never seems much more than a loyal supporter of whatever position her husband espouses. When Bernard's daughter Delia visits Hugh's family, for example, the women broach the subject of politics jokingly. Delia says that she expects that she will love Douglas if he is like her father, but Hugh's wife says that she would prefer that her son be like his own father, whom she prefers above all men—including the President, "the most elegant, agreeable old gentleman, that ever [she] saw" (55). Although Mrs. Trevor seems to separate the President's personality from his politics, Delia has been raised to distrust

122   *Will the Circle be Unbroken?*

Van Buren and oppose his political positions. Accordingly, she objects to any comparison between any family member and the president. Hugh breaks the tension by praising Delia's father (54–56)—a difficult matter for him because he is self-conscious about his own status with respect to Bernard (45–46). Hugh's response, however, is sufficient for his wife: She believes him faultless and incapable of error, and she immediately decides that she will say no more about politics until she ascertains his views (56). We shall see that this places her in contrast with her sister-in-law, Bernard's wife. While Judge Baker speaks on behalf of his son in most of his appearances with Van Buren, he appears more of a broker than a father as he tries to secure favor for his son. That is, he wants to obtain for his son something to which neither of them is entitled; Hugh appears before Van Buren as an advocate and grieving father asking that the President free his son out of respect for the Trevors' integrity. It may be that such fine distinctions as his led Tucker to see Hugh in more positive terms than did his older brother.

While Tucker through his unnamed narrator, told his readers about Hugh Trevor, he showed the older brother in action only in three brief passages: the one in which he quells the women's political tensions, one in which Douglas explains to him the confrontation at the falls of the James, and one in which he goes to the White House with Delia to plead for Douglas's life. In the meantime, Bernard is shown interacting with his wife, his daughters, his nephews, an old friend, a group of neighbors, and a Union army officer. As a result of this more detailed treatment, Bernard is the most fully developed character in the work. Because his character is revealed in a range of interactions, he is also the most sympathetic and trustworthy figure.

Bernard is a faithful man in the sense of the familial paradigm. He recognizes a myriad of ties to those around him, as is evident from his greetings of Douglas and Delia on their arrival. In the same passage, he recalls, in some detail, their childhood associations with specific slaves. While some commentators have examined Tucker's representation of loyal slaves, they typically focus on the slave militia that Bernard has formed. They overlook that Bernard locates Douglas in the family by referring to the young man's long associations with slaves. This practice relates the family to the broader community, particularly considering the use of family terms in referring to some of the slaves. Moreover, when this practice turns the conversation between Bernard and Douglas to slavery, Bernard refuses to engage in a discussion that could risk pitting son against father or duty to principle ahead of duty to family (Tucker 95–101). Clearly then, Bernard is a man of affection with a keen sense of the obligations that affection imposes throughout the social and familial hierarchy. Bernard's refusal to allow Delia to marry Douglas while he remains in the army is likewise founded on his paternal affections. While he recognizes that she loves Douglas, he also recognizes that she is bound to her parents as the Tucker

The Family Restructured: The Partisan Leader   *123*

brothers were bound to each other by ties of birth. Marriage to a Union soldier could pit her duty to her husband against her duty to her parents, and he hopes to spare her this (107–110).

Bernard is careful in respecting the rights and prerogatives of others. As we have seen, he refuses to discuss with Douglas subjects on which he and Hugh disagree. The same meticulous care is evident during the election in which he wins a place in the legislature. As indicated earlier, Van Buren has sent soldiers to ensure that one candidate will be elected without votes cast in opposition. If Van Buren's supporter wins, the victory can be presented to support the argument that Virginia stands behind the president; otherwise, the defeat of the president's candidate can be presented as evidence that his opponents manipulated the election, which in turn can be used to justify further suppression. Bernard, on the other hand, refuses to permit this, insisting that even those men who oppose him vote their convictions (175–181). While this may be read as an effort to thwart Van Buren's scheme, the concern that Bernard has already shown for the prerogatives and views of others precludes labeling his action at the election as a matter of connivance; it seems, rather, an act of principle, and it reinforces the notion that Bernard is a man to be admired and trusted. Moreover, he consults often with Mr. B___, a man whom he regards as wiser than himself (121).

Thus far, we have seen Bernard as a father and a man only peripherally connected to the political activity of the novel. On the strength of this, he does not appear as a ruler-father, but Tucker ensures that he has some claim to the title. On the day of the election, Bernard goes to vote and finds that the anti-administration candidate has been intimidated by Van Buren's supporters and the Union troops. Accordingly, he offers himself as a candidate and is elected. If Tucker had not wished to invoke the familial paradigm by intertwining the characteristics of the father with those of the ruler, he would have had no need to make Bernard a successful candidate for office. After all, Bernard could demonstrate his principles by speaking against the irregularities of the election and remaining at the polling place—as he does—without becoming a candidate himself. Once he is elected, however, he has some claim to bring the familial paradigm to the government. Granted, there is considerable distance between the president and the House of Representatives, but Tucker could not have Bernard elected president without diminishing the dramatic impact of Van Buren's monarchical tenure in the office or proposing the overthrow of the United States government, a course that he did not wish to advocate and one that he did not equate with secession.

Bernard's opposite number, President Martin Van Buren, is shown in limited detail and consistently seems unsympathetic and untrustworthy. He never appears with nor speaks of any relative, a feature that could make him seem untrustworthy in a culture that saw kinship as locating family members in the larger community and imposing standards of behavior on

124   *Will the Circle be Unbroken?*

them (Wyatt-Brown 119). To make matters worse, the portrait of Van Buren is even less flattering than the one of the Jackson-like Governor Berkley in *Cavaliers of Virginia*. The president has all of the defects of Berkley: He is self-centered and oblivious to the wishes or well-being of those he governs. Beyond this, he is quite flexible: He can be an "elegant, agreeable old gentleman," as he seems to Hugh Trevor's wife, or he can be a tyrannical usurper of his office, bent on "endeavoring to subdue the spirit and tame down the State pride of Virginia" (Tucker 55, 38). Seeking to quell open, armed rebellion through use of force, as Berkley does in *Cavaliers,* might arguably be the act of a faithful ruler seeking to maintain the divinely imposed order that has placed him in office and to protect the interests of his people. Van Buren, however, seeks to suppress the spirit and pride that might promote rebellion, and that is a different matter. Rather than fostering public spirit and a sense of interdependency among the people he leads, Van Buren remains in the White House, where his sycophants come to flatter him and do his will. He is willing to undercut supporters, to pit subordinates against each other, and, despite his democratic protestations, to disenfranchise whole states to continue his power. Tucker uses diction related to monarchy and empire to further suggest the gap that separates Van Buren from the electorate.

Van Buren's earliest direct appearance in the novel comes when he writes to Hugh, advising him that his explanation of Douglas's behavior toward Phillip Baker is satisfactory to him, but not to friends with whom the President feels he must consult (Tucker 111). Thus, this President, who has claimed monarchical status, is unable to form his own conclusion with respect to issues of right and wrong. In terms of the familial paradigm, this is an unpardonable failing in one who, like a father, must serve as an example for those of lesser estate (Yazawa 25). The difficulties with this letter go still further: Fathers and rulers were supposed to answer always to God, the power above them in the universal hierarchy, but in this instance, Van Buren answers to those below him.

When Van Buren actually appears, he is portrayed as a rather nervous middle-aged man from whose appearance character cannot be deduced. His manner provides some clarification: "His whole manner was that of a man who is somewhat at a loss to know what may be best for others, but finds full consolation in knowing precisely what is best for himself" (Tucker 132–133). Because he does not know the interests of others, he cannot possibly have the regard for them that affectionate subject—children had the right to expect of their faithful ruler-father. Moreover, he has used the mechanics of democracy as a basis to seize power from the electorate and set up what amounts to a monarchy in its place. When others are present, he sets aside his customary behavior and demonstrates gravity and dignity. This seems to fool Baker, who takes Van Buren, or at least Van Buren's power, quite seriously and sees him as a means of securing advancement.

The Family Restructured: The Partisan Leader 125

Bernard—and his political views—become more agreeable because the character has kinship connections as inviolable as those of which the author wrote in his letter to his brother Henry. It seems likely that this point would have been clear to readers who regarded family as placing members within the community and setting for each member standards of accomplishment, status, and character (Wyatt-Brown 119). Within the Trevor family, the potential for tension is great; after all, Hugh and Bernard disagree on most political matters. Nevertheless, they avoid permanent estrangement through conscious effort and painstaking tolerance for each other's opinions. As Tucker's narrator explains it, "Difference of political opinion had produced no estrangement [between the brothers], though it had interrupted their intercourse by making it less agreeable" (Tucker 52). Before the difference between his wife and his niece can flare into an argument, Hugh steps in to praise Bernard's wisdom, nobility, and generosity, and this praise seems sincere enough, despite Hugh's reluctance to acknowledge the rightness of Bernard's views (56, 46). While this course of action cannot produce unanimity or even compromise, it maintains the peace, and the affection between the family members can continue, despite disagreement, until they reach some accord.

Bernard follows a similar policy when Douglas accompanies Delia back to her home at the end of her visit to Hugh's home. Douglas has hardly greeted his uncle before the subject of politics arises. In the course of his military duty, he has traveled extensively outside of the South, but he retains his love of his home state and her culture. He has not thought much about politics, and he expresses the hope that Bernard will help him inform himself (Tucker 99–100). Bernard refuses to do so, however, because "There are some subjects . . . on which it is better to be in error than to differ, totally and conscientiously, from a father" (Tucker 100). Here again, Tucker privileges the family relationship: He makes Bernard so punctilious in this that he requires consent from Hugh before advising Douglas with respect to his submission to a court or resignation from the army. This contrasts with Van Buren, who explicitly applauds Owen Trevor for disagreeing with his father and supporting the Union without question (144).

Van Buren's praise disrupts the social order because it reduces the status of the parent-child relationship. In Tucker's hierarchical society, the relationship between parent and child, must be placed above all others. Melvin Yazawa, recognizing that Massachusetts colonial law allowed the death penalty for children who cursed their natural parents, has argued that "a society [such as the one in colonial Massachusetts, or, for that matter, the one that Tucker envisioned] founded on the primacy of domestic affections cannot afford to treat the cursing of one's parents lightly [and] the ultimate penalty was thus prescribed for an ultimate crime" (92). Tucker expresses the same view in more positive terms: Parenthood in the family or the commonwealth is so privileged that its prerogatives cannot be assumed by anyone else, even affectionate relatives.

All in all, the Trevor brothers maintain their relationship because they painstakingly respect each other's views and spheres of influence. Tucker regarded peaceable secession as possible, provided that the states showed similar tolerance and recognized the limits expressed in the Kentucky and Virginia Resolutions. Those resolutions, however, had attracted little support outside of Kentucky and Virginia in 1798. Whether they would provide a solution to the tensions forming thirty-eight years later seemed doubtful. Duty to state would be pitted against duty to country, and the nature of affectionate ties would require further examination, but *The Partisan Leader* had raised in concrete terms the prospect of war between the states.

Yet there were weaknesses in Tucker's conceptions of the novel and secession. While the Federal government had made little effort to retain the Southern states in the Union at the time of their secession in the novel, war still comes about as a result of the free trade treaty between the Southern states and England. The tension between Virginia and North Carolina before secession of the former suggests that the Southern confederacy may not be able to unify, especially considering that the North Carolinians' concerns about trade remain unanswered at the end of the novel, having been dropped without resolution almost as soon as they were raised. Even within the Trevor family, issues are left hanging at the end of the novel: There is no clear indication of whether Douglas will be rescued, released, or executed. Hugh has already lost one son, Owen. How will that affect the structure of the family when the emergency of Douglas's capture has ended? Delia, daughter of one secessionist and wife of another, may be widowed: Will her stronger ties be with her ardently secessionist father or with her uncle, the reluctant secessionist?

Tucker's letters indicate that he may have intended to address matters like these in a sequel to *The Partisan Leader,* but there is no indication that he ever began work on the continuation of the story. As a result, the novel stands as a campaign piece, aimed at Martin Van Buren, and presenting a somewhat incomplete picture. Taken with the treatise on authority offered in *George Balcombe,* however, some of Tucker's objections to the Democratic program and to Van Buren in particular become clearer. Also clearer was the division between the urban industrial Whigs, such as Kennedy, and the agrarian Whigs, such as Tucker, which made unlikely successful opposition to the Jacksonian Democrats.

CHAPTER EIGHT

Mistaken Identity: *Rob of the Bowl*

Although *Rob of the Bowl* was published in December 1838, John Pendleton Kennedy had been at work on it since 29 September 1835—slightly more than a year before the end of Jackson's administration and the election that placed Martin Van Buren in the presidency. Some scholars have argued that Kennedy's enjoyment of the historical research for this novel extended the time that he took to complete it, but this overlooks the considerable difference between the book that Kennedy described in his journal in September 1835 and the work published by Carey and Lea thirty-nine months later. In 1835, Kennedy recorded in his journal that he had "not yet fixed the story, but [meant] to put it upon the Chesapeake just before the revolution around 1774 perhaps." The proposed work would "introduce Billy of the Bowl, the pirate or buccaneer and smuggler, Cocklescruggs, a family of old maids" and a parson who conducted worship services with pistols on his lectern.[1] The case for writing a work set around the time of the Revolution was strong; Kennedy had enjoyed success with such a novel in *Horse-Shoe Robinson,* and the Revolutionary period still attracted readers. The characters, with buccaneers or smugglers, were ideal for a novel of adventure. In the end, however, Kennedy set his novel in colonial Maryland in 1684, a period of considerable tension between the Catholic Lords Proprietary and the increasingly Protestant populace. The Maryland colony of Kennedy's novel, deeply divided as it is, stands in danger from internal and external threats, and the divisions, like those of the United States in the Jacksonian years, must have seemed almost irreconcilable to those living through them. They leave the ruler-father, the Lord Proprietary, careworn as they almost come to overshadow his consciousness. The tensions of the times in the novel are made worse because the members of the community refuse to recognize their common concerns and the ruler-father's faithfulness. They are thus made easy prey for an outsider, the pirate Richard Cocklescraft, who, with his crew, repre-

128   *Will the Circle be Unbroken?*

sents the Brotherhood of the Coast, a loose association of freebooters, pirates, and smugglers. With this bitter struggle as a backdrop, Kennedy wrote a novel in which he could point to differences between "natural" and "artificial" families and address issues of nature and nurture that had political ramifications.

Rob of the Bowl offered readers a large cast of characters representing all sorts and conditions of humanity, generally arranged in an orderly hierarchy. At the top of the hierarchy stands Charles Calvert, Lord Baltimore, the Lord Proprietary of the province of Maryland, along with his family: his wife, his sister Maria, and his ward, Benedict Leonard. While his inner circle of council members—aristocrats who advise the Proprietary—make appearances, they play less important roles in the plot than do figures of the next lower tier, the professional class that directly serves the ruler and his council. This professional class includes such figures as Albert Verheyden, the Proprietary's young secretary, a young man highly regarded in the town despite uncertainty concerning the gentility of his birth, and Jasper Dauntrees, a companionable aging military veteran who commands the militia detachment at St. Mary's City, the colonial capital. Another functionary at roughly the same level is Anthony Warden, Collector of the Port of St. Mary's and the father of Blanche, "the Rose of St. Mary's," with whom Albert falls in love and marries at the end of the work. These figures, too, are assisted within the plot by yeoman figures from the next lower tier, such as Arnold de la Grange, a woodsman; Simon Fluke, a fisherman; Garret Weasel, a taverner; and a number of sturdy women, such as Dorothy Weasel, Garret's wife and the *de facto* ruler of the Crow and Archer tavern, and Bridget Coldcale, the cook at Anthony Warden's home, Rose Croft. Of figures from the lowest class Kennedy provided a host, featuring the simple-minded and virtuous Wise Watkin and peripatetic fiddler Willie of the Flats.

Given this range of characters, Kennedy's tale of St. Inigoe's could have been nothing more than a lively account of interactions between tolerant, intelligent topping and middling folk and the laughable poor and yeomanry with whom they come in contact as they all try to establish a colony in North America. Like colonial society, however, Kennedy's novel included another class, this one comprising outlaws and outcasts operating outside of the orderly hierarchy. The members of this class, led by Robert Swale, an amputee called "Rob of the Bowl," "Trencher Rob," or simply "the Cripple"; and Captain Richard Cocklescraft, actively engage in smuggling and piracy respectively. While both of these characters seem to have accumulated some wealth, neither has a place in Maryland society. Both have set themselves at the margin of that society, participating in it only as much as they must to get their livings. Rob is a fugitive who left England after killing a man he suspected of having an affair and fathering a child with his wife. On his voyage to the colonies, Rob was shipwrecked and lost both of

Mistaken Identity: Rob of the Bowl   129

his legs. His limited mobility and his guilt keep him out of the colonial society, but he earns a living by purchasing stolen goods from Cocklescraft and selling them to the colonists without charging duties. Cocklescraft poses as a merchant captain bringing legitimate goods from Europe, but he is actually a pirate trained by the legendary Morgan. On his voyages, he purchases some cargo, seizes more from legitimate vessels, deposits some of his goods with Rob for sale, and takes the remainder to the port of St. Mary's. There he sells goods with all lawful duties, but as we shall see, he explicitly rejects the authority and structure of the colonial community.

At the beginning of the novel, the colony of Maryland faces a number of dangers, internal and external. Indian tribes on the northern border are rumored to be preparing an uprising. Everyone in the colony may be in danger from these uprisings: Protestants blame the unrest on Catholics and Catholics blame it on Protestants. The resulting tension is manifest in the plans of some Protestants to mount an uprising of their own against the Catholic governor, the Proprietary. Their uprising, however, may not be necessary: the Proprietary has received orders from the Board of Trade and Plantations to remove all Catholics from office in the colony and replace them with Protestants. The governor has always based his appointments on merit and ability rather than religion, and he and the council have therefore agreed to resist the Board's order. Nevertheless, the order has been signed by the king, and it threatens to disrupt the governmental operations in the colony and disrupt, if not destroy, the social structure. As if these problems were not sufficient to provide tension for a single novel, the colony also seems to face supernatural dangers at a fisherman's house that has become known as the Wizard's Chapel. People passing the house at night have heard noises there and seen strange lights and faces that they believe to be goblins.

Still more trouble is on the way. Rumor has it that the brigantine *Olive Branch*, under command of Captain Richard Cocklescraft, is approaching. The word of Cocklescraft's arrival, as usual, reaches town well in advance of the *Olive Branch* because the skipper stops to put some goods ashore at the Wizard's Chapel with Rob Swale, the amputee known as Rob of the Bowl. Rob is a shrewd man, quite capable of arranging pyrotechnic displays, noises, and the appearance of bizarre faces at Wizard's Chapel, all of which serve to keep a superstitious populace away from the smuggled goods stored in the old building. On this particular voyage, Cocklescraft is especially eager to reach St. Mary's City because he believes that he is in love with Blanche Warden, daughter of the Port Collector. Blanche, in turn, is strongly attracted to the Proprietary's secretary, Albert Verheyden. The resolution of this romance ultimately allows Kennedy to draw together all of the political tensions of the novel.

The tension arising from the conflicts in the colony is not enough to preclude a good time, however. Blanche is about to reach her eighteenth birth-

130   *Will the Circle be Unbroken?*

day, and at the behest of the young women of the town, Lady Maria Calvert, sister of the Proprietary, arranges a party at Rose Croft that involves almost the entire population of St. Mary's City. Even people of the lowest class can participate in the festivities by gathering to watch the invited guests arrive and saluting such figures as the Proprietary.[2] Everyone in the community seems to anticipate the party eagerly, but Blanche approaches it with dread, partly because of her usual reticence and partly because her father, without consultation, has invited Cocklescraft to the party. Her concerns are well-founded: Before the party ends, Anthony Warden refuses to allow Cocklescraft to marry Blanche, and the skipper quietly challenges Verheyden to a duel.

Verheyden wins the duel bloodlessly, and Cocklescraft vows that he will have revenge, not simply on the secretary, but on the entire community. Although he is a lifelong Catholic who has promised a substantial donation to the St. Mary's City parish, he joins a Protestant conspiracy to overthrow Lord Baltimore. This, he must expect, will topple the social structure of the community and place him on an equal footing with Albert and Anthony. He is thus willing to take action against his principles for selfish and pragmatic reasons. In doing so, however, he allows his loyalties to be divided in just the way that Douglas Trevor avoided in *The Partisan Leader*. Based on espionage by Captain Dauntrees, evidence of the plot is assembled and the leading conspirators are jailed, but Cocklescraft decides to kidnap Blanche before making his escape. Before he can implement his plan, however, he kills a fisherman and a hue and cry is raised to track down the murderer. While Albert rides to join in this pursuit, Cocklescraft and his crew hold revels at Wizard's Chapel, and through a complex chain of events, Albert inadvertently takes shelter there and is captured. Rob, who is really Albert's father, recognizes his son on the basis of a miniature that he wears. On the strength of their kinship, Rob seeks to save Albert's life, and he offers to oversee the young man's execution but instead helps him escape. By recognizing his kinship with Albert, Rob also recognizes his connection to the community at large, and he acts on this connection by taking command of the brigantine, ostensibly so that Cocklescraft can make a quick escape after seizing Blanche. Once again, though, the assistance that Rob offers is a betrayal of the buccaneers, who are captured after a long chase on the water and overland. Rob's action to protect his son, then, parallels his action to protect the larger community.

This does not quite end the action, although the appearance of the pirates and their captain under guard in St. Mary's suggests that the outcome is all but certain. Rob testifies that he is really Major William Weatherby, Albert's genteel father. He also testifies against Cocklescraft. Because of Rob's obvious remorse and his testimony against the others, Lord Baltimore declines to punish him. After Cocklescraft and his men are brought in, however, the skipper seizes a dagger, stabs the amputee, and

Mistaken Identity: Rob of the Bowl   *131*

escapes with his crew in the commotion that follows. Although the Protestants assist his escape by blocking the path of the pursuing militiamen, Cocklescraft does not return to help them in their insurrection, which disintegrates. Albert and Blanche are married, and they use much of the fortune that Albert inherits from Rob in charitable works, thereby rehabilitating the fortune and, to some extent, Rob's name.

Kennedy's publishers were eager to place *Rob of the Bowl* on their shelves and paid him more than he had received for the publishing rights to *Swallow Barn*, but reviews were poor and sales were similarly unsatisfying. Reviewers seized on literary devices, such as the epigraphs at the heads of chapters, as reasons for disliking the book. The reviewer for the *New York Review* found the book packed with material: "It was said of a late opera, that it had material enough in it for a dozen modern operas, and so it [can] be said of the characters that Mr. Kennedy has collected in *Rob of the Bowl*" (quoted in Osborne 14). An unidentified reviewer even complained that the epigraphs for the chapters were taken from the works of English poets and thus inappropriate for an American work (Osborne 14). Reviews such as these suggest that Kennedy's busy plot impeded interpretation. The *New York Review* writer may have indicated a widely held view when he wrote "that the book leaves no very distinct impression on the mind" (quoted in Osborne 99): Focusing on a central issue may have proven to be a problem, and Kennedy's apparent wish to handle a host of issues may have slowed the resolution of the plot.

The absence of a clear impression of plot or character extends to modern commentators, as well. The most extensive discussion of the work is found in Charles Bohner's biography, *John Pendleton Kennedy: Gentleman from Baltimore*. Bohner noted that Kennedy had written of his pride in the "antiquarian labor" that the work had required, and he also noted the author's observation that the book had "as much history as it has invention" (102–103). He did not, however, indicate any sense of what the readers of Kennedy's day found in the novel, a question that he apparently dismissed by pointing out the novel's slow sales. Vernon Parrington called the work "light and whimsical cavalier romance, all atmosphere and small talk," but he added that ". . . [i]t is in this . . . book . . . that Kennedy really found himself" (48–49). This suggests that Parrington may have regarded Kennedy as a man of atmosphere and small talk, but perhaps insubstantial—an argument supported further by Parrington's contention that Kennedy "was ill fitted to deal with rollicking action of picaresque adventure; he preferred the leisurely, discursive romantic, subdued to gentle raillery or humorous tenderness" (51). This temperament, Parrington believed, kept Kennedy from adequately exploring the cavalier romantic strain that he had opened in *Rob of the Bowl*. After all, Parrington contends, Kennedy had in the work "the raw stuff of a true bloody-bones thriller" and produced instead a book in which "the action is deliberately subdued to the

132   *Will the Circle be Unbroken?*

humoresque; atmosphere is studiously created; adventure is held in strict subjection to the whimsical; and a mellow old-time flavor is imprisoned in the leisurely pages" (51).

Kennedy had produced bloody bones and thrills in some passages of *Horse-Shoe Robinson,* which suggests that it was not his temperament that kept him from doing so in *Rob of the Bowl.* On the contrary, he may have sought to produce tension and conflict of other sorts and deliberately suppressed the swashbuckling aspects of the tale.[3] Jay Hubbell dismissed the work with a single sentence: "*Rob of the Bowl* (1838), though it brought Kennedy twice as much money as *Swallow Barn,* seems to have attracted less attention than its predecessors" (486). The lack of attention that Hubbell noted has continued: William R. Taylor, Ritchie Watson, and Kathryn Seidel make no mention of the book. Yet what seems a wistful romance looking back to a simpler era is hardly a simple work.

At the end of *Rob of the Bowl,* questions remain unresolved. Kennedy provides an eight-paragraph closing chapter introduced as follows: "Here ends my tale. We have no longer an interest to follow the fortunes of the personages who have been brought to view in this motleyed narrative of trivial and tragic events. A brief memorandum will tell all that remains to gratify the inquiries of my readers" (362).

But the remaining paragraphs of the conclusion hardly gratify the inquiries that readers of any era might make: Some plots remain unresolved. First, readers learn that Albert and Blanche were married shortly after the events of the novel and that they inherited from Rob/Weatherby a sizable estate which they dispensed in charity and hospitality to bring about "purification of the more than doubtful uncleanness of the Cripple's wealth" (362). Next, Kennedy turns to the Protestant conspirators, but he mentions only four of their leaders. While their sentences involved long imprisonment and heavy fines, in no case was the death penalty carried out, despite the serious charges arising from the conspiracy to overthrow the lawful authority of the colony. Finally, Kennedy acknowledges that no records remained of the other conspirators—except for the bibulous Corporal Edward Abbott, who was released from prison by Lord Baltimore's order because he confessed his crimes and held that he was too drunk to recall anything that had been said or done in the conspiracy. This conclusion, which claims to "tell all that remains to gratify the inquiries of . . . readers" includes no reference whatsoever to the piratical Richard Cocklescraft, from whose actions much of the tension of the plot develops. While Cocklescraft and his men escaped from St. Mary's, the question of their possible return remains open. What efforts, if any, did Lord Baltimore make to capture and try those who had disrupted the peace of his colony? Did Cocklescraft return to St. Mary's or cause trouble elsewhere? In other words, Kennedy leaves a murderer who has scoffed at the order of society unrepentant, unpunished, and even unfettered. Perhaps the issues of the plot were com-

Mistaken Identity: Rob of the Bowl 133

plex, as were those facing the nation, and neither set had yet been resolved in the author's mind.

The writing of *Rob of the Bowl* took place through a period, 1835–1838, during which some historians believe that the tensions of the Jacksonian period shifted away from the character and style of the president and came to rest instead on economic and social issues. To rehearse the history of Jacksonian economic policy is beyond the scope of this study; however, it is important to recognize how it may have posed a dilemma for men like Kennedy. Jackson's policies contributed to the Panic of 1837, in its time the worst economic crisis to befall the United States since the Declaration of Independence. Still, those policies did not cause the panic, nor did any one of the other numerous contributing factors. No longer could a man or a party or a policy be isolated as the cause of a problem. Doing so could lead to precisely the sort of tension extant between Protestants and Catholics in *Rob of the Bowl*. Unity and cooperation, on the other hand, might rescue the nation.

Jackson's economic policy revolved to a great extent around his dislike of the Bank of the United States, the charter for which expired in 1836. He regarded the bank as an unconstitutional placement of public power in private hands, and in some respects, the bank's management of government funds, payment of government debts, and provision of currency for the government did place the bank in the position of governing the government. Nevertheless, when Jackson's adversaries in Congress voted to recharter the bank in 1832, three years before the existing charter was due to expire, Jackson vetoed the bill. By late 1833, he had begun to withdraw federal funds from the Bank of the United States and to deposit them in state banks that were generally known to be friendly to his administration.[4] Jackson was not unaware of the shortcomings of the state banks as depositories, and he preferred establishing a government bank that was a branch of the Treasury Department without a business charter, the power to make loans or hold property, or stockholders (Feller 169–172).

While Jackson was opposing rechartering, state legislatures were hurrying to charter new banks, and the number of financial institutions with state charters doubled between 1830 and 1835 (Feller 172). These banks had few restraints, and the government deposits gave them plenty of money to lend; moreover, cotton exports were doubling in value between 1833 and 1836, prompting planters and textile manufacturers to seek loans for expansion (136). Prices and interest rates crept higher, and predictions circulated to the effect that a bad end would follow the expansion of the early 1830's (172). Finally, the end came: Crops failed in 1835, and farmers were unable to pay merchants or speculators, who in turn needed to pay banks (Schlesinger 217). By 1837, contraction of the money market had led to widespread unemployment, and prices of some foods more than doubled between March 1835 and March 1837 (218). The *New Era* mourned that

134   *Will the Circle be Unbroken?*

at least in New York, "'At no period of . . . history has there been as great a degree of general distress as there is at this day'" (quoted in Schlesinger 220). This Panic of 1837 would be followed by another panic in 1839, and national recovery would not be complete until the mid-1840's.

This distress could not be traced to any single act or actor. While Jackson's shifting of the deposits may have weakened the currency, some state banks had been irresponsibly run, especially in the west and the south (Pessen 146). As Edward Pessen has observed,

> Trade Jacksonians blamed Biddle; agrarian Jacksonians blamed banks; Whigs blamed Democrats or Jackson, in general, and the Bank War, the removal of the deposits and the Specie Circular, in particular. Fatalists blamed the Great Fire that devastated New York City. Abolitionists blamed slavery. Sensible eclectics, while inevitably assigning different weights to different causes, would include the rage for improvements, the era's bank practices, the speculation in land, the economy's great reliance on a European capital over whose removal Americans had no control, the too great reliance on one crop as the means of raising foreign specie, the Hessian fly for its effect on American crops, and in sum the abandon with which too many Americans had pursued wealth during the era (147).

Regardless of where blame was placed, most of the nation seemed to be suffering, and theories concerning the causes and cures for the distress gave impetus to the formation of a host of groups and organizations in society. While these groups generally expressed positive aims, many of them relied on rituals and secrets that could be seen as fragmenting society in a time when unity was crucial, especially to a nationalist like Kennedy, who attacked these constructed communities in *Rob of the Bowl*. To understand this attack, it is first necessary to understand those communities. From perfectionist communities to benevolent organizations, the range is too great to examine in detail here; however, the evangelical religions provide some insight into how many of these constructed brotherhoods operated. They have been discussed in detail in *And They All Sang Hallelujah: Plain-Folk Camp-Meeting Religion, 1800–1845,* by Dickson D. Bruce, Jr.

The evangelicals and other organizations attracted the socially and politically marginalized classes who suffered most during the Panic (Bruce 5), classes that Kennedy had represented as equally capable of virtue or vice in *Horse-Shoe Robinson*. It is important to recognize that some of the benevolent and perfectionist organizations formed by the less marginalized elements of society functioned in similar ways. The distinctive feature of evangelical religion was the camp meeting, and Bruce argued that the experience of this ritual assisted participants in organizing their other experiences and gave them a sense of hope and empowerment. In these respects, they resembled similar rituals of numerous other organizations springing up away from the frontier areas where the evangelicals flourished. By joining any of these movements and becoming brothers or sisters, people gained a sense of belonging as well as a way of comprehending reality that was shared with

Mistaken Identity: Rob of the Bowl

and supported by the other members. While the new fraternal bonds offered by such organizations may have been attractive to the marginalized, they looked less attractive to outsiders.[5] Perhaps the best-known example of this involved a purely fraternal organization without religious connections, the order of Freemasons. Although many prominent men, including Washington, had been Masons, Feller points out that the "carefully guarded secret rites [that] fostered comradeship among members . . . invited outsiders' resentment and suspicion" (102)—just as the evangelicals' rituals did. This suspicion led, in some cases, to organized opposition, such as the Antimasonic movement, which eventually attacked all secret societies, political establishments, and other exclusive organizations (103). Moreover, Kennedy was familiar with the Antimasonic movement; his friend William Wirt had run for President as the Antimasonic candidate in 1832 (103).

These artificial brotherhoods flourished because they seemed to meet people's needs, and they took on increased importance as economic insecurities increased, such as those extant in Virginia with the decline of the tobacco economy and throughout the nation with the advent of the Panic of 1837 (Bruce 29). For insiders, evangelical religions—and other artificial brotherhoods—offered a means of maintaining a balance in the community as well as a new way of looking at the world and human relationships (35). What is important in the context of the present study is that this new way of perceiving used the vocabulary of the family to express and organize fundamental relationships outside of the household and outside of kinship structures. As Bruce pointed out, "many people who took part in the camp-meeting did so without assuming any kind of leadership role, but they were still church members who had undergone conversion. They referred to themselves in terms which indicated both their solidarity and their special status, using expressions which have had a long currency among sectarian Christians. They addressed each other as 'Brother' and 'Sister,' and thought of themselves, collectively, as 'Brethren,'—all terms which had been used by the earliest Christians" (77).

As the sinner progressed toward salvation in evangelical bodies and the new member joined fraternal groups, distinctions between the sinful and the saved—the insider and the outsider—became clear, with members exhorting and ministering to the initiates who were moving toward full brotherhood (Bruce 74–75). Ultimately, the conventional distinctions of race and sex could be swept away, and the old order could be replaced with a new order (76). Thus, the insider's loyalty might be divided, or his primary allegiance might slip from the community at large to the constructed brotherhood.

For camp-meeting evangelicals, converts followed a strictly prescribed course from sinfulness to conviction (an explicit rejection of the would-be convert's previous worldly life and reaching toward religion) to conversion (in which the convert placed absolute reliance on the mercy of God and

136   *Will the Circle be Unbroken?*

became alienated from the past) (Bruce 63–66). As this process took place in churches and camp meetings, the physical layout of the area replaced existing social structures, including families, with new structures (72). Men and women sat in separate areas, a contrast with the family seating practices of the liturgical religions. In addition, black participants were separated from white participants, and the social order of the community was thus disrupted, at least until the converts answered the altar call and met at the mourner's bench (Bruce 73–74). It is entirely reasonable to view this transition as a movement from an earthly order necessary because of Adamic sin, such as the Whigs imagined (and such as Yazawa proposed), to a heavenly order in which there was no sin but only various orders of closeness to God.

At the most elemental level, the new conceptualizations that the evangelicals offered expressed a sibling relation among the converted under the fatherhood of God. This fatherhood went beyond acknowledgment of God as creator; the act of conversion that brought the convicted into full fellowship with the brethren was an act of dependency upon a narrow group rather than the broader community in which the brotherhood existed. It was, in a sense, a rejection of an existing community for one that outsiders might see as artificial and disordered or misordered. That is, it bore strong effective resemblance to Cocklescraft's rejection of the Proprietary and allegiance to the Brothers of the Coast. Once converted, the new brothers and sisters in any of these groups, like those in the evangelical movement, were subject to discipline within the organization as well as to expulsion at some points (Bruce 48). In a sense, the rules of the constructed community supplanted the laws of the broader community, but these fraternal laws, unlike civil and criminal law, left open the hope of forgiveness and reconciliation. Because of this, the brotherhood could appear to operate according to different and looser standards than the community as a whole.

These constructed brotherhoods, then, provide additional insight into the familial paradigm, and they reflect another inadequacy of Melvin Yazawa's formulation. While the filial dependency among the members of a "natural" community was generalized, the fraternal dependency within constructed community was specific: The converted brethren needed each other to progress spiritually (and, presumably, temporally once the necessary spiritual progress had been made). The roles in a structure of filial affection and interdependency had to be fixed; that is, a town drunk had always to be the town drunk, a constant example of the dangers of weak character. On the other hand, fraternal dependency allowed for the possibility of change: when an evangelical brother or sister prayed over a converting sinner, both must have recognized that at some future time, their positions might be reversed.

Fraternal ties were not, of course, limited to evangelical communities; in that arena, they may have been somewhat more readily accepted by out-

Mistaken Identity: Rob of the Bowl

siders than, say, Freemasonry or a radical perfectionist community. The sibling relationship was also the model for the ties within social organizations and even some craft organizations. All of these groups, like evangelical Christians, admitted members who passed through an initiation that amounted to a ritualized restructuring of their worldview. After becoming part of the new brotherhood, the initiate was subject to a set of regulations that supplanted the laws of the broader community. Shared experiences and secrets distinguished members from outsiders and connected each member with the fraternal order, but not to the community in which it existed. At the head of the order was not a ruler-father but a first-among-equals, an elder brother who would, at some point, surrender office and, in effect, return to the rank-and-file of membership.[6]

The most obvious fraternal group in *Rob of the Bowl* is the one to which Cocklescraft and his cutthroats belong, the Brothers of the Coast. This group appears loosely organized; at least, Kennedy provides little information on its structure. This "tribe of desperate men," as Kennedy describes it, appears to be a haphazard group of pirates noteworthy primarily for sacking South and Central American cities (156). Cocklescraft became a part of the group as a child, although the details of his affiliation are sketchy: His "first breath was drawn upon the billows of the ocean, and his infancy was nursed in the haunts of the buccaneers" (156). Even this sketchy description suggests less-than-genteel breeding and associates Cocklescraft with the marginalized class that was especially susceptible to the attractions of artificial fraternal groups. He has no family to provide kinship ties and a place in the natural community. Thus deprived, while he was still young, Cocklescraft caught the attention of Captain Morgan, who "was charmed with the precocious relish for rapine conspicuous in the character of the boy" (156). Morgan kept the youngster near him in a ceremonial capacity, "that of a page or armor-bearer, according to the yet lingering forms of chivalry" (156). Thus Kennedy associates this with a ritual of initiation—the passage of page to knight.

The Brothers of the Coast may be an egalitarian lot, but their leaders seem lacking in both faithfulness and authority, and order in their brotherhood is tenuous at best. While Morgan is introduced as Cocklescraft's mentor, Kennedy does not identify him as a leader of the brotherhood; on the other hand, he makes clear that after the sack of Panama, "The Welsh Captain, laden with spoils of untold value, played false to his comrades, by stealing off with the lion's share of the booty," thereby teaching young Cocklescraft that the first among equals could claim entitlement to a disproportionate share of spoils (Kennedy 157). Morgan's authority, limited though it may be, seems to rest entirely upon his force, and his connections to the brotherhood are tenuous. At the time of his retirement, however, Morgan simply abandoned his young protégé (157).

138   Will the Circle be Unbroken?

While Cocklescraft is the skipper of his brigantine, the *Olive Branch,* he demonstrates little in the way of authority. His claim to command seems to rest on pragmatic grounds: He supplies the ship, one that he seized from a merchant; he selected the "crew of trusty cut-throats"; and his relationship with Rob ensures that voyages will be profitable (Kennedy 158). But his crew's acceptance of his authority is shaky at best. At the end of the revels at Wizard's Chapel, for example, he gives orders for his crewmen to return to the ship while he rests at Rob's hut (302). Despite these orders, when Rob returns to the "haunted" house to retrieve his account book, he encounters a group of the sailors who have arrived in search of another drink (305). Although several sailors hear Cocklescraft give Rob instructions as to where the *Olive Branch* should anchor while he is kidnapping Blanche, the Cripple, who would have little chance in combat with an able-bodied sailor, manages to have the crew sail the ship and anchor elsewhere (317, 318). Even when Rob brings the vessel upstream and it must be clear that his actions will work against Cocklescraft, the crewmen apparently make no effort to oppose the actions that can lead to their captain's betrayal.

The reason for Rob's successful leadership is not made explicit in the novel. He lacks the Proprietary's patience and gentle touch with subordinates. Lord Baltimore, for example, takes it upon himself to provide a new hat for Arnold de la Grange, a forester in his service. This generosity contrasts with Rob's close dealing with two merchants who come to buy goods from him. He is careful to show only samples of his wares so that he can set prices based on alleged shortages rather than actual supplies. Despite Rob's shrewdness, the sailors who make brief appearances seem to trust him. The two assigned to assist him in killing Albert are presented in more detail than the others, and they are duped into believing that the young man has fallen overboard and drowned. Their desire to return through stormy waters to the shore leads them to accept Rob's word without investigation (Kennedy 314). Had they paused a moment to investigate, as Cocklescraft does when they reach shore, they, too, might have found beneath the seat of the boat the stone that they had prepared to tie around their victim's neck (315). The basis for Rob's authority, then, is unclear, but the fact remains that he may have an aura of command that serves him well. Despite his long career as a smuggler, he is, by birth a member of a class that has been raised to exercise authority, and as a military officer, he has been trained to use authority. In this connection, it is important to note that Rob only directs the pirates successfully *after* he has recognized Albert and his own connection with the community—and with that connection, his place in the social hierarchy.

Cocklescraft's pirates have much in common with the Tory guerrillas Kennedy had created for *Horse-Shoe Robinson.* Both groups appear to draw their members from the lowest stratum of society. Neither has strong, capable leadership, and members of both quickly lose sight of their objec-

Mistaken Identity: Rob of the Bowl 139

tives. Neither group can claim any noteworthy victory: even when they gain some temporary advantage, their prisoners escape and the cutthroat bands must flee or disintegrate. In *Rob of the Bowl,* however, Kennedy made the Brothers of the Coast members of a group that explicitly set itself apart from the "natural" community of St. Mary's City. In *Horse-Shoe Robinson,* the guerrillas at least paid lip service to the regular authority represented by British officers, but the pirates, represented by their captain, know no allegiance except to Rob of the Trencher—the man who betrays them as soon as he recognizes his own connection through Albert to the community. And while Kennedy made the Tories coarse and bloodthirsty, he made his pirates almost animalistic: "'Perros, a la savannah'"—"Dogs, to the field"—is their often-repeated motto. This figure of speech makes them more than outcasts; it makes them a breed apart, capable only of threatening an established order. In a time of great tension, such as the time of the novel—or, for that matter, the late 1830s—these artificial brotherhoods, with their initiations and professed separateness from the community at large, could appear to be real threats indeed.

Moreover, deny it though they will, the rogues are in a dependent relationship with the inhabitants of St. Mary's City. The community, however, does not reject Rob and Cocklescraft, although it holds them at a distance. Their illicit trade goes on fairly openly, as Kennedy shows early in the novel. Discussion between Dauntrees and Weasel demonstrates that there exists a body of informed consumers who know that smuggled goods sell for lower prices than those legally imported through the Collector of the Port. Even though nothing in the novel suggests an interest on the part of the Proprietary in stopping the illicit activity, merchants recognize that dealing in these goods has risks that they are willing to take. As a result, Rob, Cocklescraft, and the pirates are not absolute outcasts, but neither are they full members of the community. Cocklescraft seeks to marry Blanche, and he talks of giving up piracy, but he has not earned or been born to the standing that would make him acceptable to her or her father. When they reject him, he seeks to overthrow the order of the community by agreeing to aid in a Protestant uprising against the Proprietary. It is Cocklescraft's refusal to accept the structure of the community—not his misdeeds against specific laws or members of the community—that dictates that at best, he must leave and never return at the end of the novel.

The community and the pirate brotherhood are finally set against each other after a series of events in which the skipper proves repeatedly that he is and will remain an outsider. When Cocklescraft becomes enamored of Blanche Warden, he makes a clumsy attempt to follow courtship rituals by approaching her father. Anthony and Cocklescraft might be adversaries because the former is a customs official and the latter a smuggler, but the collector's tolerance is such that he invites the buccaneer to Blanche's birthday celebration. This, however, does not make Cocklescraft an acceptable suitor and Anthony rejects him emphatically. Next, Cocklescraft seeks to

140   *Will the Circle be Unbroken?*

kidnap Blanche, assisted by his crew. Captured before he can succeed in that crime and facing a death sentence, the piratical skipper tells Lord Baltimore "'I never acknowledged your Lordship's laws. . . . I have lived above them—coming when I would and going when it pleased me. . . . I have but one master here—Old Rob of the Trencher'" (358). In other words, his rejection of connection with the community that has purchased his goods actually goes beyond rejection to a final, flagrant affront to the interdependency of that well-ordered organic community. It is a falsehood, a denial that the community has allowed him a place in its operations, regardless of any suspicions about his business. This affront places the skipper far outside the pale; he cannot be corrected by a ruler-father whose authority he does not accept. But Cocklescraft has—or believes he has— status within the community of his crew, apparent outcasts from several nations, who like their captain, acknowledge no law nor social position outside of their indistinctly drawn Brotherhood of the Coast. In addition, Cocklescraft, although a Roman Catholic, allies himself with another con-structed community, a group of Protestants including the Fendall brothers, as well as John Coode, and Parson Yeo. Kennedy avoids placing these char-acters clearly in any social class, but instead separates them from the mainstream community as he does the pirates. This similarity is hardly accidental; the two fraternities resemble each other in their determination to overthrow the orderly system of the colony as represented by the more sympathetic figures. These outsiders make up artificial brotherhoods, con-structed and maintained self-consciously, in contrast with the "natural" families of Lord Baltimore, Anthony Warden, and Garret Weasel, which are created through birth and marriage. While the latter provide the community's structure and organization, the former threaten both and exacerbate any problem that arises.

     This loose collection of rogues stands in contrast to the well-organized citizens of St. Mary's City and its environs. As we observed earlier, they represent all social classes, and they recognize social distinctions without regarding them as barriers. When the elite of the town gather to celebrate Blanche's birthday, the "humbler ranks" are present for the celebration, just as the gentry are, even though the former are not included in the guest list (Kennedy 193). Willy of the Flats, the town's peripatetic fiddler, organ-izes the humble people to doff their caps when the Proprietary arrives, and those in the crowd actually seem to take pleasure in this gesture—even when the vehicle taken for the coach at a distance turns out to be Dorothy and Garret Weasel on a cart carrying food and drink to the gathering (196). Blanche, of course, has taken pains to invite all whose status entitles them to attend, including some guests who may be marginal. Similarly, the mem-bers of the natural community support each other in times of need. When Albert, somewhat unpracticed in fencing, is challenged to a duel, he needs only awaken Captain Dauntrees for assistance. Similarly, when Simon Fluke, a poor fisherman who lives a distance from St. Mary's City, is murdered,

Mistaken Identity: Rob of the Bowl

the town turns out, first to console his family and then to pursue the murderer. Such foibles as Dauntrees' superstitions concerning the Wizard's Castle can be tolerated by the gentry, provided, of course, that these beliefs do not interfere with the duty that Dauntrees owes the Proprietary.

Thus, at a time when the Jacksonians were increasingly pointing to the "unproductive" upper class as inimical to workers, Kennedy depicts a stratified society as a peaceable kingdom. To eliminate natural social distinction, as the pirates do with their artificial brotherhood, would risk anarchy because it would strip away the natural basis for paternal faithfulness and filial affection that legitimated authority. Within the natural organic community, the classes could cooperate and thereby survive difficult times. Still, the unfinished plot lines of the novel suggest that Kennedy was less able than before to conceptualize clear answers to problems. The old generation of political leaders—men of such stature as Washington, the Adamses, Jefferson, Madison, Monroe, and Jackson—were giving way to a new generation of men such as Van Buren, who had not been alive at the time of the Revolution and had not had any part in the founding of the country. The generational progression to which Kennedy had pointed hopefully in *Swallow Barn* did not appear to have taken the direction that he had hoped. With these newer leaders, it became more difficult to suggest, as he had in *Horse-Shoe Robinson,* that new leadership would resolve difficulties that plagued the nation as a whole. One part of Kennedy's nationalistic view, however, remained intact through the Panic of 1837 and the apparent threats of social fragmentation and chaos: The United States was still a single entity in which inflation, lack of credit, and joblessness did not observe sectional or social boundaries. On the contrary, they set up conditions in which the structure of society could be disrupted by artificial brotherhoods that ignored interdependencies and undermined even the authority of a faithful ruler-father.

CHAPTER NINE
To the West:
Knights of the Horse-shoe

In an addendum to *Cavaliers of Virginia, or the Recluse of Jamestown* (1835), William A. Caruthers promised readers that he would soon offer them another novel, this one focusing on the exploits of the band of Virginian adventurers who in 1716 accompanied Governor Alexander Spotswood on an expedition to the crest of the Blue Ridge Mountains.[1] That story, *The Knights of the Horse-Shoe: A Traditionary Tale of the Cocked-Hat Gentry,* did not appear until 1841, however; Caruthers's relocations from New York City to Lexington, Virginia, in 1835 and from Lexington to Savannah, Georgia, in 1837 may have interrupted his work, and a fire in his Lexington home in the spring of 1837 destroyed his manuscript (Davis, "Introduction" viii–ix). As a result, the work promised in 1835 was delayed: after serial publication in *The Magnolia: or, Southern Monthly* in 1841, still more time lapsed before the work was finally published in two volumes in 1845. Moreover, *The Knights of the Golden Horse-Shoe* was not published by the Harper Brothers, who had published Caruthers' earlier novels, but by Charles Yancey of Wetumpka, Alabama, (Davis, Introduction xxix)a house that lacked the Harpers' ability to distribute books throughout the United States.

There may have been several reasons why Caruthers placed *The Knights of the Golden Horse-Shoe* with Yancey. The Panic of 1837 had probably forced the Harpers to reduce their list of offerings, and in a tight economy, reprints of English favorites seemed safer and more attractive to publishers than the works of American authors (Davis, *Chronicler* 200). The decision that the Harpers would not publish a third Caruthers novel, then, may have been the publisher's and not the author's. Curtis Carroll Davis has speculated that Caruthers placed the work with a small Southern publisher "probably on grounds of sectional pride" (Davis, "Introduction" x), and it is true that Caruthers wrote to Charles Campbell, a historian who had assisted him in research, that Yancey "'[was] about to try *very patri-*

143

144   *Will the Circle be Unbroken?*

otically to establish a Southern Publish [sic] House . . . No one would rejoice more than I would at his success, but it is next to impossible unless he has got a large fortune to back him'" (quoted in Davis *Chronicler* 203). But Caruthers, in the same passage of the same letter showed that he had reservations concerning Yancey's success, and those reservations were founded on experience: "'I have warned him of the consequences and attempted to describe to him what a complicated and ramified affair one of the great northern houses is . . .'" (quoted in Davis, *Chronicler* 203) Clearly, Caruthers knew that Southern publishing success was not likely to come quickly, and he must have recognized, as well, that Yancey's limited distribution capability would mean limited financial success for the author.

Nevertheless, it is undeniable that by the 1840s Southerners had begun to call for a Southern literature and support for Southern publishers. Wetumpka may have seemed as likely a place as any other for these calls to be answered. The established cities of Richmond, Charleston, and Savannah had not supported a strong publishing industry, but Wetumpka, incorporated in 1834, did not have the history of false starts that the older cities had accumulated. The growing town offered water transportation, and the publisher, Charles Yancey, already owned and edited a fairly successful newspaper. He hoped to establish a publishing center, and the prospect of publishing a novel by an author whose work had already been offered by a major New York house must have been attractive to him (Davis, *Chronicler* 201–202). He may have succeeded in persuading Caruthers to give him *Knights* because the author, now living in the South for the first time, wished to address southern readers more directly, calling on them to lead a unified nation into the sparsely populated West. The effort to go west, Caruthers suggests in the novel, would bind the opposing factions (or force them out) in fulfillment of their common national destiny, and it could be undertaken successfully as soon as a visionary leader—a ruler-father—stepped forward and led people to recognize the fraternal ties that bound them. The fulfillment of this destiny was the next step in national maturation.

While Caruthers' title, *Knights of the Horse-Shoe* or *Knights of the Golden Horse-Shoe,* suggests that the novel's plot revolves around the Spotswood tramontane expedition of 1716,[2] the bulk of the work treats events that occur before that expedition, and much of the business of the plot must be completed in order for the expedition to occur. At the beginning of the novel, Governor Alexander Spotswood is at his summer residence, Temple Farm, near Yorktown, Virginia. The historical Spotswood was a bachelor at the time of his service as governor, but Caruthers provides him a family consisting of a wife; two daughters, Kate and Dorothea; and two sons, John and Robert. The elder daughter, Kate, is a marriageable young woman of seventeen, well educated, devoutly religious, talented in music, and deeply interested in caring for the sick (Caruthers 3–4, 8, 11,

To the West: Knights of the Horse-shoe   145

44–45). Dorothea is two years younger, her father's pet, and ever ready to use her privileged status as a base from which to attack anyone whom she finds remotely pretentious (3–4, 19, 45–46). Their brother, John, is the oldest Spotswood child. In his mid-twenties, he is captain of the Rangers, a standing military force deployed along the frontier (4). Although he has followed his father in pursuing a military career, he is nevertheless a rebellious and self-indulgent young man who succumbs to alcohol and sexual passion and thereby seals his ruin. Robert is far younger, and beyond requiring a tutor, his role in the plot is minimal.

The Spotswood family is further augmented by the presence of several figures who are not blood relatives but enjoy such intimacy that they function as family members. These include Commissary James Blair, the head of the Anglican Church in Virginia (and, historically, an opponent of Alexander Spotswood who was instrumental in bringing about the governor's dismissal in 1722) and Dr. Evylin, a venerable Williamsburg physician (Caruthers 5), whose daughter, Ellen, is a close friend of Kate Spotswood and comes to play a prominent role in the plot. These figures interact closely with the Spotswoods in such ways as assisting the governor in the secret burial of the governor's half-brother, and Caruthers points out the affection that the Spotswood daughters feel for them. Blair and Evylin can be described as performing avuncular roles, and as we shall see, Ellen Evylin performs a sisterly role, particularly to Kate. Another character who may be considered a marginal member of the household, Bernard Moore, is one of Kate's suitors. During the early part of the novel, the governor employs a tutor (who becomes a major figure) as well. We have seen, in considering the Tucker family, that tutors sometimes were on terms of considerable intimacy with their employers' families, and this tutor quickly reaches this status.

All is not idyllic for Governor Spotswood at Temple Farm as the novel begins. Tensions overseas have interfered with his administration, but he remains committed to a tramontane expedition to the western lands, and he is busy with measures to ensure that the House of Burgesses will authorize the expedition and provide support for it at their next session. One night, while the governor and his household are visiting neighbors, a mysterious party of two men and a woman in masks comes to the farm seeking shelter from a storm, and they leave behind a mysterious sealed packet for the governor. The governor and his family search unsuccessfully for the three strangers the next day, but Spotswood does meet a twenty-four-year-old man called Henry Hall, and he hires him as tutor to young Robert (Caruthers 22). This apparently impoverished young man quickly becomes a favorite of the entire household because of his gentlemanly erudition, skill with the short sword, military insight, and politeness (22, 25, 26, 39). Meanwhile, John Spotswood returns to Williamsburg and learns that his brief dalliance with Wingina, the sister of the governor's Shawnee inter-

146   *Will the Circle be Unbroken?*

preter, has left her pregnant and in grave danger of being abandoned by her family as well as the white people with whom she has associated. The couple can find no solution to this dilemma except death or an escape to the mountains, and John's guilt plunges him into an alcoholic binge followed by hallucinations and serious illness (12, 62–64, 66–70).

In the meantime, two more characters have arrived at Temple Farm: Harry Lee and Ellen Evylin. Harry and his older brother Frank, heirs to one of the greatest fortunes in Virginia, were orphaned at an early age and grew up in the home of Dr. Evylin. After his brother was reported to have been killed in Scotland, Harry not only claimed the estate that Frank had inherited from their father, but he tried to claim his brother's relationship with Ellen, even though she finds him tedious, tiresome, and persecuting (Caruthers 31, 23). Harry comes to Temple Farm because he is a member of the House of Burgesses and Governor Spotswood needs his vote in favor of the tramontane expedition (41).

Caruthers introduces Harry in a letter from Ellen to her father. This unflattering introduction gains reinforcement when Dorothea Spotswood lampoons Harry on the way home from church before the character actually appears in the text. Consequently, when Harry first appears in the novel, readers already believe that he is jealous to a fault, that he loves himself more than he loves others, and he is silent, cautious, given to pomp and vanity, affected, and unable to take a joke (Caruthers 32–33). Were it not for the indirect introduction, readers might conclude that Harry is not an absolute blackguard: After all, he learns that the new tutor has the same name as a relative to whom he is trying to turn over an inheritance from a recently deceased aunt, and he promptly gives the tutor a portion of the estate without requiring proof of identity (53–54). This gesture surprises some members of the household because it seems out of character (54).

Ellen has been described as a typical Caruthers heroine because she is "small, blonde, and blue-eyed" (Davis, "Introduction" xii), but her similarities to Caruthers's other heroines are more extensive than this. Like Frances St. Clair in *The Kentuckian in New-York*, Ellen is given to fainting, and her physical fragility has its origins in family issues: While the Lee brothers lived with Dr. Evylin, Frank developed into a particularly engaging young man—good-natured, loyal, and thoughtful. When Harry recognized that most people showed Frank partiality, he accused Dr. Evylin of trying to arrange a marriage between Ellen and Frank in order to get control of the Lee fortune (Caruthers 33). This led to an argument between the brothers as well as a premature engagement between Ellen and Frank Lee (33–35). Dr. Evylin, seeking to reduce the conflict between the two brothers and postpone the marriage, sent Frank to Edinburgh to continue his education, but while there, the young man became involved in the political intrigues that have bedeviled Governor Spotswood and is rumored to have been killed in an unsuccessful attempt to rescue a political prisoner (36).

To the West: Knights of the Horse-shoe   147

Ellen has come to Temple Farm in hope of seeing papers in the governor's possession that may confirm or refute reports of Frank's death (36–37).

By the time of Harry Lee's arrival, the tutor has already become a favorite of the women of the household and indispensable to the governor, assisting substantially in the efforts to arrange the tramontane expedition. He reveals to Ellen that he was, in Scotland, a close friend of his kinsman, Frank Lee. This revelation forms the basis for increasing intimacy between Ellen and the tutor, and Harry finds worrisome the tutor's favored position in the Spotswood household and with Ellen. While the governor is in Williamsburg tending to John during his illness, Harry begins a series of efforts to discredit the young immigrant as an impostor.

The tutor is, in fact, Frank Lee, but this information only emerges through a series of legal and social trials. First, Harry Lee demands that the tutor repay the money that he has been advanced from the estate; this is impossible for the impoverished young man. When this leads to the tutor's imprisonment, Ellen sends the money to pay the debt, and the prisoner is freed. Harry's plan appears to have unraveled, and the tutor heads west toward the frontier, where he expects to live free of the concerns that have beset him. He stops at Germana, a fortified way-station, on the same night that John Spotswood and Wingina, in their flight to the frontier for similar reasons, arrive there. Harry Lee arrives shortly thereafter, and during the night, someone murders John Spotswood. The tutor is suspected immediately, and Harry Lee, having the highest social status of anyone on the scene, has him arrested. Taken back to Williamsburg in chains, the tutor is tried and convicted, but before he can be sentenced and executed Wingina arrives to testify that she saw her brother, Chunoluskee, murder Spotswood. The tutor is freed, but when Governor Spotswood organizes the gentry for the tramontane expedition, Harry Lee charges that his rival is an impostor and ineligible to take part in the expedition. Once again, it appears that he has a powerful case: He promises to provide the real Henry Hall, recently arrived from Scotland.

When Harry makes his charges, however, the community is stunned to learn that the young tutor is actually Frank Lee, who took the name of his kinsman, Henry Hall, to ensure his escape from Scotland and charges of treason. The queen, however, has died, and the new king has pardoned him, restoring him to his rightful place as the Lee heir and a reputable and estimable man in the community. Harry Lee is discredited, not to mention deeply in financial debt to his brother, whose estate he has been spending for some time. At this point in the novel, the last barrier to the marriage of Ellen and Frank is removed. Kit Carter, rival of Bernard Moore for Kate's hand in marriage, has also discredited himself by his support of Harry Lee. The story could end at this point with a double marriage, and in doing so, it would follow the pattern that Caruthers had established in *The Kentuckian in New-York*. On the other hand, it would then be little more

148   *Will the Circle be Unbroken?*

than a costumed courtship story, and its link to the events of the period in which it was written would be tenuous. Such a work might have made for diverting reading, but it would not have made a comment on the western expansion, a subject about which Caruthers had powerful feelings.

At a time when the question of the annexation of Texas had brought the issue of western expansion to increasing attention, Caruthers appears to have had a point to make by connecting the familial relations developed in the part of the novel described so far to the western expansion and Manifest Destiny. Governor Spotswood, accompanied by Frank Lee, Bernard Moore, Kit Carter, Nathaniel Dandridge and a host of gentlemen, follows a scout named Joe Jarvis to the crest of the Blue Ridge Mountains. On the way, they must learn that the west is a different land, not simply an extension of the east; that is, they must shoe their horses, which have not required shoes in the soft soil of Tidewater Virginia. They must also pursue Native American raiders who have kidnapped Wingina from Dr. Evylin's home and taken Eugenia Elliot, the governor's niece, prisoner at Germana. Those raiders, some of whom seemed tractable and cooperative back in Williamsburg, prove hostile and resourceful when the white men encounter them on their own ground, and Spotswood and his company must fight their way through a mountain pass to see the Valley of Virginia. They are able to accomplish all of this because Spotswood proves himself the model of the ruler-father of the familial paradigm. Moreover, Caruthers uses other dimensions of the familial paradigm as well: After the successful expedition, Spotswood declares the members of the expedition to be members of a fraternal order, the Knights of the Golden Horseshoe. In addition, the letters that pass between Frank and his betrothed Ellen, suggest the nature of the ideal union between man and woman and also suggest the flaws of honor as determinant of human behavior. Finally, those letters outline something of the relationship between generations. Thus, *Knights of the Golden Horse-Shoe* marks the end of the Jacksonian era in Virginian literature by weaving together the threads of the familial paradigm.

Knights of the Horse-Shoe attracted little attention when it was first published. Curtis Davis says that "only five press notices of *The Knights of the Golden Horse-Shoe* have been uncovered, and of those, only one, that in the Charleston *Southern Quarterly Review,* can qualify as a critique" (Introduction x); consequently, reconstructing how Caruthers's original audience read the work is virtually impossible. Similarly, the lack of surviving comments by the author rules out the possibility of establishing how he hoped that his work would be understood. It fell to Curtis Davis to attempt the first detailed discussion of the novel in his biography of Caruthers (*Chronicler* 197).[3]

Davis pointed out that the tramontane expedition "constituted a skein of events almost ready-cut for custom tailoring by some writer of fiction," and Caruthers, writing the first full-length book ever written about the

To the West: Knights of the Horse-shoe   149

expedition glamorized the governor and his men (*Chronicler* 205). For Davis, the expedition is the force that unifies the subplots revolving around Frank Lee's identity and John Spotswood's indiscretions with Wingina. As he sees it, the courtship plots "make for suspense in their own right"—even though the ordering of events in the plot suggests that Caruthers saw connections between the expedition and the romantic lives of his characters. Harry Lee, the thoroughly dastardly villain, helps to make the work "an archetype of the swords-and-cloaks romance" (206–207), but Davis struggles with the idea of *The Knights of the Golden Horse-Shoe* as romance. While he appeared to take issue with the commentators who disparaged the historical inaccuracies of the work, he was still careful in his own reading to point out the major differences between Caruthers's representation and what the author had found in the sources he is known to have consulted.[4]

According to Davis, Caruthers' departures from the historical record were improvements on the original circumstances because they helped to make *Knights* more popular than Caruthers' earlier works—and popular enough to be reprinted five times between 1845 and 1928. There is, of course, no way to be sure that the changes had any effect at all on the popularity or republication of Caruthers' work. Moreover, although no sales figures for Yancey's original book publication have been discovered, it seems implausible that the work could have had greater popularity than Caruthers' other novels. Davis explains some of these "improvements" by pointing out their presence in the sources on which Caruthers relied, but others remain unexplained, even though Davis says that "Many of [the errors] were dictated by sound fictional strategy" (*Chronicler* 216). To understand that strategy, it is necessary first to consider how the westward expansion was progressing when Caruthers wrote the novel.

The composition and publication of *The Knights of the Golden Horse-Shoe* coincide roughly with two events that drew American attention away from the political and economic issues of the East and into the West. In 1836, expatriate Americans in the Mexican state of Texas declared their independence from Mexico and prosecuted a successful war for independence that culminated when Virginia-born Sam Houston defeated Mexican forces under Antonio Lopez de Santa Anna at the battle of San Jacinto. Caruthers' awareness of this event is quite clear; he refers specifically to San Jacinto in his comment on a series of toasts by members of the governor's party just at the edge of the mountains (Caruthers 212–213). In 1845, the year in which *The Knights of the Golden Horse-Shoe* was first published as a book, the Republic of Texas became part of the United States by annexation, and roughly a year later, American armies commanded by Virginians Zachary Taylor and Winfield Scott would invade Mexico to fix the southern boundary of the United States at the Rio Grande River.

150   *Will the Circle be Unbroken?*

The now-well-known phrase "Manifest Destiny" does not appear to have come into use before 1845, when John L. O'Sullivan used it to describe the responsibility of the United States, as "the nation of progress," to spread freedom of conscience, freedom of person, and freedom of trade and business pursuits, as well as equality, throughout the world by first spreading it across the North American continent (Schlesinger 427). Caruthers appears to have believed passionately in this idea; William R. Taylor speculates that for the impecunious author, the West offered an escape from the failures that he suffered in the East (196–197). For many Americans, "*Manifest Destiny* signified a glowing faith in democracy and a passionate desire that it rule the world" (Schlesinger 1953 427; italics in original). Still, the political parties divided on the subject of Texas annexation, the dominating question of Western expansion in the period during which Caruthers was writing.[5] Many Democrats believed in expansion by any means; others, including Van Buren, believed in expansion but opposed annexation of Texas (428). The division did not follow the fault-lines established by some of the previous debates of the Jacksonians: Jackson, living out his last years at the Hermitage, favored annexation; Van Buren, his ally and hand-picked successor, opposed it (Feller 203). Similar division occurred among the Whigs: Northern Whigs opposed annexation, but John Tyler, a Virginian Whig, approved it after succeeding William Henry Harrison in the White House (Van Buren's successor) (Feller 203; Schlesinger 428). As Daniel Feller has pointed out, Whigs "wanted to integrate the republic, not distend it. Their hopes for a more moral, harmonious, and refined society called for connecting Americans instead of dispersing them" (203). For Caruthers, however, the process of expansion could be unifying and refining for the entire nation. This becomes clear when we consider the familial relations—courtship, paternal-filial, and fraternal—that relate to the tramontane expedition in *The Knights of the Horse-Shoe*.

Governor Alexander Spotswood is a convenient figure with whom to begin because he can be compared readily with other ruler-fathers previously discussed in this study. Davis has observed that Spotswood is the opposite of Sir William Berkley, Caruthers's Virginia governor in *The Cavaliers of Virginia* (Davis, *Chronicler* 229). Berkley never appears in any interaction with anyone outside of the genteel class, but Spotswood talks amiably with Joe Jarvis, the lower-class scout, on a number of occasions. These two men from opposite ends of colonial society can even joke about the appropriateness of Jarvis's horse or the clothing worn by the young gentry for the rigors of the expedition (Caruthers 176). Their camaraderie is strengthened when Jarvis teaches the governor how to shoe horses (Caruthers 212). Given this easy interaction, readers can accept Caruthers' assertions that Spotswood is popular with the middle and lower classes, perhaps more popular with them than with the gentry (See, for example,

To the West: Knights of the Horse-shoe   151

42, 120). Nevertheless, Spotswood maintains his sense of class; Jarvis receives a plantation for his services, but he does not receive the golden horseshoe badge that identifies the genteel members of the Tramontane Order.

Unlike Berkley and Tucker's representation of Van Buren in *The Partisan Leader,* Spotswood is a democratic politician. When the Burgesses' approval of the expedition is in doubt, the governor takes his case to the people (Caruthers 120). He may, behind the closed doors of Temple Farm, discuss political strategy with trusted advisors, just as Van Buren meets secretly with political allies in the White House in *The Partisan Leader,* but Spotswood's meetings develop strategies to mobilize the polity to act on their existing views; Van Buren's meetings, on the other hand, focus on the means of manipulating the polity. This approach to politics is not entirely natural to Spotswood; after all, he needs advice from Frank Lee, Commissary Blair, and Doctor Evylin to guide him (see, for example, 7, 27). Still, he is able to take his case to the people fairly effectively; he is ineffective in the political strategy of cultivating favor with royal ministers and courtiers in London (Caruthers 26; Davis says that "in his aggressiveness to get things done [Spotswood] is himself too apt to sweep aside the opinions of others," (*Chronicler* 229–230) but he presents no evidence on this point). Can this suggest that Spotswood, in his attentiveness to his subordinates, has democratic leanings and might even be analogous to Jackson? I think not. Like Caruthers' Bacon, Tucker's George Balcombe and Bernard Trevor, and Kennedy's Charles Calvert, Spotswood is a model ruler-father, attending to his duties with a tender regard for the interests of his subordinates and children, his place and the places of those around him, and he can manage association with subordinates without adopting equality. Indeed, he must do so in order to know their needs and concerns.

Curtis Carroll Davis has pointed out that Spotswood, in the novel, is a father. By no means does the plot of the work dictate that Caruthers give his governor a family with four children eight years earlier than his historical counterpart was married. But the presence of Spotswood's family, and particularly his children, allows the author to show parallels between the characteristics of the ruler and those of the father. In other words, the presence of Spotswood's family allows Caruthers to demonstrate the paternal dimension of the familial paradigm. Davis says that Spotswood's "family interests are tender and deep: for the benefit of his offspring, 'he became a child among children, in order that they might become men'" (Davis *Chronicler* 229). Early in the work, Caruthers shows a governor who encourages his children to join in conversation at the table with him and with his guests and, in most cases, he enjoys these conversations (Davis *Chronicler* 10). The result of this affectionate, as opposed to authoritative, upbringing is that Kate and Dorothea, the teenage daughters, have become well-educated, independent young women with interests and opinions of

152   *Will the Circle be Unbroken?*

their own. Kate figures more prominently than Spotswood's other children
in the plot. She plays an especially important part in Caruthers' representation of sibling relations, and we will examine her in detail in that context.

Examination of Dorothea's character, on the other hand, contributes to
our understanding of paternal authority in Caruthers' representation of the
familial paradigm. Like her sister, Dorothea, as the governor's daughter,
occupies a position "a little different from that of other young ladies, even
among the gentry . . . [being] more bound than any other young lady, to
present a model even more blameless than common, inasmuch as her example is looked up to and followed by those, who are beneath her in rank and
position" (Caruthers 216). It seems safe to assume that the consciousness
of this position, which Kate expresses in a letter to Bernard, extends to
Dorothea and that the governor and Lady Spotswood, with an even more
mature awareness of their daughters' position, have encouraged the daughters to be self-conscious and satisfactory models.

Dorothea, at fifteen, is Spotswood's pet, apparently because her demon-
strative temperament and ready wit help him to set aside the cares of his
office. In the privacy of Temple Farm, when her father enters a room and
others bow, she runs to him and throws herself into his arms (Caruthers 5).
When the household members attend church together, she obviously pays
attention to the sermon; had she not done so, she would hardly have been
able to regale those in the coach with her on the ride home with a witty
commentary on how the sermon on humility might apply to the pompous
Harry Lee (46). Granted, her mother and Commissary Blair have to silence
her before others catch them laughing, and she is sufficiently astute as a
politician's daughter to know that she must not repeat her performance for
Bernard Moore when Harry Lee is near: "'Don't you know,' she whispered,
'that Mr. Lee has a vote in the house of Burgesses.' Papa says I must learn
to be a politician, or I shall frighten away all his political *friends*" (46).[6] It
is also Dorothea who mobilizes the women to oppose Harry Lee's snubbing
of the tutor (90). In other words, Dorothea has "a habit of saying sometimes very pungent things in her demure way," and her parents and friends
not only tolerate but seem to encourage her to question and poke fun at
anything that seems pretentious (4). Although she is the younger daughter
and perhaps occupies a low position (if a privileged one) in the family
hierarchy, she is confident that she will not be corrected or punished for
expressing her views. As the newly arrived tutor does in discussing the
expedition (27), as Doctor Evylin and Commissary Blair do in discussing
the disposition of General Elliot's body (7), Dorothea speaks freely—and,
in the return from church passage discussed here, Caruthers even connects
her with political concerns. It is with Dorothea that we may most clearly
see the governor as an affectionate father who "became a child among children": "it was no uncommon thing to see them sitting quite apart from the

To the West: Knights of the Horse-shoe 153

company, she chatting away most volubly, and he bursting every now and then into a laugh" (4).

For all of Spotswood's fatherly attention to his children, he has not been successful in raising all of them to be such exemplary young adults. His son John might be offered as evidence that the affectionate childrearing of the Spotswood household does not always succeed. While Kate, Dorothea, and Robert all seem devoted to each other and their parents, John is seldom present at the family fireside; on the contrary, at breakfast, "he scarcely [notices] his sisters, whose still clinging affection he [seems] to loathe. His mother he [avoids] on all possible occasions, and for those general family meetings in the country he [has] an especial abhorrence" (10). But John, through his dissipation, has rejected the family almost as clearly as Cocklescraft rejects the community in *Rob of the Bowl*. The primary difference is that John was born a member of the family and has rejected it for reasons that Caruthers leaves unspecified. Cocklescraft has not been a member of the community, and whether he genuinely wished to be is not clear. John never appears in conversation with any blood relative; on the contrary, readers learn that Kate attends him in his alcohol-induced illness and talks to him, but Caruthers never makes readers privy to these conversations. John appears in conversation only with Bernard Moore and Wingina, and his conversations with the former seem designed by the strongly pro-temperance Caruthers to convince readers that John Spotswood is an alcoholic suffering from hallucinations. His conversations with Wingina demonstrate his inability to make and act on decisions. John Spotswood is hardly a fully developed character; Caruthers developed him to provide a contrast with such characters as Frank Lee and Bernard Moore (who have stronger relations with the governor than John ever displays) and to be killed so that the tutor can be accused of a murder that Harry Lee or Chunoluskee might have committed. What is more important for our purposes here, however, is that Caruthers also presented John as having isolated himself from his family, and this wayward son cannot enter the promised land of the west.

Whatever his failings, John retains the loyalty of his family; they do not reject him. When he suffers alcohol-induced hallucinations at Williamsburg, Bernard sends to Temple Farm for Dr. Evylin, but the young man is uncertain of whether he can appropriately interrupt the governor's work toward the tramontane expedition for this family emergency. Consequently, he leaves it to the doctor to tell the rest of the family, and Governor Spotswood and Kate choose to accompany the doctor back to town to assist in John's care. When John seems to have recovered, they take him back to the farm to complete his convalescence and to allow the family to see him before they return to Williamsburg (98). His violent death plunges the family into profound mourning, and Wingina's appearance and explanation of John's murder, while upsetting to the family, do not diminish their loyalty (151, 158). Susan J. Tracy has written one of the most recent studies to include examination of *Knights of the Golden Horse-Shoe* (and the only one that I have found in which the relationship between John and Wingina is treated at all); she points out that Caruthers presents the social arguments that southerners might have used to justify John's refusal to marry the woman he has ruined. As Tracy puts it, "Wingina is an outlaw on two accounts. First, as a woman, she thwarted male-dominated society (her brother, in this case) by having an independent sexual life; worse, she has chosen a person of another race" (98). At this point, too, Spotswood considers Chunoluskee, Wingina's brother, to be a loyal interpreter, so that he might take Wingina's "crime" against her brother as a crime against himself. Moreover, Wingina's independent sexual life, if it is as independent and abhorrent to Southerners as Tracy claims, has led to the death of the governor's son. Surely this would justify the Spotswood family in shunning her, but their response is the opposite. Kate, with her father's approval and input, writes to Ellen, explaining that Wingina's association with John and his murder makes contact with her painful for the governor's family, but she hopes that Ellen will give the Indian woman comfort and assistance (Caruthers 158–159). And the governor later agrees that he will give a handsome settlement to Joe Jarvis if he marries Wingina so that the child that John fathered will be provided for (185). Caruthers, in summary, shows no reason for the Spotswoods to extend any assistance to Wingina; on the contrary, they have ample cause to have nothing to do with her or her child. Still, because of their loyalty to John, they are unwilling to leave the mother of his child to her own devices. Differences within this idealized family, unlike those in the Trevor family in *The Partisan Leader*, need not bring about rejection.

The governor, as father, allows John to follow his dissolute course, apparently never attempting to interfere with his son's route to ruin. But he and his family never reject John. Similarly, the governor as ruler allows mercy to temper his judgment during the tramontane expedition. When Caesar, a slave belonging to Harry Lee, is captured while helping a party of Native Americans to harass the expedition, Frank argues that the black man ought to be hanged at once, but the governor rejects the idea (Caruthers 200). The governor explains that the hanging would jeopardize the success of the mission—although he does not specify and it is difficult to imagine how it could present a significant risk. He also says that he wishes to investigate the matter upon his return to Williamsburg—although the case seems clear-cut: Caesar has been caught in the company of the Native American raiders, and he has paddled a boat to assist them (199–200). After hearing the governor's plans for the disposition of the prisoner, Frank writes to his brother and offers him an opportunity: Frank cannot forgive Harry for his actions against the tutor, but he can forgive the debt that his brother has built up. If Harry leaves Virginia forever and takes

To the West: Knights of the Horse-shoe
155

Caesar with him, Frank will forgive the debt. Frank does not think that the governor will be much displeased to find both Harry and Caesar absent upon his return (203). At no point does Caruthers make explicit that Spotswood intended for Caesar to escape punishment; however, the governor's character makes such conjecture on the part of readers eminently possible. Moreover, this disposition of the matter is entirely in keeping with the dispassionate discipline associated with the familial paradigm.

Governor Spotswood, then, is an exemplary ruler-father. Davis holds that the character "was a man almost too *good* to be true" (*Chronicler* 229)—an assessment that we have seen applied to George Balcombe—but this seems to overstate the governor's character. In his public life, he resembles Caruthers's Nathaniel Bacon and Kennedy's Lord Baltimore, both of whom also interact easily with subordinates and thereby gain their support. He also possesses George Balcombe's discernment and ability to mobilize public spirit. In his family, he enjoys affection similar to what Balcombe receives. He might be regarded as a less parochial Frank Meriwether—a pleasant man at the center of a community centered on his family, earnestly trying to do what he can to advance the interests of all of the members of that community, even when the members, such as his wayward son, cannot recognize this. Under his leadership, the members of the younger generation—or the young nation—form a strong (if not all-inclusive) network of sibling cooperation.

Knights of the Golden Horse-Shoe includes two pairs of siblings who play prominent roles in the plot: the Lee brothers and the Spotswood sisters. We have seen that the Lee brothers are opposites in personality, and the same may be said of the Spotswood sisters. Dorothea's personality is almost the opposite of her older sister, Kate, and Caruthers is careful at almost every opportunity to show that the Lee and Spotswood siblings are very different people. Kate is tall and graceful; Dorothea is short and bouncy (Caruthers 4). Dorothea manages the dairy at Temple Farm; Kate tends to the sick, and because she is slightly older, she extends this work to the broader community (8–10). While it appears that Harry and Frank Lee were close in their childhood, Harry's jealousy has broken their relationship; Harry has for some time been more silent, more cautious, and more given to pomp and vanity than his older brother. During their student days, Harry picked fights, but Frank usually did the fighting (Caruthers 32). Despite differences in sex, these two pairs of siblings represent what Caruthers must have regarded as unsatisfactory and satisfactory sibling relations. The satisfactory relationship of the Spotswood sisters endures while the unsatisfactory relationship of the Lee brothers ends with Frank, calling on his authority as the head of the family, effectively banishing Harry to Europe. The sisters accept differences in status; Harry is not willing to recognize that Frank is more accepted than he because of personality differences. Because they are brothers, Harry believes they should be equal in all respects—a position that Southerners, concerned about the North's grow-

156   *Will the Circle be Unbroken?*

ing population and wealth, were increasingly willing to adopt with respect to their sibling states.

What makes the relationships different is the roles that the siblings take with respect to each other. As we have already noted briefly, the Lee brothers have grown up in the household of Dr. Evylin and at first, Ellen could see little difference between them (Caruthers 31). By the time the two reach adolescence, however, it is clear that Harry is jealous. He has inherited from his mother an estate sufficient to secure his independence, but he is angry that Frank has inherited their father's estate, which is larger. He also resents Frank's position as head of the family and relationship with Ellen (32–33). This jealousy, of course, is undesirable, particularly because it focuses on matters over which Frank has no control: His father wrote the will that made Frank a wealthy young man, and his position and status within the family derive from birth order and, perhaps, his impressive maturity (32). Harry envies Frank, in other words, for being what he cannot: a young man of wealth whose natural social graces earn him the affection of his elders (the governor and Dr. Evylin), women of all ages (Lady Spotswood, her daughters, and, of course, Ellen Evylin), men of his own age and social position (Bernard Moore), and social inferiors (Joe Jarvis, the scout for the expedition). At first, this seems a far cry from the other estranged brothers whom we have seen in this study, Douglas and Owen Trevor. The Trevors part company over political allegiance, not over an estate or a woman, and Owen, the Unionist, places loyalty to the President above loyalty to family or loyalty to principles. In doing so, he also takes a step that he expects will contribute to the success of his military career (although his death in combat eventually precludes this). All things considered, Owen's dedicated but unprincipled pursuit of his own objectives, which carries him to military ranks for which he is not truly qualified, differs little from Harry's unprincipled pursuit of what is rightfully Frank's. While Harry Lee does not die, as Owen does, he is disgraced.

This envy, however unseemly or indecorous, might be written off as a quirk if matters went no further, but Harry Lee's jealousy becomes the driving force of his personality as Caruthers reveals it. The problem is not that Harry tries to have his brother tried and punished for indebtedness, fraud, and murder; he does all of this, after all, believing that the man he is harassing is truly an impostor.[7] This may indicate that Frank's experiences in England have altered his appearance, or it may indicate that Harry is so self-absorbed that he cannot identify his own brother. Far worse, Harry lies in order to win what he cannot legitimately earn: Ellen Evylin's love. While Frank is in Edinburgh, Harry writes to explain that: "He [expects] to marry [Ellen] before [Frank's] return, . . . he [has] already obtained her father's consent, and only [waits] to break down the obstacles which young maidens love to gather round themselves; that they [are] already giving way, and [will] soon totally disappear before the warmth of his suit" (75).

To the West: Knights of the Horse-shoe   157

It is true that Harry has spoken with Dr. Evylin about marriage to Ellen, but the doctor has left the question to his daughter; she, however, has not given him an answer and is actually "endeavoring to teach [herself] to look upon him in the light of a brother"—an undertaking that ultimately proves unsuccessful and leads her to adopt an icy reserve when Harry is present (75). Harry, despite his protestations concerning the tutor's pedigree, proves no gentleman in matters of integrity. It is not clear, in the end, that he has actually sent the slave, Caesar, to assist in the harassment of the expedition and perhaps the murder of his brother, but it seems unlikely that Caesar, a long-time household servant, would escape and undertake such an errand on his own. Harry, in other words, follows the pattern of Owen Trevor in putting his own material advancement ahead of family loyalties and integrity.

This contrasts strongly with the Spotswood sisters, Kate and Dorothea. That the two young women have different interests cannot be denied: Kate cares for the sick, and Dorothea manages the dairy at Temple Farm. In both of these roles, they are accepting the role of genteel young women in the antebellum South: They are learning to perform some of the duties that will be theirs when they are married. More important, they are accepting their places within the household and within society. Each, in her own way, con-tributes to the well-being of all, and each takes some pride in her abilities. Consequently, there is no jealousy between them; on the contrary, there is cooperation. Unlike the other sisters we have seen in this study, Lucy and Victorine Meriwether and Bel and Catharine Tracy, Kate and Dorothea have work to do; their work gives them a sense of worth and a place in the household and society, and they accept their positions without any appar-ent jealousy or ill will. They are not simply decorative, and their presence in the novel serves to emphasize that the westward expansion will draw together all Americans. They take into their sisterhood Ellen Evylin, as well, and she, too, seems to feel no particular jealousy.

On the contrary, the women of this sisterly triad assist each other when necessary: When Harry Lee denounces the tutor to Ellen and Lady Spots-wood, Dorothea refuses to cut the tutor out of the conversation at supper and then tells Ellen that she should have slapped Harry and treated the tutor kindly (Caruthers 91). To do this, Dorothea must ignore her mother's example, an act that requires some confidence in her own perceptions as well as in her parents' willingness to accept disagreement from their chil-dren. She must also have some confidence in her ability to persuade her friend. Similarly, Kate has long discussions with Ellen in which she attempts to restore the doctor's daughter to a cheerful and optimistic demeanor by reminding her of her native character. In these conversations, the two young women also discuss Kate's character, thereby suggesting that siblings play a part in defining each other's identities. By the time Caruthers was writing *Knights of the Golden Horse-Shoe*, it appeared to many that the Northern states were seeking to redefine their Southern sisters on the issue of slavery, which was increasingly coming to differentiate the sections. In response to the moral suasion of Lewis Tappan and other evangelical abolitionists, Southerners had sought to set up barriers against what they regarded as meddling. Ellen accepts the "assistance" of the Spotswoods in part because they make clear that they wish to help her and not necessarily themselves. Another factor in her acceptance may be that these sisterly relationships carry considerable reciprocity. When Ellen arrives at Temple Farm, Kate takes the semi-invalid young woman under her medical care; in Williamsburg, when she needs someone to assist Wingina, she does not hesitate to call upon Ellen, who accepts the task without question or complaint.

Ellen's sisterhood with the Spotswood daughters suggests yet again the notion that familial relations need not be based on blood ties but can be based on some demonstration of affection in the sense that Yazawa uses the term. Similarly, the Tramontane Order is a brotherhood based upon the shared experience of traveling west to the crest of the mountains. But it is not like the Brothers of the Coast in *Rob of the Bowl*. On the contrary, the Tramontane Order exists at the direction of the Governor, who, presumably, has the authority to establish such an order and select its members (Caruthers, 245n, raises the issue of the governor's authority to form the order; Davis's Introduction, xxi, discusses the matter briefly.) Moreover, the constructed fraternity of *The Knights of the Golden Horse-Shoe* is based upon experience—not declaration.

The process of formation, however, is more consequential than the governor's authority to form the group. Initially, the governor calls upon the young gentry to express support for the tramontane expedition (and obtain generous land grants) by recruiting and equipping fifty men each and leading them to Williamsburg. The young men respond, and it becomes necessary to establish organization—to establish, that is, the type of formal organization that the Brothers of the Coast rejected and could not successfully oppose in the end (Caruthers 113, 162). In responding to the governor's call, moreover, they demonstrate that they have stature within their communities: When they lead, their neighbors will follow. This fraternity does not present an alternative to the structure of the community as a whole. Rather, it reflects and reinforces that structure.

The Brothers of the Coast seem to have simply come into being, with little attention to who might be a member. While the Tramontane Order is formed at the governor's calling, there is still debate over who may be a member: Simply wanting to risk one's life on an arduous trip to the crest of the mountains is not sufficient. The governor opposes the proposal from Harry Lee and Kit Carter that members be "of gentle blood," preferring that gentlemen of good reputation and the officers of the Rangers will be brought into the expedition so that the basis for a military chain of command can exist (Caruthers 162). The distinction is not, in itself, important, but Caruthers uses this scene to restate the Whiggish principle concerning

To the West: Knights of the Horse-shoe 159

class distinctions revealed in *Horse-Shoe Robinson:* All are welcome, but inequality is the natural order. The Carter-Lee faction opposing the governor argues that the governor's position will allow even the noncommissioned officers of the Rangers to demand a place in the order (162). As Bernard Moore points out, however, the governor's plan emphasizes merit rather than pedigree (163); to the idealized ruler-father, then, recent and current actions are more important than the bloodlines of previous generations in defining the relationships among subordinates.

In the end, Caruthers escapes the potentially egalitarian implications of the governor's position by having Harry Lee explain that his objective is keeping the tutor out of the order and having the tutor explain that he has no objection to Lee's proposal; after all, he is, beneath the wig that disguises him, a Lee and entitled to membership on the basis of blood *and* reputation (Caruthers 164). Even with this sticking point resolved, a complex process of voting is required to nominate members, and even this only admits one to candidacy (164). Ultimately, no one receives the badge of membership without completing the expedition and returning to Williamsburg. All of this seems a striking contrast to the Brotherhood of the Coast: The membership requirements are never stated, but the artificial brotherhood in *Rob of the Bowl* seems to accept all comers, and many of the comers seem to have been rejected everywhere else. The members refer to their brotherhood, but their actions suggest that they have no particular loyalty to each other.

For all that the Tramontane Order is discussed by name throughout the work, it comes into existence only some time after the expedition has returned to Williamsburg, when the members gather in the Burgesses' chamber to receive the golden horseshoe that indicates their membership. At this point, as the governor points out, they have a symbol of their order that they can pass with pride to their descendants (Caruthers 245). Moreover, while the horseshoes symbolize a shared experience, they also bind the members to future service if it should be asked of them (245). Thus, the order derives its purpose from a visionary governor, takes measures to ensure organization that will support its primary undertaking, admits men on the basis of character (of which pedigree is necessarily a part), and then celebrates success by pledging to be available for future service. There are no such characteristics of the Brotherhood of the Coast. It exists to serve only the immediate purposes of the members, most of whom seem to have little interest in pursuing any long-term activity. In *Rob of the Bowl,* the allegiance of the members of the brotherhood shifts quickly. When Cocklescraft orders two of his men to execute Albert, the sailors hardly hesitate to accept instead Rob's plan to row the secretary into stormy waters and drown him—even though Rob, unlike Cocklescraft, is not one of their Brothers of the Coast. The drunkenness of the sailors is no explanation for this lapse in discipline, either; Governor Spotswood's men drink regularly (despite their author's emphatic support of temperance (Davis Chronicler 276)), and tempers sometimes flare, as they do between Bernard

160   *Will the Circle be Unbroken?*

Moore and his rival for Kate's hand, Kit Carter (Caruthers 206–207). These episodes, unlike the drunken revels at Wizard's Chapel in *Rob of the Bowl,* do not distract the tramontane brotherhood from its primary objective.

While it was possible to characterize the relations among the states or sections as sibling relations and indissoluble, however, it was equally possible to characterize them as marital relations and voluntary, as Caruthers had done in *The Kentuckian in New-York.* For Caruthers, the difference between filial love and marital love may have been slight (at least in terms of abiding power): While Kate is returning to Williamsburg after seeing Bernard off at the beginning of the expedition, Frank sees her crying and teases her that he will tell her beloved about her tears in camp. Kate's response—"'Filial tears, filial tears, Mr. Lee'" (Caruthers 180)—suggests that these two types of affections have similar emotional strength and may at times appear in such similar ways as to be indistinguishable. In *The Knights of the Horse-Shoe,* the courtship plot is finally resolved with a triple wedding of Frank Lee to Ellen Evylin, Bernard Moore to Kate Spotswood, and Henry Hall to Eugenia Elliot. The first two couples by far eclipse the third in importance in the plot, and they provide far more insight into how relationships, according to Caruthers, should be conducted.

Unlike *The Kentuckian in New-York, The Knights of the Golden Horse-Shoe* does not include the first meetings of the couples whose marriages end the work. Caruthers, as a result, does not seem to be interested in the origins of relationships but in their successful continuation, particularly during difficult times. Given Ellen Evylin's physical illness at the beginning of the novel, when she believes that her beloved Frank has been killed (Caruthers 23),[8] it appears that this question is particularly important: the disruption of such a relationship, even if it had not yet been celebrated or consummated, was devastating, so relationships needed to be carefully preserved. When Ellen sees the tutor, who is actually Frank posing as Henry Hall, her reaction is powerful: she almost faints when she recognizes a similarity between his voice and Frank's, and Kate believes that she should be taken to another room (25). Clearly, this relationship is critical: Without it, Frank wishes to die and Ellen does not wish to live. In other words, the partners have discovered their interdependency, just as did the couples in Caruther's earlier works.

The nature and extent of their dependency become clear as the novel progresses: Frank and Ellen, the idealized couple of the novel, are two halves of a whole. While Ellen is physically frail, Frank is sturdy (if not robust). Frank is a philosophical young man, given to contemplation of the human condition, and Ellen has come to the same sort of musings. It is important to note that she sees this as a masculine pastime and fears that such conversations somehow diminish her femininity. Frank, still disguised as a tutor, tells her that "'whatever relates to our higher sentiments and our spiritual natures, certainly belongs in common to the sexes, and if man has usurped the whole claim to discuss them, he assuredly has no right to do

To the West: Knights of the Horse-shoe   161

so'" (Caruthers 94–95). This might not be particularly revealing in terms of political tensions; after all, it seems a simple expression of an argument against a difference between the sexes—except for a later, similar occurrence. Toward the end of the expedition, couriers bring Spotswood and his men letters from their loved ones. Frank receives a letter from Ellen because the two are honoring their commitment to exchange letters by each opportunity. They are, that is, maintaining an agreement to serve as each other's eyes and ears during a separation. Ellen, although prohibited from going on the expedition, can still experience it, in a sense, through Frank's eyes.

What she writes to him is not so much an account of what is going on in Williamsburg, although she does tell him of some events, but one side of a conversation. She points out in the course of this epistle that she is concerned about the conception of the gentleman held by some men: "The conscience of a gentleman of honor substitutes what others think of us for that unerring monitor within our own bosoms. Indeed, the conventional conscience often silences the still, small voice of the inward man, and this, too, often in supposed deference to the opinions of [women]" (216).

In short, Ellen hopes that Frank will be guided by conscience, the internal arbiter of right and wrong, rather than honor, an external system in which the opinion of others mediated between individual and community (Wyatt-Brown 14). Charity, she points out, is the moral guide of a Christian gentleman—a higher standard than honor provides (Caruthers 216). The immediate impetus for these musings is the possibility that Kit Carter, rejected by Kate, will challenge Bernard Moore to a duel and Bernard will accept. Ellen also rejoices that she and Frank share an unrestricted confidence that allows her to express forthrightly her view of morality, and she is confident that Frank will be guided by her wishes—not because she is the moral center of the relationship, but because he values the intimacy of the relationship (217).

In proposing intimate equality as a characteristic of ideal relationships, Caruthers was tapping at a barrier that had, by this time, begun to hinder the South in dealing with northern abolitionist attacks on slavery. So far, at the time of *The Knights of the Golden Horse-Shoe,* the abolitionists believed that moral suasion could lead the southern slaveholders to free their slaves, but the southerners saw their efforts as affronts to Southern honor and collective self-esteem (Wyatt-Brown 29). During 1835 and 1836, the years when Caruthers began writing *The Knights of the Golden Horse-Shoe,* the American Anti-Slavery Society had begun shipping antislavery literature into the South, and southerners had responded by seizing the offensive pamphlets and publicly burning them. Similarly, Southerners had stifled discussion of slavery in Congress by forcing adoption of a gag rule. This rule did not stop the petitions that the American Anti-Slavery Society was sending to Congress (Sydnor 233, 234), but it limited productive discussion of this issue, which was becoming increasingly important as slaveholders began to move toward new territory.

162   *Will the Circle be Unbroken?*

In this context, Ellen's praise of unreserved communication and trust between partners who are in some respects the opposites of each other takes on additional weight; it clearly carries political echoes, particularly when we consider that Bernard and Kit never duel. There is therefore no need in terms of the plot for Caruthers to raise the matter of communication between partners. But raise it he does, and he also makes the point that this trust does not come about in an instant when a couple are married, but actually must predate the marriage (Caruthers 216). This assertion in Ellen's letter arguably speaks to the opposing theories on the nature of the Union. If the trust and communication that make a marriage successful emerge gradually without reference to the ceremony, then it matters little whether the Union was created by the states or the people: A unity of purpose led to its formation and unity of purpose, rather than a specific action, such as ratification of the Constitution, would serve as the bond that held the Union together.

That bond, however, was imperfect. It could not bind the members of the Spotswood family, and John was lost. Those who did not accept the values of the family, then, could have no part in the promised land of the west. Others, such as Dorothea and Nathaniel Dandridge, are not yet ready to be bound together and despite indications of adolescent courtship, their story remains unfinished at the end of the novel. Similarly, Caruthers specifically leaves open the ending of Joe Jarvis's story: The scout may have married a Native American woman and had children, or he may not have. Considering the care with which Caruthers had closed the plots of his previous novels, this openness seems to reflect an uncertainty. While the settlement of the west might well strengthen the Union, Caruthers seems to have recognized that this was not a perfect solution. The novel may not be, as William R. Taylor argued, the author's escape from his own failures; neither does it offer an escape from the political tensions of the Jacksonian era.

It is, perhaps, revealing, that at the end of *The Knights of the Golden Horse-Shoe,* readers learned the destinations of the principal characters and that descendants of those characters still lived, but Caruthers supplied little more detail. The novel appeared at the end of the Jacksonian era, at a time that Daniel Feller has characterized in a chapter title as "The Descent into Discord" (183).

CHAPTER TEN
Conclusion

During the month before William Alexander Caruthers agreed to allow Charles Yancey to publish *Knights of the Horse-Shoe*, the Old Hero, Andrew Jackson, died at his Tennessee plantation. He had lived there as an elder statesman and gentleman farmer since leaving office in 1837, but he had remained a national presence so long as his hand-picked successor, Van Buren, remained on the national scene. By 1840, however, the political party systems that Jackson and Van Buren had done much to create could use conventions to nominate and state and county organizations and newspapers to promote and elect. These candidates did not capture the imagination as Jackson had; unlike Old Hickory, they could not, by their mere participation, organize debate.

Without such leaders, it was perhaps inevitable that people would see fewer similarities between the family and the commonwealth. As we have seen, the ruler-father figure in the later novels of this study becomes a problem figure. George Balcombe and Alexander Spotswood are developed in some detail, but both seemed, at least to some readers, too good to be believed. The Proprietary in *Rob of the Bowl* is more sketchily developed, and he is never referred to by name. That is, he must give up personal identity to be the ruler-father. Consequently, he seems almost a functionary intended to advance matters of plot and characterization. But in a nation with urgent problems, real leadership seemed necessary. The powerful and affable figure of Frank Meriwether in *Swallow Barn* is presented as the object of Kennedy's gentle satire; his day has passed, and the future of Swallow Barn lies in the hands of Ned Hazard, who has put aside the colorful finery of his youth for more sedate clothing and his antic behavior for demonstrations of seriousness. He is on the way to becoming an able administrator, but hardly a captivating patriarch. Nathaniel Bacon, having overthrown Governor William Berkley in *Cavaliers of Virginia,* has the personal force of a Balcombe or Spotswood, and he proves capable of organ-

163

164   *Will the Circle be Unbroken?*

izing and advancing the interests of subordinates, even when doing so is contrary to his own interests. Nevertheless, when his narrowly defined mission—defense of the colony against Native American uprisings—is fulfilled, he is eager to step down, and he rejects the authority that has fallen into his hands. In the only novel of this study without a clear ruler-father, *Horse-Shoe Robinson*, Kennedy's aristocratic father, Phillip Lindsay, plays the most important role in advancing the plot, but Allen Musgrave, as we have seen, has closer relations with his subordinates and can better direct their activities toward successful outcomes. Imposing though he is, however, Musgrave has no desire to take charge: He regards human events as directed by God and asks only to be shown his part in those events, and he would be far less likely than Nathaniel Bacon to assume a position of leadership outside of his family. At the end of the work, he does not resolve the tensions of the plot; that falls to the title character and a number of sketchily drawn Whig military leaders.

Yazawa argued that in a republic, "political authority was less personal and less affectionate. The exercise of discretion in civil or judicial matters, especially, smacked too much of a paternalistic monarchy and seemed to close to ruling by arbitrary will to be condoned" (112). In the republic, that is, there was no king except the law, and that law was not to be an evolving and organic body of customs, statutes, and institutions, as was the English constitution, but rather a conscientiously debated constitution—a machine that would run of itself. But the framers of the Constitution had been unable to resolve every issue and every ambiguity, and these Founding Fathers had, in a sense, deferred some of the thorniest issues for another generation to resolve. It is perhaps merely a coincidence that they permitted the international slave trade to continue until 1808, twenty-one years, and just slightly more than the conventional length of a generation, after ratification of the Constitution. And the framers of state constitutions had done little better; indeed, during 1820s and 1830s new state constitutions were rewritten or old constitutions extensively revised. In many instances, these constitutional revisions occurred precisely because of the need to balance power between eastern and western portions of a state. (See Ford 106–107 for discussion of how this occurred in South Carolina; Sydnor 276–293 traces the causes and effects of this movement.)

The solution for the Virginian Whigs whose works we have been examining was an aristocratic class to provide leadership. Of course, men such as Ned Hazard, born to this class, might have to learn new technical skills from the likes of Frank Meriwether, but even Southerners of a more radical stripe than these authors were hardly averse to employing new technological developments. (Ford 17–18 points out the willingness of South Carolinians to construct a canal system, a novelty at the time; Ford also points out that in 1842, the South Carolina legislature had commissioned Edmund Ruffin to conduct agricultural and geological surveys aimed at

Conclusion   165

improving the agricultural base of the state's economy.) But, as we have observed, the characters who represent this class either prove somewhat inept (as do Arthur Butler and Philip Lindsay) or impossible to believe (as do George Balcombe, Alexander Spotswood, and to a lesser extent, the Proprietary).

This ruler-father, like Balcombe and Spotswood, would have to recognize and coordinate the interests of his subordinates, but his efforts in this regard would fail if the subordinates could not recognize that they had reconcilable interests. But what ties bound those subordinates? The authors considered here appear to have struggled unsuccessfully with this question, never quite resolving it.

Because the Constitution was a self-consciously constructed document rather than an organic body of laws, the relations between the states could be represented metaphorically by courtships and the resolution of their differences by marriages. This is clearly what Caruthers intended in *The Kentuckian in New-York*, where North, South, West, and middle states are joined in multiple marriages. Similarly, the resolution of *The Cavaliers of Virginia* includes Bacon's marriage to Virginia Fairfax, and the story of *The Knights of the Golden Horse-Shoe* ends with no fewer than three marriages. These marriages suggest that not all relationships among the states could be equally close, but the novels do not make this clear, and such a reading could suggest that some ties among states, like marriage in some states, was impermanent. Moreover, the evolving notion of affectionate marriage emphasized the importance of romantic love, and this mystical force left open the question of what might happen if the irresistible force became resistible—if, for example, one lover took actions contrary to the interests of the other. If marriage was a contract, it could be dissolved; if it was the manifestation of a mystical force, then a rift might indicate that the force had been misinterpreted in the first place. No nationalist such as Caruthers would willingly accept such an idea.

Kennedy also struggled with marriages. Ned Hazard and Bel Tracy vanish from the scene just before their marriage, and their courtship in *Swallow Barn* suggests little more than the need for those in courtship or marriage to tolerate each other's foibles as they mature together. *Horse-Shoe Robinson*, on the other hand, indicates more clearly that maintaining these relationships sometimes demands that partners step outside of their normal roles, as do Mary Musgrave and Mildred Lindsay. Here, however, Kennedy's insistence upon realism dictates that Mary lose her fiancé with John Ramsay's death. Was it possible that these relationships might be destroyed despite the efforts of both parties? And what of the strange and dysfunctional family of Wat Adair, all of the members of which seemed entirely disconnected from each other? *Rob of the Bowl* shed little light on the subject, despite the fact that it revolved in large measure around the courtship of Blanche Warden and Albert Verheyden. Blanche, the Rose of

St. Mary's, is a passive flower who is the object of the struggle between Albert and Captain Cocklescraft, and Cocklescraft loses her in part because he lacks the appropriate social situation to marry her. Was there any faction or state that would accept such a passive role?

From the marriages of Tucker's novels we learn little. Granted, Douglas and Delia represent the two factions of the Trevor family, and those factions, at the beginning of the novel, represent opposing political views, but as the novel progresses, Delia plays a less important role. After she and Douglas are married, she disappears until the end of the work, when she appears with her father-in-law, Hugh, now a convert to secession, to plead for the life of her husband before President Van Buren. She hardly seems the daughter of her mother, the educated and politically astute and active wife of Bernard Trevor and friend of Mr. B___. Was the message that partners supported each other only in times of crisis? And why, when many of Douglas's men have brought their wives to the guerrillas' sylvan camp, has their leader left his wife in South Carolina? By the same token, little is gained through the study of marriage in *George Balcombe*. The title character praises his wife at every opportunity, but he praises her for the passivity that she displays throughout the work. She is a woman who stays out of her husband's way, always eager to express support and encouragement for him, but again, she has little role in the outcome of the work and little influence on the plot. The courtship of Napier and Ann also reveals little: The novel turns around the Napiers' effort to protect their union against external threat—Montague's refusal to return the inheritance that is rightfully theirs.

Sibling relations seemed to take into account that the colonies had formed on the same continent and had early on established relations with each other. The sister states, growing up like Lucy and Victorine Meriwether of Swallow Barn, were inseparable and bound by common interests. This view, however, overlooked the complications of the relationship that were growing steadily more evident. Siblings played no part in *The Kentuckian in New-York* and *The Cavaliers of Virginia,* but they reappeared in a different form in *Horse-Shoe Robinson.* Here Kennedy created Mildred Lindsay and her brother Henry, siblings opposite in sex but bound by fraternal ties as well as by their loyalty to the cause of American independence—Whiggery. They take different roles for the cause, each bound by sex and gender, and this relationship suggests that the Union can accommodate (and indeed requires) a range of different capabilities—a view consistent with Caruther's notion that sectionalism was necessary and healthy. But in developing the characters, Kennedy makes Henry almost childish and Mildred almost maternal in her relationship with him. She becomes, in other words, a figure of parental authority and almost a surrogate father and mother for her younger brother—a superior. Among factions or states, this represented a claim of precisely the sort that provoked tension.

Conclusion   167

Something very similar happens in *George Balcombe,* when Napier must point out his sister's failings to her. If she is to be kept from interfering with his efforts to reclaim their inheritance, he must reproach her for her selfishness and insist that she consider others. In doing so, as we have seen, he took the role of father-ruler, the first instance in which he claims his place. Thus she is relegated to a subordinate position and the representation of sibling relations fail once again as a model for relations among groups within the polity. In *The Partisan Leader* and *The Knights of the Golden Horse-Shoe,* tension among brothers comes close to fratricide. Sisters fare better, and Caruthers made a muted plea for female equality through Dr. Evylin's conversation with Harry Lee, but again, the sisters are far behind in Williamsburg at the climactic moment when Spotswood and his men look into the Valley of Virginia.

A curious hybrid, one that may have seemed especially accessible in an era when fraternal associations were undergoing tremendous growth and playing an increasing role in developing individual identity, was the artificial brotherhood such as we have seen in *Rob of the Bowl* and *The Knights of the Golden Horse-Shoe.* In the former, the Brothers of the Coast are a force in the work, but Kennedy wrote little about this brotherhood because he saw it as divisive and thus negative, and it is most clearly developed through comparison with the Tramontane Order in Caruthers' work. The elitist nature of this latter order meant that those of democratic leanings would consider it an unacceptable model for anything in the nineteenth century. Moreover, the Tramontane Order was so formally constituted that it bore little resemblance to the realities of family life in any section.

There were other flaws in the family model as well. The children with whom we have been concerned here have been, for the most part, of marriageable age. That is, they were old enough to choose whether they would remain dependent upon a parent or independent. Younger children were shadows: In *Swallow Barn,* Kennedy did not even name the younger Meriwethers, nor did he have them participate in the action in any significant way. While Dorothea Spotswood is the younger sister and has the childlike functions of providing affection and entertainment, she is also approaching marriageable age. Robert, her younger brother, figures little in the plot. The children may have been "Heaven's best gifts," as they were for the North Carolinians of Jane Censer's study (24–25), but the authors discussed here seem to have had difficulty integrating the younger ones into their family model of society.

As the western expansion continued and new territories became populous enough to be considered for statehood, the same difficulty would arise: How would territories be organized? What would be their relationships to existing states and the central government? The question of slavery in the territories, when it arose, could have been cast as a question of parent-child relations. The older siblings, however, struggled over how the

168   *Will the Circle be Unbroken?*

younger should be brought into the family. This, in turn, placed a premium on political technique. A hard working technician such as Steven A. Douglas might struggle against the statesmanlike eloquence of Abraham Lincoln, but Douglas was elected to and effective in the Senate; Lincoln was not. And while Lincoln is best remembered today as a statesman for his achievements as President, he clearly understood political technique. He, like Spotswood, Bacon, Balcombe, and the Proprietary, understood how to gain and preserve popular support. While Union troops might march singing "We are coming, Father Abraham," Lincoln's public image was not that of a ruler-father born to his place.

Thus there was no clear role for children and a diminishing role for the conventional Whig ruler-father. Similarly, there were only sketchy roles for women and African Americans in the family model on which the familial paradigm operated. Even the abolitionists struggled with the question of what to do with freed slaves—and what role women could have in the effort to free the slaves. Still, publication of fugitive slave narratives and women's statements, such as the Seneca Falls Declaration of Sentiments pointed out that families were more than fathers and marriageable children—and society might be more than the white men who held political and economic power.

So as the tension intensified, the familial paradigm proved less useful as a means of interpreting the Union. Ruler-fathers to whom all might look for definition of the relevant terms were replaced with technicians such as Van Buren, Harrison, Tyler, and Polk. These men, like Steven A. Douglas of the 1850s, proved skillful at breaking down major issues into minor ones, the better to assemble temporary coalitions. In the end, however, these technicians seemed less trustworthy than their predecessors—and perhaps less trustworthy than Jackson, who, once he finally declared himself, would not be moved. They proved incapable of resolving what Hinton Helper and David M. Potter have called The Impending Crisis.

At the same time, the family took a less prominent place in the Southern novel. John Esten Cooke, the next successful Virginian novelist to follow those with whom we have been concerned, hardly treated family issues at all (except courtship), and his novels often seem to be nostalgic longings for an historical past that was heavily romanticized. Unlike some of the families of the novels we have examined, Cooke's families do not leave Virginia or interact extensively with non-Virginians. Similar isolation may be seen in the refusal of Virginia to align herself with the seceding states or the Union in the secession winter of 1860–1861. While other states seceded, Virginia sent a peace delegation to Washington, D.C. to bring about a settlement that would allow the seceded states to leave the Union peaceably while Virginia remained behind. The effort failed, however, and Virginians joined other Southerners marching into conflict identifying themselves as "a band of brothers, and native to the soil."

Conclusion

169

In the post-Reconstruction period, Thomas Nelson Page looked back at the plantation family as the core of Southern society and culture. For him the ruler-father was a less central figure than the pre-war Whigs had made him. In *Social Life in Old Virginia Before the War*, Page treated the plantation mistress as the dominant figure. In that work, she is "mentioned first, as she was the most important personage about the home" (34). She had full responsibility and authority within the household and was "mistress, manager, doctor, nurse, counselor, seamstress, teacher, housekeeper, slave all at one" (37–38). Page characterizes her in terms of the work that she does and the roles that she fulfills. The plantation owner is a more abstract figure and characterized in terms of beliefs, attitudes, and personality rather than action. In this respect, he is similar to some of the women in the earlier works. His ideas were often supported by classical writers filtered through his grandfather's Revolutionary generation and his father's generation, which had constructed the United States. The sons of plantation owners were not so admirable as their fathers; they were self-indulgent, wasteful, and "addicted to the pursuit of pleasure" (51), but they were also brave, generous, and high spirited. They were suitable men for war, but Page gives no indication of how they would fare in peacetime when their generation had to provide leadership. Unlike Ned Hazard and Napier, they show no signs of increasing readiness to assume authority, nor is it clear that they would relinquish it as readily as Bacon does. The daughters of plantation owners were images of their mothers. Thus, the family that Page presents is matriocentric rather that patriarchal, and except for entertaining and visiting, it is self-contained, with no strong connections outside of the community or region. Thus it was little understood outside of the South and, when misrepresented in *Uncle Tom's Cabin*, became an object of hatred in the North (1–2). After the war, its characters became the object of caricature (3–4).

The deterioration of the familial paradigm is also apparent in Page's *Red Rock: A Chronicle of Reconstruction*. This novel traces events in the community of Brutusville from the time of the secession debate until roughly 1870. While it features a community threatened with disorder and disunity and many other features of the antebellum Virginia novels, in this case familial relations cannot provide models for the preservation of order and prosperity. The community, at the beginning of the novel, is a quiet and prosperous place located, according to its minister, near the site of the original garden of Eden and somewhat remote despite its rail connections. There are three major planters in the area: Mr. Gray, Dr. Cary, and Mr. Legaie, and the social and cultural life of the community seem to revolve around them. War and secession rupture the national community, but the unity of Brutusville remain intact. Indeed, Cary and Legaie, who have disagreed strongly on the subject of secession, enlist and serve through the war together, their differences moot. During the war, Mr. Gray is killed while

170   *Will the Circle be Unbroken?*

leading his regiment and his son, Jacquelin, returns home weakened by wounds and imprisonment. He finds that his father's overseer, Hiram Still, has made loans to many men within the county, including his father, and is acquiring property as his debtors default in the postwar economic upheaval. At the same time, Union occupation provides the means for Jonadab Leech, a carpetbagger, to seize political power. Cary and Legaie are unable to oppose Leech and Still successfully. Leadership of the opposition falls to Mr. Gray's former ward, Steve Allen, who grew up as something of a spoiled rascal at the Gray's Red Rock plantation but matured somewhat as a major in the Confederate army. Because the local people accept Steve's leadership, he becomes a convenient target for the usurpers. In the end, however, his sudden marriage to Ruth Welch (daughter of a former Union officer who has come south to look after his business dealings there) prevents Leech from imprisoning him. Caught in a fraud, Still returns Red Rock to Jacquelin Gray. With these events, the community takes its first steps toward restoration of order and prosperity.

There is no single male character in *Red Rock* who embodies, as Balcombe or the Proprietary, the ruler-father. Dr. Cary and Mr. Legaie have the years, wisdom, and stature based on faithfulness, but they are repeatedly outmaneuvered by Hiram Still and Jonadab Leech, who represent a subordinate tier of society. Indeed, the faithfulness and affection of the established community leaders is little more than an inconvenience to these avaricious but technically skillful manipulators. Unlike the ruler-father characters in the earlier novels, Dr. Cary dies before he can see order restored in the community. The younger generation, represented by Steve Allen and Jacquelin Gray, can mount more active resistance to usurpers, but they, too, are outmaneuvered until they receive assistance from outsiders such as Major Welch and Senator Rockfield. These outsiders act out of respect for the moral leadership that Cary and Legaie provided, but the fact remains that moral leadership without access to legal or political power has not prevailed over treachery.

The younger men of *Red Rock*, Steve Allen and Jacquelin Gray, are best described as leaders in training. They do not have the stature to lead the community; the night riders who seize the weapons from the homes of Leech's black militiamen develop into a branch of the Ku Klux Klan despite Steve's refusal to join and his protests that the organization is unnecessary. Jacquelin is not able to carry out his father's injunction to hold onto Red Rock. When he tries to reclaim it legally, his efforts are thwarted, partly because the war disrupted the transmission of culture: He has not learned all of his own family's tales and cannot refute Hiram Still's claim to the plantation.

The failures of the ruler-fathers of the Brutusville community occur in part because the law fails them. After the war, officials who had served the Confederacy are cast out of office. Lawyers are not permitted to practice until they have sworn the Oath of Allegiance, and they must practice before

Conclusion   171

courts where judges place more weight on the parties' political loyalties than on the evidence and rules of procedure. Thus, Page represents in his novel a tension that Yazawa suggests must have occurred in the early days of the republic. In Page's formulation, as in Yazawa's, however, the law and the ruler-father cannot coexist because of the impersonality of the former and the potential for abuse in the latter.

Although the Union was undergoing reconstruction during the period represented in *Red Rock*, marriage carries little thematic weight in the novel. The characters involved do not represent contending factions or regions, and their courtships are not presented in sufficient detail to suggest the bases of their attractions to each other. Jonadab Leech's failed marriage underscores his failings as a social creature, but it does not relate directly to his political abuses. Steve Allen's courtship of Ruth Welch leads to an intersectional marriage, and that in turn leads to the first cracks in the power structure that Leech and Still have established. Ruth, as Steve's wife, cannot be compelled to testify against him, and without her testimony, the usurpers cannot imprison him. Nevertheless, this would be little more than a temporary impediment to Leech and Still without Senator Rockfield's timely intervention, which promises to break their power. Similarly, Jacquelin Gray and Blair Cary, briefly identified as a Democrat and a Whig respectively, are likely to marry at the end of the novel, and the course of their courtship has been routh throughout the novel. Their reconciliation is not tied to any political shift but to correction of trivial misunderstandings.

Blair, in fact, seems to violate some conventions of the southern belle. While she is attractive, lively, and flirtatious, she is also a skillful cook and housekeeper. Also a scholar, she excels in Latin and later works as a school-teacher to earn money for her family. When the Ku Klux Klan sets out to destroy another school in the community, Blair intervenes and sends the riders home. Her father praises the women of the community for their courage; it seems that Blair retains this characteristic through Recon-struction. In this respect, she resembles Mildred Lindsey, but in her rela-tions with Jacquelin and Steve, she is more like Bel Tracy. If, as Seidel has argued, she reflects her author's view of the South, the South grew stronger and more independent during Reconstruction while retaining its charm; this is clearly not what Page meant to portray.

Sibling relations in *Red Rock* are similarly unimportant. Jacquelin Gray and Steve Allen may regard each other as brothers, but the tension in their relationship does not correspond to any tensions in the community or nation. These tensions arise solely from Jacquelin's mistaken belief that Steve and Blair Cary are in love. They are never sufficient to interfere with the legal work that the two men do, and Steve dispatches them immediately when the subject is finally broached. Between Jacquelin and his younger brother, Rupert, the sibling relationship seems almost coincidental. Jacquelin says he wants to regain Red Rock for his brother, and Rupert participates in resist-

172   *Will the Circle be Unbroken?*

ance against Leech and Still as much as his years allow. There is nothing, however, to indicate that these fraternal relations were intended as a model for relations among states or sections of the Union. They may, rather, be a call for the young to preserve Southern distinctiveness.

Artificial brotherhoods in *Red Rock*, as in *Rob of the Bowl*, are represented as a threat to social order and unity. The local organization of the Ku Klux Klan begins as a group of Confederate veterans seeking to restore order by disarming Leech's black militia and restoring a balance of power between the races and between the people of Brutusville and the Union military government. Disarming an ill-disciplined band commanded by a self-serving, avaricious outsider hardly seems a reprehensible act, particularly when the group responsible seems to be a well-disciplined force with clearly defined objectives. Later, however, when the group has aligned itself with the Ku Klux Klan and claims the right to execute Leech under its own laws, Page couches Steve's denunciation in terms that make clear the danger arising from such alternative communities and laws.

At the end of the novel, peace has returned to Red Rock. Northerners such as the Welches, Lawrence Middleton, Reely Thurston, and Senator Rockfield have become better acquainted with the character of Southerners and developed respect for them. On the other hand, Dr. Cary, who led the Whigs of Brutusville before secession and always served as a voice for moderation, has died. Mr. Legaie and Mr. Bagby, who had been the leading lawyers of the town, have been supplanted by Steve and Jacquelin. The transfer of cultural knowledge to this generation has been interrupted by war and affected by Reconstruction and the arrival of Northerners in the community. The South that they build seems likely to have little resemblance to the antebellum South, although it may have "left its benignant influence behind it to sweeten and sustain its children" (*Social Life* 104).

The antebellum novel, then, gave way to what might be termed a plantation romance, a work in which social commentary was limited to longing for a supposedly simpler past that had been destroyed by those who could not see its strengths and virtues. These romances did not address overarching questions of structure and responsibility; those matters, perhaps, had been settled by the war. The plantation romance, however, has remained a staple of writing in the United States, through such works as *Gone with the Wind* and a host of other historical romances set in the antebellum South. These more recent works, like the caricatures of Page's time, often seem less substantial and more escapist than earlier works. The predecessors of these romances, the works of Kennedy, Caruthers, and Tucker, however, continue to offer insights into the mind of the Old South.

Notes

Notes to Chapter One—Introduction

[1] Susan Tracy's recent work, *In the Master's Eye: Representations of Women, Blacks, and Poor Whites in Antebellum Southern Literature* (1995) argues that these works by white authors represent slaves and other socially marginalized figures in ways calculated to perpetuate the power of the white male aristocracy. As we shall see, this reading is not inconsistent with the reading to be proposed here; the principal difference is in whether the authors represented the plantation gentry and why the perpetuation of power seemed important to the authors.

[2] The order adopted for this study is the order of publication: Kennedy's *Swallow Barn* (1832), Caruthers's *The Kentuckian in New-York* (1834) and *Cavaliers of Virginia* (1834–35), Kennedy's *Horse-Shoe Robinson* (1835), Tucker's *George Balcombe* (1836) and *The Partisan Leader* (1836), Kennedy's *Rob of the Bowl* (1838), and Caruthers's *The Knights of the Golden Horse-Shoe* (1841, 1845).

[3] Factual inaccuracies in Watson's discussion of *Swallow Barn* lead one to question his conclusions. See, for a clear example, Watson's attribution of the exploits of Ned Hazard to Frank Meriwether (84), who represents, at least in my mind, a completely different type of character.

Notes to Chapter Two—Generational Progress in *Swallow Barn*

[1] The standard biography of John Pendleton Kennedy is Charles Bohner's *John Pendleton Kennedy, Gentleman from Baltimore*. Kennedy's papers are in the Maryland Historical Society; they are also available on microfilm.

[2] What Kennedy meant by "writing the last impression for the press" is not clear. While he may have put what he regarded as finishing touches on the work in the fall of 1830, there is no indication that he pursued publication until 1832.

[3] Frank's opinions with respect to steamboats and internal improvements are the opposite of Kennedy's, although both opposed Adams in 1828. Most readers of 1832, however, could not have known this, and what is more important is that staying out of politics allows Frank to tend carefully to the stewardship of Swallow Barn in the interest of future generations.

174   *Notes to Chapter Five*

NOTES TO CHAPTER THREE—"AN ARDENT DESIRE": *KENTUCKIAN IN NEW-YORK*

[1] Ned's behavior, of course, cannot be attributed to inexperience; as pointed out in the previous chapter, he has traveled and experienced more than the other characters. At Swallow Barn, he is temporarily somewhat like a belle figure in that he has little to do and an unclear role in the family and community. It is useful to note that no one depends upon him or Virginia Bell for anything until midway through the works in which they appear.

[2] Victor comes from a malarial region of South Carolina, where the gentry must leave their plantations for summer homes to avoid disease. Moreover, physicians of Caruthers' period believed that the diseases (and treatments) differed from one region to another, with southern diseases being more severe than their northern counterparts (McMillen 11). This would account, at least in part, for Victor's curiosity.

[3] The standard biography of Caruthers is Curtis Carroll Davis, *Chronicler of the Cavaliers: A Life of the Virginia Novelist, Dr. William A. Caruthers*, which includes detailed examinations of all of Caruthers' novels. Davis developed his biographical information from census, tax, court, and vital records because only three letters from Caruthers have survived. So scant is conventional biographical evidence on Caruthers that the place of his burial is unknown.

[4] This road may well be the National Road, which was the primary east-west route in this area. Caruthers does not name it, however; he may have regarded the specific identification as superfluous for an audience who would not have required it. To raise the National Road by name would bring up, by implication, the Maysville Road controversy and might alienate readers early in the work.

[5] Caruthers never makes the nature of Beverley's illness explicit, but as a physician, he must have known malaria to be a prevalent disease of the coastal South (McMillen 141–142). Given this, he would have known also the recurring nature of the disease. If Beverley suffers from malaria, as I believe he does, his dependency upon Virginia Bell will occur again and again for the rest of his life.

NOTES TO CHAPTER FOUR—AUTHORITY AND AFFECTION: *CAVALIERS OF VIRGINIA*

[1] There are in existence only three letters in Caruthers' hand. None of them relate to this subject or, for that matter, to political issues.

NOTES TO CHAPTER FIVE—WHIGS AND COVERT MISSIONS: *HORSE-SHOE ROBINSON*

[1] Caruthers left no document that presents his political views as clearly as *Defense of the Whigs*, but his Governor Berkley strongly resembles the Tory of Kennedy's formulation. This lends additional weight to the argument that Berkley was meant as a critique of Jackson.

[2] Kennedy normally uses "Tories" in *Horse-Shoe Robinson*, even in cases in which "British" might be more correct. In an effort to maintain some historical accuracy without sacrificing Kennedy's conception of the Revolution, I use the term "Royalist" to include both British troops and their American supporters and "Tory" to refer specifically to Americans supporting the British regime.

Notes to Chapter Eight 175

NOTES TO CHAPTER SIX—BIRTHRIGHT AND AUTHORITY: *GEORGE BALCOMBE*

[1] In a sample of 750 Southern planters born between 1765 and 1815, Catherine Clinton found that cousin marriage occurred at a rate of 12.3 percent for women and 12.4 percent for men; it did not occur at all in her sample of 100 members of the Hudson Valley Dutch elite born during the same period (Clinton 233). In Jane Censer's sample of 124 North Carolinian families, 7.9 percent of the women and 14.3 percent of the men married first or second cousins (Censer 84, n. 39). While not uniformly accepted, even within these small samples, cousin marriage occurred, at least among Censer's North Carolinians, in older established communities where a limited number of planters with a large number of descendants made kinship ties among any two members more likely, and in isolated communities where the number of potential marriage partners was limited. The Tidewater community in which *George Balcombe* takes place seems to fit the latter description. It is impossible to ascertain what Tucker's original readers may have made of the relationship between Napier and Ann.

[2] The Coleman-Tucker Collection at Swem Library of the College of William and Mary contains a wealth of archival material from Beverley Tucker, his ancestors, and his descendants. Consequently, new works on Tucker subjects are almost always in progress. Robert Brugger's psychobiography, *Nathaniel Beverley Tucker: Heart over Head in the Old South* is the standard biography.

[3] The model of female education that Napier proposes and Balcombe rejects is identical to the model that Yazawa associates with Revolutionary republican thought; Balcombe's model is similar to the model that Kennedy praises through Mark Littleton in *Swallow Barn*. Caruthers, on the other hand, accepted the republican model, and in *Knights of the Golden Horse-Shoe* argued through Dr. Evylin for female equality.

NOTES TO CHAPTER SEVEN—THE FAMILY RESTRUCTURED: *THE PARTISAN LEADER*

[1] Tucker wrote to his brother Henry in 1837 that he "had said to General Jackson (March 1833) that if a government of opinion was to be exchanged for a Government of force (he] prayed God that the people might lose no time, in bringing to the only arbitrament the question 'Whether they can be governed by force.'"

NOTES TO CHAPTER EIGHT—MISTAKEN IDENTITY: *ROB OF THE BOWL*

[1] Kennedy's punctuation in this journal entry leaves unclear the reference of some phrases here. If, for example, "a family of old maids" refers to Cocklescruggs, which seems to have shifted to Cocklescraft, the difference between the rough plan of 1835 and the finished novel is even greater than what is discussed here. The shift of a century in setting and changes in the characters lend force to the argument that Kennedy was aiming to produce something more than a swashbuckler.

[2] It is particularly interesting that Kennedy builds a somewhat humorous scene around this ritual of obeisance—precisely the same type of ritual upon which Yazawa seized in his discussion of filial demeanor (Yazawa 33–39). While in Kennedy's time these rituals may not have carried exactly the meaning they had carried before the Revolution, books of etiquette in the nineteenth century still

176 *Notes to Chapter Nine*

devoted considerable space to the giving and receiving of such courtesies (Kasson 40–46).

[3] The statement that Kennedy *deliberately* suppressed some material here suggests that the work was carefully and self-consciously developed, a view that seems at odds with Kennedy's own statement that he had written the book in haste: He wrote to his uncle Phillip Pendleton, in December 1838, "My book wore the heart out of me, in a bloody labour of forty days and forty nights during which I sweated as never did Jonah in the whale's belly" (quoted in Osborne 99). This statement, however, contradicts the evidence from Kennedy's journal, cited earlier in this chapter, to the effect that he began work on the novel in 1835. What seems most likely is that Kennedy worked intensively for a short period to finish a work that he had worked on less intensely for much longer. This does not rule out careful, self-conscious work, in keeping with the practice Kennedy had established in *Swallow Barn,* especially during the final stages of the effort.

[4] It was this that provoked John Pendleton Kennedy's dismay during the period when he was completing *Horse-Shoe Robinson* and beginning *Rob of the Bowl.* The basis for Kennedy's disapproval was not specified in the journal entry on this subject quoted earlier in this study. Nevertheless, as one involved in law, politics, commerce, and business (through his father-in-law's mills), Kennedy surely recognized that the Bank of the United States was a proven financial institution regulated by law, while the state banks were often unsanctioned, unregulated, and operated by inexperienced officials (Feller 171).

[5] An example of this appears in *George Balcombe,* where the worship at the camp meeting so disgusts Napier that he cannot effectively pursue Montague there. The young man believes that he approaches the meeting without prejudice, but he is sickened by what he sees there.

[6] It is interesting, at this point, to note that Nathaniel Beverley Tucker applied the fraternal paradigm to the community of lawyers. Brugger points out that Tucker saw himself, during his years on the bench in Missouri, as an elder brother to the lawyers there. He may be referring to a passage in Tucker's later introductory lecture for law students at the College of William and Mary: "The beautiful fiction of Law, by which the members of the profession are considered as brethren, of whom the judge is but the elder, hardly deserves the name of fiction. There is no corps animated by a spirit so truly fraternal, nor is there any member of it to whose comfort this spirit is so essential, as the judge himself" (Tucker 600).

This provides an instance of a Whig who had cut ties with the conservative Democrats specifically invoking the fraternal metaphor.

NOTES TO CHAPTER NINE—TO THE WEST: *KNIGHTS OF THE HORSE-SHOE*

[1] Caruthers dates the expedition as occurring in 1714; this is one of numerous inaccurate representations of historical fact in *Knights of the Horse-Shoe.* To discuss all of these errors in detail is beyond the scope of this work; accordingly, only those errors that relate to representations of the family are discussed.

[2] Both titles were used during Caruthers's lifetime: *The Magnolia* used the title *The Knights of the Golden Horse-Shoe*; the Charles Yancey edition was sold as *The Knights of the Horse Shoe.* The latter title was used for 1882, 1909, and 1928 editions. The 1970 reprint used in this study reproduces the text for the first book edition of 1845, but the editor restored "Golden" to the title. No case can be made for either title as better representing the author's intent.

Notes to Chapter Nine 177

[3] Other modern commentators include those cited elsewhere in this study: Jay B. Hubbell, William R. Taylor, J.V. Ridgely, and Ritchie D. Watson. While all agree with Davis's view that *Knights of the Golden Horse-Shoe* is Caruthers's best and (in some unspecified sense) most important work, none elaborate significantly on Davis's discussion. To review their readings here, consequently, seems superfluous.

[4] Most of these inaccuracies are irrelevant to the familial paradigm. Those listed by Davis include the size of the expedition, the assertion that the horses had not been shod before the journey, the adequacy of food and drink, the danger from Native Americans, and the year of the expedition (*Chronicler* 212–213).

[5] The term "Manifest Destiny," of course, embraces more than the annexation of Texas, but the repeated references to Texas and Mexico in *The Knights of the Golden Horse-Shoe* indicate that Caruthers's attention, when he wrote the novel, was fixed on Texas to the exclusion of California and the Oregon Territory. In the novel, Caruthers mentions Texas repeatedly, but he also offers glowing descriptions of the land to the west of the mountains, a phrase embracing the entire west and making Texas exemplary of the destiny to move westward and possess the land.

[6] The use of quotation marks here reflects the 1845 edition, which appears incorrect. This edition contains numerous errors and inconsistencies such as this which appear to have minimal relevance, if any, to the meaning of the novel, and which probably suggest more about the quality of typesetting available in Wetumpka, Alabama, in 1845.

[7] Davis finds it remarkable that Frank, by wearing a wig, manages to hide his identity from the governor, Kate, and Henry (*Chronicler* 207); there is no clear indication in the text that the governor and Kate had a particularly close relationship with Frank before his departure for England. Moreover, the tutor wears heavy whiskers. Caruthers was familiar with eighteenth-century portraits of Virginians and must have known that beards were unusual, at least among the upper class. He may also have realized that a beard, in such circumstances, would draw attention away from other features. Moreover, when he returns, Frank has a facial scar that seems to dominate his features.

[8] Throughout the latter part of the novel, Frank expresses pleasure that Ellen recognized him despite his disguise and kept his secret to keep him safe. Ellen never makes any response when he says this in her presence, and I have found nothing in the text to suggest that she *did* recognize him before he revealed his identity. While this issue is peripheral to this study, it seems reasonable that Caruthers has Frank believe that Ellen recognized him in order to suggest the intimacy that the couple feel.

Works Cited

Adams, John. "Letter to Abigail Adams." 1780

Bakker, Jan. *Pastoral in Antebellum Southern Romance*. Baton Rouge, LA: Louisiana State University Press, 1989.

Bardaglio, Peter. *Reconstructing the Household: Families, Sex, and the Law in the Nineteenth-Century South*. Chapel Hill: University of North Carolina Press, 1995.

Bohner, Charles H. *John Pendleton Kennedy: Gentleman From Baltimore*. Baltimore, MD: Johns Hopkins University Press, 1961.

Brugger, Robert J. *Beverley Tucker: Heart Over Head In The Old Dominion*. Baltimore, MD: Johns Hopkins University Press, 1978.

Bryan, E.T. "Letter to Nathaniel Beverley Tucker." Coleman-Tucker Collection, Swem Library, College of William and Mary, 1836.

Bryan, E.T. "My Own Views of the Will Case." Coleman-Tucker Collection, Swem Library, College of William and Mary, 1836.

Carey, Henry. "Letter to John Pendleton Kennedy." John Pendleton Kennedy Papers, Enoch Pratt Free Library, 1832.

Caruthers, William Alexander. *Knights of the Golden Horse-Shoe*. Chapel Hill, NC: University of North Carolina Press, 1970 (1845).

Censer, Jane Turner. *North Carolina Planters and Their Children, 1800–1860*. Baton Rouge, LA: Louisiana State University Press, 1984.

Charvat, William. *The Profession of Authorship in America, 1800–1870*. New York: Columbia University Press, 1992.

Clinton, Catherine. *The Plantation Mistress: Woman's World in the Old South*. New York, NY: Pantheon Books, 1982.

Coalter, St. George. "Letter to Nathaniel Beverley Tucker." Coleman-Tucker Collection, Swem Library, College of William and Mary, 1837.

Conway, Martin. *Harper's Ferry: Time Remembered*. Reston, VA: Carabelle Books, 1981.

Cowie, Alexander. *Rise of the American Novel*. New York: American Book Company, 1948.

Davis, Curtis Carroll. *Chronicler of the Cavaliers: A Life of the Virginia Novelist, Dr. William A. Caruthers*. Richmond, VA: Dietz Press, 1953.

Davis, Curtis Carroll. "Introduction to Knights of the Golden Horse-Shoe: A Traditionary Tale of the Cocked Hat Gentry in the Old Dominion, by William A. Caruthers." Chapel Hill: University of North Carolina Press, 1970.

Dickson, Frank A. "Adventures of Horse-Shoe Robinson." In *Journeys into the Past: The Anderson Region's Heritage*. NP:NP, 1975. 35–40

Ellis, Richard E. *The Union at Risk: Jacksonian Democracy, States' Rights, and the Nullification Crisis*. New York: Oxford University Press, 1987.

F.P. "Letter to Nathaniel Beverley Tucker." Coleman-Tucker Collection, Swem Library, College of William and Mary, 1837.

Feller, Daniel. *The Jacksonian Promise: America, 1815–1840*. Ed. Stanley I. Kutler. Baltimore, MD: Johns Hopkins University Press, 1995.

Fischer, David Hackett, and James C. Kelly. *Away I'm Bound Away: Virginia and the Westward Movement*. Richmond, VA: Virginia Historical Society, 1993.

Ford, Lacy K., Jr. *Origins of Southern Radicalism: The South Carolina Upcountry, 1800–1860*. New York: Oxford University Press, 1988.

Green, Duff. "Letter to Nathaniel Beverley Tucker." Coleman-Tucker Collection, Swem Library, College of William and Mary, 1837.

Grossberg, Michael. *Governing the Hearth: Law and the Family in Nineteenth-Century America*. Ed. G. Edward White. Chapel Hill: University of North Carolina Press, 1985.

Hamilton, Phillip. "Education in the St. George Tucker Household: Change and Continuity in Jeffersonian Virginia." *Virginia Magazine of History and Biography* 102. April 1994: 167–192.

Hare, John L. "St. George Tucker's Essay 'For the Old Batchellor' in Praise of Virginia Women: A Critical Edition." M.A. Thesis. College of William and Mary, 1976.

Holman, C. Hugh. "Introduction." *The Partisan Leader, by Nathaniel Beverley Tucker*. Chapel Hill: University of North Carolina Press, 1971.

Hubbell, Jay Broadus. *The South in American Literature*. Durham, NC: Duke University Press, 1954.

Isaac, Rhys. *The Transformation of Virginia, 1740–1790*. New York: W.W. Norton & Company, 1982.

Johnston, A.S. "Letter to William Preston re: *The Partisan Leader*." 1836

Kasson, John F. *Rudeness and Civility: Manners in Nineteenth-Century Urban America*. New York: Hill and Wang, 1990.

Works Cited 181

Kennedy, John Pendleton. "Defence of the Whigs." *Political and Official Papers*. New York: G.P. Putnam & Sons, 1872.

Kennedy, John Pendleton. *Horse-Shoe Robinson: A Tale of the Tory Ascendency*. New York: George P. Putnam, 1835.

Kennedy, John Pendleton. John Pendleton Kennedy Papers. Enoch Pratt Free Library.

Kennedy, John Pendleton. *Rob of the Bowl: A Legend of St. Inigoe's*. New Haven, CT: College & University Press, 1838.

Kennedy, John Pendleton. *Swallow Barn, or A Sojourn in the Old Dominion*. New York, NY: G.P. Putnam & Company, 1853.

Kerber, Linda K. *Women of the Republic: Intellect and Ideology in Revolutionary America*. New York: W.W. Norton and Company, 1980.

Lebsock, Suzanne. *The Free Women of Petersburg*. New York: W.W. Norton & Son, 1984.

Lewis, Jan. *The Pursuit of Happiness: Family and Values In Jefferson's Virginia*. New York: Cambridge University Press, 1983.

Livingston, Paisley. "Convention and Literary Explanations" in *Rules and Conventions: Literature, Philosophy, Social Theory*. Ed. Mette Hjort. Baltimore, MD: Johns Hopkins University Press, 1992. 67–94.

Mapp, Alf J. *The Virginia Experiment: The Old Dominion's Role in the Making of America, 1607–1781*. 3rd ed. Lanham, MD: Hamilton Press, 1985.

McMillen, Sally G. *Motherhood in the Old South: Pregnancy, Childbirth, and Infant Rearing*. Baton Rouge: Louisiana State University Press, 1990.

Norton, Mary Beth. *Liberty's Daughters: The Revolutionary Experience of American Women, 1750–1800*. Boston: Little, Brown and Company, 1980

Osborne, William S. "Introduction." *Rob of the Bowl: A Legend of St. Inigoe's*. New Haven, CT: College and University Press, 1965. 5–27.

Osborne, William S. "John Pendleton Kennedy's *Horse-Shoe Robinson*: A Novel with 'Utmost Historical Accuracy'." *Maryland Historical Magazine 59*. September 1964, 286–296.

Page, Thomas Nelson. *Red Rock: A Chronicle of Reconstruction*. Ridgewood, NJ: Gregg Press, 1967.

Page, Thomas Nelson. *Social Life in Old Virginia Before the War*. New York: Charles Scribner's Sons, 1897.

Parrington, Vernon L. *The Romantic Revolution in America*. New York: Harvest Books, 1927.

Pessen, Edward. *Jacksonian America: Society, Personality, and Politics*. Urbana: University of Illinois Press. 1978.

Preston, W.C. "Letter to Nathaniel Beverley Tucker." Coleman-Tucker Collection, Swem Library, College of William and Mary.

182 *Works Cited*

Remini, Robert V. *Life of Andrew Jackson*. New York: Penguin Books, 1988.

Ridgely, Joseph V. *Nineteenth-Century Southern Literature*. Lexington: University Press of Kentucky. 1980.

Ringe, Donald A. "The American Revolution in American Romance." *American Literature* 49. November 1977: 352–365.

Robinson, T.M. [?] "Letter to Nathaniel Beverley Tucker." Coleman-Tucker Collection, Swem Library, College of William and Mary. 1837.

Rubin, Louis. "The Literary Community in the Old South." *The Writer in the South*. Athens: University of Georgia Press, 1972: 1–33.

Schlesinger, Arthur M., Jr. *The Age of Jackson*. Boston: Little, Brown And Company, 1953.

Seidel, Kathryn Lee. *The Southern Belle in the American Novel*. Tampa, FL: University of South Florida Press, 1985.

Smith, Daniel Blake. *Inside the Great House: Planter Family Life in Eighteenth-Century Chesapeake Society*. Ithaca, NY: Cornell University Press, 1980.

Stowe, Steven. *Intimacy and Power in the Old South: Ritual in the Lives of the Planters*. Baltimore, MD: Johns Hopkins University Press, 1987.

Sydnor, Charles S. *The Development of Southern Sectionalism, 1819–1848*. Eds. Wendell Holmes Stephenson and E. Merton Coulter. Vol. 5. Baton Rouge: Louisiana State University Press, 1948. 10 vols.

Taylor, William R. *Cavalier and Yankee: The Old South in American National Character*. New York, NY: Doubleday Anchor Books, 1961.

Tracy, Susan J. *In the Master's Eye: Representations of Women, Blacks, and Poor Whites in Antebellum Southern Literature*. Amherst, MA: University of Massachusetts Press, 1995.

Tucker, Henry St. George. "Letter to Nathaniel Beverley Tucker." Coleman-Tucker Collection, Swem Library, College of William and Mary. 1837.

Tucker, Nathaniel Beverley. *George Balcombe: A Novel*. New York: Harper & Brothers, 1836.

Tucker, Nathaniel Beverley. "Letter to General Thomas A. Smith." Coleman-Tucker Collection, Swem Library, College of William and Mary. 1833.

Tucker, Nathaniel Beverley. "Letter to Henry St. George Tucker." Coleman-Tucker Collection, Swem Library, College of William and Mary. 1837.

Tucker, Nathaniel Beverley. "Letter to Lucy Tucker." Coleman-Tucker Collection, Swem Library, College of William and Mary. 1835.

Tucker, Nathaniel Beverley. *The Partisan Leader*. Washington, DC: Duff Green, 1836.

Tucker, Nathaniel Beverley. "Valedictory Address to his Class." *Southern Literary Messenger* 1 (1835): 600.

Upshur, Abel. "Letter to Nathaniel Beverley Tucker." Coleman-Tucker Collection, Swem Library, College of William and Mary. 1837.

Works Cited

Ward, John William. *Andrew Jackson-Symbol for an Age*. New York: Oxford University Press, 1955.

Watson, Ritchie D. *The Cavalier in American Fiction*. Baton Rouge: Louisiana State University Press, 1985.

Wentworth, Linda Clark. "Childrearing in the Early Chesapeake: The Tucker Family and the Rise of Republican Parenthood." M.A. Thesis. College of William and Mary in Virginia. 1984.

Wyatt-Brown, Bertram. *Southern Honor: Ethics and Behavior in the Old South*. New York: Oxford University Press, 1982.

Yazawa, Melvin. *From Colonies to Commonwealth: Familial Ideology and the Beginnings of the American Republic*. Ed. Thomas Bender. Baltimore, MD: Johns Hopkins University Press, 1985.

[Caruthers, William A.] *Cavaliers of Virginia, or the Recluse of Jamestown*. New York: Harper & Brothers, 1834–1835.

[Caruthers, William A.]. *The Kentuckian in New-York*. New York: Harper and Brothers, 1834.

Index

abolitionism, 161
Adair family, 78
Adair, Wat, 78, 80, 81, 83
Adams, John, 18
Adams, John Quincy, 69
Allen, Steve, 170, 171
American Quarterly Review , review
    of Kentuckian, 34
American System, 79, 113
antebellum era, in Parrington, 2
anti-Jacksonianism, in Cavaliers of
    Virginia, 51
artificial brotherhoods, 134–136,
    140, 158, 167; and social class,
    137; in Knights of the Horse-
    Shoe, 167; in Red Rock, 172; in
    Rob of the Bowl, 167; loyalty
    among members,137
authority: and republicanism, 164; in
    Horse-Shoe Robinson, 77–78; in
    Knights of the Horse-Shoe,152,
    158

Bacon, Nathaniel, 64, 155, 163
Baker, Judge, 122
Baker, Phillip, 109, 120
Bakker, Jan, on Swallow Barn, 16
Balcombe family, 95–96

Baltimore (Maryland), in Kentuckian,
    42
Bank of the United States, 133
Bardaglio, Peter, 10
belle figure, 174 (n.1)
Berkley, Gov. William,62, 150, 163; as
    ruler-father, 63–64; as Yankee
    figure, 65; compared to Jackson,
    62–63; usurpation of power, 66
Blair, James, 145
Bohner, Charles: on Horse-Shoe
    Robinson, 71; on Rob of the
    Bowl, 131
Brothers of the Coast, 137, 139, 158,
    159
Brugger, Robert, 89, 113, 117
Bryan, Elizabeth Tucker, 94, 112
Butler, Arthur, 73, 76, 77, 79

Calvert, Charles (The Proprietary),
    128, 137, 163
Calvert, Maria, 128, 130
Carey, Henry: and sectionalism, 23,
    26; and Swallow Barn, 23
Carey, Mathew, 23
Carter, Kit, 147
Caruthers, William A., 33, 143; and
    brother John, 40; and

185

186   *Index*

Caruthers, William A., *(continued)*
    Nullification, 31; biography of,
    174 (n.3); dependency of, 41;
    familial experience of, 40–41;
    in Hubbell, 3; in Parrington, 3;
    in Taylor, 4; in Watson, 5;
    Indebtedness, 41; life of, 39–40;
    marriage in works of, 165;
    marriage of, 40, 60; siblings in
    works of, 167; travels of, 40
Cary, Blair, 171
Cary, Dr. John, 169
Cavalier figure, 5, 55
Cavaliers of Virginia, 124;
    characterizations, 52;
    composition of, 51–52; conflict
    in, 52; contemporary reviews of,
    54; familial paradigm in, 68;
    historical setting, 60–61; Native
    American characters, 57; ruler-
    father in, 68; setting, 61, 62;
    sources on Bacon's Rebellion,
    60–61; summary, 52–54
Chevillere, Victor, 35; on sectionalism,
    42–43; Taylor on, 35
Chevillere, Virginia Bell, 36, 39, 45,
    46
children, 82
chivalry, 74
Coalter, John, 96
Coalter, St. George, 93, 112
Cocklescraft, Richard, 128, 129, 130,
    137, 140, 153
Coldcale, Bridget, 128
colonial tensions, in Rob of the Bowl,
    129
community, structure of, 87
Constitution of the United States, 164
constitutions, state, 164
convention, literary, 6
Cooke, John Esten, 168
Cooper, James Fenimore, 71
courtship, 66; in familial paradigm, 11;
    in Kentuckian, 11, 37–38, 44–45;
    in Red Rock, 171; in Rob of the

Bowl, 139; in Swallow Barn, 27;
    parental roles, 66

Damon, Montgomery, 36, 40, 83
Dauntrees, Jasper, 128, 139
Davis, Curtis Carroll: on Cavaliers of
    Virginia, 51, 52; on Kentuckian,
    34; on Knights of the Horse-Shoe,
    143, 148
de la Grange, Arnold, 128
Defence of the Whigs, 75
demeanor, 8, 140, 175
Democrats, 72, 77
discipline, 8, 154
Douglas, Steven, 168

Election of 1828, 173 (n.3)
Election of 1836, 114
Elliott, Eugenia, 148
evangelicals, 134–136
Evylin, Dr., 145, 146
Evylin, Ellen, 145, 146, 157, 156, 161

Fairfax, Emily, 65
Fairfax, Gideon, 66
Fairfax, Virginia, 64, 66–67
familial ideology, in Seidel, 6
familial paradigm, 118, 125, 136,
    171; and Nullification, 31; and
    republicanism, 9; and
    sectionalism, 160; as national
    metaphor, 9; courtship in, 11;
    discipline in, 8; durability, 9–10,
    61–62; generational progression,
    18; in Cavaliers of Virginia,
    67–68; in George Balcombe, 96,
    102, 105; in Horse-Shoe
    Robinson, 83; in Kentuckian,
    48–49; in Knights of the Horse-
    Shoe, 148, 150, 155, 162; in
    Partisan Leader, 116, 119, 124; in
    Swallow Barn, 24; in Virginia
    novels, 10, 11–12; in Yazawa, 8;
    Interdependency, 31; marriage in,
    165; organic community in,

Index

187

22–23, 40; ruler-father, 23; sibling relations in, 11, 157, 165–166; slavery and, 122; weaknesses of, 167, 168

family, 123; extended, 66; identity and, 97, 99; in Knights of the Horse-Shoe, 153

fathers, 81

female characters, 46; in Knights of the Horse-Shoe, 151, 155; in Partisan Leader, 121; in Kentuckian in New-York, 76

gender roles, 39, 45

generational progression, 27, 169; in Rob of the Bowl, 141; in Swallow Barn, 18, 24–25

George Balcombe: Brugger on, 95; composition of, 89, 95; contemporary reviews of, 93, 94; familial paradigm in, 102, 105; inheritance in, 11; popularity of, 94; Ridgely on, 95; ruler-father in, 90; summary, 89–92; Taylor on, 94

George Balcombe (character): 90, 92, 93,98–99, 100, 103–104, 155, 163

Gideon Fairfax, 64

Gray, Jacquelin, 170, 171

Green, Duff, 111

Hall, Henry, 147

Harper Brothers, 143

Harper's Ferry (Virginia), 41–42

Hazard, Ned, 25, 163; and Rip Meriwether, 28; and sectionalism, 26; as cavalier, 26–27; courtship of, 27; description of, 27; maturation of, 27

Holman, C. Hugh, on Partisan Leader, 113

Horse-Shoe Robinson, 70, 137, children in, 82; chivalry in, 74; composition of, 70; familial

paradigm in, 83; fathers in, 81; female characters, 75; hospitality in, 81; Hubbell on, 74; marriage in, 83; Osborne on, 75; popularity of, 73; reception in England, 74; Ridgely on, 74; Ringe on, 75, scholarship, 74; summary, 73; Taylor on, 74; Watson on, 74; Whig values in, 82, 84; Whigs in, 70; women's roles in, 84

Hubbell, Jay B., 3–4; on George Balcombe, 94; on Horse-Shoe Robinson, 74; on Kentuckian, 34; on Partisan Leader, 113; on Rob of the Bowl, 132; on Swallow Barn in, 16

Indian policy: in Cavaliers of Virginia, 58; legal cases, 58–59; tribal sovereignty, 58

Indians, 103

inheritance: in George Balcombe, 11; in Swallow Barn, 10; in Virginia novels, 10–11

initiation rituals, 135

in-laws: in Kentuckian, 43; in Swallow Barn, 15; of John Pendleton Kennedy, 17

interdependency, 140, 160

internal improvements, 173 (n.1)

Isaac, Rhys, 7

Jackson, Andrew, 102; and Revolutionary War, 72; and Virginia novels, 12; career as Indian fighter, 57; death of, 163, economic policy, 133; election of 1832, 69; Indian policy, 57–58; Maysville Road veto, 20; opposition to, 30; political career, 56, 76; public image, 55, 56; use of veto, 56–57, 71; views on Federal authority, 19

Jacksonian democracy, 16

Jarvis, Joe, 148, 150, 154
Johnston, A.S., 112

Keizer, John, 93, 100, 103
Kennedy, John Pendleton, 99; and election of 1830, 20; and political process, 20; and Union Bank, 72; biography of, 173 (n.1); Defence of the Whigs, 71; extended family, 17; family experience, 16–17, 82; in Hubbell, 3; in Parrington, 3; in Taylor, 4; in-laws of, 17; marriage in, 165; Maysville Road veto, 20, 21; on Henry Clay, 21; on Nullification, 20; on Swallow Barn, 13; parents of, 16; political views, 18, 19, 20, 21, 70, 71, 72, 74, 76, 80; siblings in works of, 165; views on Federal authority, 19
Kentuckian in New-York, 160; and sectionalism, 31; characterizations, 35; contemporary reviews of, 33–34; courtship in, 11, 31, 44–45; Davis on, 34; familial paradigm in, 48–49; female characters, 35–36; gender roles in, 39; Harper's Ferry (Virginia) in, 41–42; Hubbell on, 34; in-laws in, 43; marriage in, 38–39, 43–46; medicine in, 37–38; organic community in, 40; Parrington on, 34; Ridgely on, 34; scholarship, 34; sectionalism in, 42, 47–48; slavery in, 38, 48–49; summary, 36–38; Taylor on, 34; travels in, 36–38, 41; types in, 35; Virginia (state) in, 38
Kentucky and Virginia Resolutions, 118
Kerber, Linda K., 84
Knickerbocker: review of Cavaliers of Virginia, 54; review of Kentuckian; 34

Knights of the Horse-Shoe: artificial brotherhoods in, 167; authority in, 152; composition of, 143; conclusion of, 162; contemporary reviews of, 148; Davis on, 148; familial paradigm in, 148, 150, 155, 162; family in, 153; female characters, 151; marriage in, 147, 160, 162; popularity of, 149; publication of, 143; representation of history in, 149; ruler-father in, 148; scholarship, 177 (n.3); siblings in, 155; summary, 144–148; Texas independence in, 149
Ku Klux Klan, 170, 172

Lee brothers, 155
Lee, Frank, 146, 149, 160, 161, 177 (n.7)
Lee, Frank (as Henry Hall), 145, 147
Lee, Harry, 146, 147, 149, 156
Leech, Jonadab, 170, 171
Legaie, General, 169
Leonard, Benedict, 128
Lincoln, Abraham, 168
Lindsay family, 78, 80
Lindsay, Henry, 78, 84
Lindsay, Mildred, 73, 76, 77, 83, 84, 85
Lindsay, Philip, 73, 78, 79, 86, 164, 171
Littleton, Mark, 19, 24
Livingston, Paisley, 6
love, romantic, 68

malaria, 174 (n.5)
male characters, Red Rock, 170
Manifest Destiny, 150, 177 (n.5)
marriage, 45–46, 161; basis for, 67; conceptions of, 65; in Cavaliers of Virginia, 64–65; in familial paradigm, 164–165; in Horse-Shoe Robinson, 83; in Kentuckian; 38–39, 43–45, 46; in

Index

189

Knights of the Horse-Shoe, 147, 160, 162; in Partisan Leader, 110, 119; in Red Rock, 171; of cousins, 175, (n.1); social status of partners, 68

Maysville Road bill, 21, 174 (n.4)

medicine, 48; and sectionalism, 174 (n.2); in Kentuckian, 37–38

Meriwether family, 13–14

Meriwether, Frank, 163; and politics, 24, 26; as ruler-father, 23; description of, 25–26; on sectionalism, 24; on slavery, 19; possession of Swallow Barn, 25; provincialism of, 26

Meriwether, Lucretia, 24, 29

Meriwether, Lucy and Victorine, 157

Meriwether, Rip, 28

Meriwether, Victorine, 29

middle states, 42

Moore, Bernard, 145, 147

Mr. B___, 110

Musgrove family, 78, 80

Musgrove, Allen, 79, 164

Musgrove, Mary, 76, 80, 83, 85

Napier, William, 89, 93, 97, 100, 101

National Road, 174 (n.4)

national tensions, 30, 32, 33, 59–60, 61, 163, 171; in Partisan Leader, 107, 125; in Rob of the Bowl, 127, 141; in Swallow Barn, 23; in middle states, 42

natural community, 139

New York Review, review of Rob of the Bowl, 131

New York Times, review of Kentuckian, 34

New York Transcript, review of Kentuckian, 34

New-York American, review of Kentuckian, 34

New-York Mirror, review of Cavaliers of Virginia, 54

Norton, Mary Beth, 84

Nullification Crisis, 31, 32–33, 69, 79, 87

organic community: in Kentuckian, 40; in Swallow Barn, 22; in Swallow Barn, 24–25; Montgomery Damon in, 40

Osborne, Willam, on Horse-Shoe Robinson, 75

Page, Thomas Nelson, 169

Panic of 1837, 133, 134

Parrington, Vernon L., 2–3; on Partisan Leader, 112; on Rob of the Bowl, 131; on Swallow Barn, 16

Partisan Leader, The, 90, 130; and election of 1836, 111; Brugger on, 113, 117; composition of, 114; contemporary reviews of, 112; distribution of, 111; familial paradigm in, 116, 119, 124; female characters, 121; Holman on, 113; Hubbell on, 113; marriage in, 110, 119; national tensions in, 107, 126; popularity of, 111; publication of, 117; Ridgely on, 113; ruler-father in, 120; scholarship, 112–113; secession in, 107, 120; slavery in, 122; summary, 108; Watson on, 5

Pessen, Edward, 134

plantation romances, 172

Poe, Edgar Allen, on George Balcombe, 94

Preston, William C., 94, 112

publishing industry, 144

Ramsay family, 78

Ramsay, Andrew, 86

Ramsay, David, 79, 81, 86

Ramsay, John, 86

Randolph, Beverley, 35; courtship of, 39; illness of, 45

Randolph, John, 89, 97

190 Index

Randolph, Nancy, 93
Randolph, Richard, 94
Randolph, Theodorick, 94
Red Rock: artificial brotherhoods in, 172; conclusion of, 172; courtship in, 171; male characters in, 170; marriage in, 171; siblings in, 171; summary, 169
republican motherhood, 84
republicanism, 9, 164
Revolutionary War, as setting, 61, 71
Richmond Whig , review of Partisan Leader, 112
Ridgely, J.V.: on Cavaliers of Virginia, 52, 55; on George Balcombe, 95; on Horse-Shoe Robinson, 74; on Kentuckian, 34; on Partisan Leader, 113; on Swallow Barn, 16
Ringe, Donald, on Horse-Shoe Robinson, 75
Rob of the Bowl, artificial brotherhoods in, 167; Bohner on, 131; characters, 128; colonial tensions in, 129; composition of, 127, 133, 176 (n.3); conclusion of, 132; contemporary reviews of, 131; courtship in, 139; Hubbell on, 132; national tensions in, 127, 141; Parrington on, 131; publication of, 131; social class in, 128, 130, 140; summary, 129
Robertson, James (Horse-Shoe Robinson), 70
Robinson, Horse-Shoe (character), 72, 76, 84
Robinson, T.M., 94
Rockfield, Senator, 170, 171
Rubin, Louis D., 51
ruler-father, 23, 100, 102, 168, 169; Alexander Spotswood as, 151, 154; and Nullification, 31–32; Bernard Trevor as, 119, 122–123; failure of in Reconstruction, 170;

Frank Meriwether as, 23; George Balcombe as, 103; in Cavaliers of Virginia, 66, 68; in George Balcombe, 90; in Knights of the Horse-Shoe, 148; in Partisan Leader, 120; in Swallow Barn, 23; in Yazawa, 8; Martin Van Buren (character) as, 124

Sandford, 43
Schlesinger, Arthur, Jr., on Partisan Leader, 115
Scott, James, 92, 93
Scott, Mary, 96
secession, 87, 107, 120, 121, 168
sectionalism, 32, 79; and disease, 48; and familial paradigm, 160; and ignorance, 26, 41, 43; and medicine, 174 (n.2); in Kentuckian, 42, 47–48; in Parrington, 2, 3; in Swallow Barn, 16, 24; in Taylor, 4; in Watson, 5; middle states, 42
Seidel, Kathryn, 6, 29
Seward, William, 115
sibling relations, in familial paradigm, 11, 165
siblings, 160, 176 (n.6), in Horse-Shoe Robinson, 165; in Knights of the Horse-Shoe, 155; in Red Rock, 171
Simms, William Gilmore, on George Balcombe, 94
slavery, 161; and familial paradigm, 122; Frank Meriwether on, 19; in Kentuckian, 18–19, 38; in literary scholarship, 1, 2; in Partisan Leader, 122; in Swallow Barn, 19, 28; Mark Littleton on, 19
social class, 92, 103, 134, 150, 173 (n.1); and artificial brotherhoods, 137; and leadership, 164; in George Balcombe, 100; in Knights of the Horse-Shoe, 159;

Index

in *Partisan Leader*, 111; in *Rob of
  the Bowl*, 128, 130, 140
*Social Life in Old Virginia Before the
  War*, 169
southern belle, 29; Bel Tracy as, 15;
  Blair Cary as, 171; in Seidel, 6;
  Virginia Bell Chevillere as, 36
Southern Literary Messenger, review
  of *Partisan Leader*, 112
Southern Quarterly Review, review
  of *Knights of the Horse-Shoe*,
  148
Spotswood family, 144
Spotswood, Alexander, 144, 148, 163;
  as political leader, 151; as ruler-
  father, 150, 151, 154
Spotswood, Dorothea, 144, 145, 151,
  152, 157
Spotswood, John, 144, 145, 147, 149,
  153
Spotswood, Kate, 144, 151, 157
Spotswood, Robert, 144
St. Clair, Frances, 35–36, 38;
  courtship of, 38–39; first
  marriage, 44; flight of, 37; on
  sectionalism, 18; weakness of, 44
state banks, 133
Still, Hiram, 170
Swale, Robert ("Rob of the Bowl"),
  128, 129, 130, 137
Swallow Barn: and *Kentuckian in New-
  York*, 31; chivalry in, 15;
  composition of, 13; courtship in,
  14; familial paradigm in, 24;
  Federal authority, 19; female
  characters, 29; generational
  progression in, 18, 24–25; in
  Bakker, 16; in Hubbell, 16; in
  Parrington, 16; in Ridgely, 16; in
  Taylor, 16; in Watson, 5; in-laws
  in, 15; lawsuit in, 14, 21;
  Maysville Road veto, 21; national
  tensions in, 24; Nullification in,
  21; organic community in, 22,
  24–25; political process in, 21;

popularity of, 15–16; publication
  of, 23; references to politics,
  23–24; resolution of, 29; ruler-
  father in, 23; scholarship, 16;
  sectionalism in, 16, 24; slavery in,
  19, 28; summary, 13–15

Taylor, William R., 4–5; cavalier fig-
  ure, 25; on *Cavaliers of Virginia*,
  55, 65; on *George Balcombe*, 94;
  on *Horse-Shoe Robinson*, 74; on
  Kentuckian, 34; on Ned Hazard,
  27; on *Swallow Barn*, 16; on
  Victor Chevillere, 35; Yankee
  figure, 43
Temperance, 153
Texas, annexation of, 148, 149
Texas, war for independence, 149
The Minister, 110
Tracy family, 14
Tracy, Bel, 14, 17, 157, 171; as belle
  figure, 15, 29; courtship of, 27
Tracy, Isaac, 14, 21
Tramontane expedition, 148
Tramontane order, 158, 159
travel, in *Kentuckian*, 41
Trevor brothers, 156
Trevor family, 107, 117
Trevor, Bernard, 108, 110, 115, 120,
  122, 125; as ruler-father, 119,
  122–123
Trevor, Delia, 108, 109, 110, 119
Trevor, Douglas, 107, 108, 110, 115,
  119, 120
Trevor, Hugh, 107, 120, 122; family
  of, 108
Trevor, Owen, 110, 111, 156
Tucker family, 94, 95–96
Tucker, Henry St. George, 116; and
  Partisan Leader, 118; political
  views, 117
Tucker, Nathaniel Beverley: and
  Andrew Jackson, 115; and Martin
  Van Buren, 115; biography of,
  175 (n.2); familial paradigm in

192 *Index*

works of, 90; family experience, 95, 97, 117, 118; in Hubbell, 3; in Parrington, 2; in Taylor, 4; in Watson, 5; marriage in, 165; on
Tucker, Nathaniel Beverley, *(continued)* Partisan Leader, 114; political views, 90, 95, 102, 112, 113, 116; siblings in works of, 167
Tucker, St. George, 85, 96

Union, 68, 84
Upshur, Abel, 111

Van Buren, Martin, 90, 116
Van Buren, Martin (character), 108, 115, 120, 124, 125; as political leader, 151; as ruler-father, 124; corruption of, 109, 110
Verheyden, Albert, 128, 129
Virginia (state), 38

Waldie's, review of Kentuckian, 34
Warden, Anthony, 128, 130

Warden, Blanche, 128, 129
Watson, Ritchie D., 5, 173 (n.3); on Horse-Shoe Robinson, 74; on The Partisan Leader, 5; on Swallow Barn, 5
Weasel, Dorothy, 128
Weasel, Garret, 128, 139
Welch, Major, 170
Welch, Ruth, 170, 171
western expansion, 148, 167
Whigs, 77; election of 1836, 116; values of, 70, 72, 82, 84
Widows, 87
Wingina, 147, 149, 153–154
Women, education of, 175 (n.3) widows,
women's roles, 29, 84, 157, 165, 169, 171

Yancey, Charles, 143, 144
Yankee figure, in Kentuckian, 43
Yazawa, Melvin, 7–10, 18, 40, 102, 118, 136, 164